Isaac Deutscher is one of today's leading authorities on Russia, Communism, and Soviet society. His historical studies, STALIN: A POLITICAL BIOGRAPHY, and THE PROPHET ARMED have been acclaimed as works of major importance.

ISAAC DEUTSCHER was born in Poland in 1907. In 1949, when he became a British subject, Mr. Deutscher withdrew from regular journalism after a brilliant career. He is still a regular contributor to *The Times, The Manchester Guardian,* and *The Reporter* of New York, and his commentaries on Soviet affairs appear in the leading newspapers of fifteen countries. Mr. Deutscher also contributes to many academic periodicals. He is the author of STALIN: A POLITICAL BIOGRAPHY, SOVIET TRADE UNIONS, RUSSIA WHAT NEXT? and THE PROPHET ARMED.

RUSSIA IN TRANSITION

and other essays

RUSSIA IN TRANSITION
and other essays

BY ISAAC DEUTSCHER

COWARD-MCCANN, INC., *New York*

1281432

Contents

Preface

The essays collected in this volume describe and analyze the development and the background of Soviet society. The opening section of the book deals with the post-Stalin era and with recent developments such as Krushchev's exposure of Stalin, the Polish and Hungarian upheavals and their impact on the U.S.S.R., the "ferment of ideas" among the Soviet *intelligentsia,* the economic facts of the situation, and so on. Three further papers scrutinize the "close of the Stalin era" and trace back to that period, and to their latent state, nearly all the critical issues which have come to light since Stalin's death. In the "Historical Essays" I have attempted, *inter alia,* to correlate the experience of the Russian revolution with that of the great French revolution and to place the events of our day in deeper perspective. Finally, the closing section includes controversial writings, in which I have opposed a sociological and historical view of Soviet society and of its "inner contradictions" and conflicts, and movement to that static and "demonological" vision of it which has been so characteristic for many ex-Communist writers and which until recently enjoyed so great a vogue on both sides of the Atlantic.

Readers will find here developed even further the views I have expressed in my *Stalin, A Political Biography* (1949) and more particularly in my *Russia: What Next?* (1953). This last book appeared shortly after Stalin's death and forecast explicitly and emphatically the whole chain of events, with all its twists and turns, which is now commonly described as de-Stalinization. These forecasts were at the time received by some American critics with bitter attacks and sneers or, at best, with polite incredulity. I shall refrain from quoting back to my critics the things they wrote in 1953 and forego the all-too-easy satisfaction or amusement that could be derived therefrom. Instead, I shall only point out that the essays collected here were written at various times between 1948 and 1957 and that they are reproduced in the form in which they were originally published. (The only exception is "Mid-Century Russia" which I have redrafted from the more topically journalistic style the article had when it appeared in *The Reporter* in 1951, without, however, changing its content.) Readers are invited to check in every case the date of the original publication and to judge for themselves to what extent events have confirmed or refuted my analyses and anticipations. As to my severe critics, I shall only ask how many of them would venture to republish now in book form the views they expressed on Soviet prospects six, seven, or only three years ago?

I am greatly indebted to Mr. Donald Tyerman for giving me the benefit of his discriminating judgment and patient advice in the preparation of this volume.

My thanks are due to the Editors of *The Reporter, Foreign Affairs, World Politics, The Times* (London), *The Times Literary Supplement* (London), *The Listener* (London), and *Soviet Studies* (Glasgow), for permission to reprint articles which appeared in their papers.

I. D.

April 3, 1957
Wokingham, Berks.
England

Part One

RUSSIA
IN TRANSITION

1. Russia in Transition [1]

1

Who would still maintain nowadays that Soviet society has emerged from the Stalin era in a state of petrified immobility, decayed and incapable of inner movement and change? Yet, only a short time ago this was the opinion commonly accepted; and a writer who defied it and claimed that, despite all appearances to the contrary, the Soviet universe did move seemed to argue from mere faith or wishfulness. Yes, the Soviet universe does move. At times it even looks as if it were still a nebula unsteadily revolving around a shifting axis—a world in the making, rumbling with the tremor of inner dislocation and searching for balance and shape.

It is the twilight of totalitarianism that the U.S.S.R. is living through. Again, how many times have not "political scientists" told us that a society which has succumbed to totalitarian rule cannot disenthrall itself by its own efforts, and that such is "the structure of Soviet totalitarian power" (the like of which, it was said, history has never seen before!) that it can be overthrown only from the outside by mighty blows delivered in war. Yet, it is as a result of developments within the Soviet society that Stalinism is breaking down and dissolving; and it is the Stalinists themselves who are the subverters of their own orthodoxy.

It is nearly four years now since the U.S.S.R. has ceased to be ruled by an autocrat. None of Stalin's successors has

[1] Written January 1, 1957.

3

"stepped into Stalin's shoes." Government by committee has taken the place of government by a single dictator. A French writer, still somewhat incredulous of the change, recalls that in Rome, when a Caesar died or was assassinated, his head was struck off the public monuments but "Caesar's body" was left intact until another head was put on it. Yet, in Moscow not one but many heads have been put on Caesar's body; and perhaps even the "body" is no longer the same. It is pointless to argue that it makes no difference for a nation whether it lives under the tyranny of an autocrat or under that of a "collective leadership." The essence of collective leadership is dispersal, diffusion, and therefore limitation of power. When government passes from one hand into many hands it can no longer be exercised in the same ruthless and unscrupulous manner in which it was exercised before. It becomes subject to checks and balances.

It is not only Caesar's head that has vanished. What used to be his strong arm, the power of the political police, is broken. The people are no longer paralyzed by fear of it. The stupendous machine of terror which overwhelmed so many people with so many false accusations and extorted so many false confessions of guilt, the machine which looked like an infernal *perpetuum mobile* at last invented by Stalin, has been brought to a standstill. Stalin's successors themselves have stopped it, afraid that even they would be caught by it; and they can hardly bring it back into motion, even if they wished to do so—the rust of moral opprobrium has eaten too deep into its cogs and wheels.

Nearly dissolved is also the Stalinist *univers concentrationnaire*, that grim world of slave labor camps which in the course of several decades sucked in, absorbed, and destroyed Russia's rebellious spirits and minds, leaving the nation intellectually impoverished and morally benumbed. Rehabilitated survivors of the Great Purges of the 1930's have returned from places of exile. There are, unfortunately,

few, all too few, of them; and some may be broken and
exhausted men. Yet, few as they are and such as they are,
they are a leaven in the mind of post-Stalinist society—a
reproach and a challenge to its disturbed conscience. Multitudes of other deportees have been allowed to leave concentration camps and to settle as "free workers" in the remote
provinces of the north and the east. Temporarily or finally,
the nightmare of mass deportations has ceased to haunt
Russia.

The mind of the nation has stirred to new activity. Gone
are the days when the whole of the Soviet Union was on its
knees before the Leader and had to intone the same magic
incantations, to believe in the same bizarre myths, and to
keep its thoughts tightly closed to any impulse of doubt and
criticism. To be sure, it is only slowly and painfully that people recover in their minds from monolithic uniformity and
relearn to think for themselves and express their thoughts.
Yet, a diversity of opinion, unknown for decades, has begun
to show itself unmistakably and in many fields. A fresh gust
of wind is blowing through the lecture halls and seminars of
universities. Teachers and students are at last discussing
their problems in relative freedom from inquisitorial control
and dogmatic inhibition. The Stalinist tutelage over science
was so barbarous and wasteful, even from the State's viewpoint, that it could no longer be maintained; and so it is perhaps not surprising that scientists should have regained freedom. What is more startling and politically important is the
freedom for people to delve into the Soviet Union's recent
history—a freedom still limited yet real. In Stalin's days this
was the most closely guarded taboo, because the Stalin legend
could survive only as long as the annals of the revolution and
of the Bolshevik Party remained sealed and hidden away, especially from the young, who could find in their own memories no antidote to it.

Even now the annals have not been thrown open indiscriminately. They are being unsealed guardedly, one by one.

The historians reveal their contents only gradually and in small doses. (The history of the October Revolution is still told in such a way that the giant figure of Trotsky is kept out of it—only his shadow is allowed to be shown casually, on the fringe of the revolutionary scene. But if Hamlet is still acted without the Prince of Denmark, the text of the play is becoming more and more authentic, while in Stalin's days the whole play, with the Prince cast as the villain, was apocryphal.) Every tiny particle of historical truth, wrested from the archives, is political dynamite, destructive not only of the Stalin myth proper, but also of those elements of orthodoxy which Stalin's epigoni are anxious to conserve. The old-Bolshevik heresies, of which even the middle-aged Russian of our days has known next to nothing, and the authors of those heresies, the ghostly apostates and traitors of the Stalin era, are suddenly revealed in a new light: the heresies can be seen as currents of legitimate Bolshevik thought and as part and parcel of Russia's revolutionary heritage; and the traitors —as great, perhaps tragic, figures of the revolution.

The rehabilitation, even partial, of past heresy militates against wholesale condemnation of present and future heresy. It corrodes the very core of orthodoxy to such an extent that the ruling group shrinks from the consequences. But the ruling group is no longer in a position to stop the process of Russia's historical education which forms now the quintessence of her political education.[2]

This is not the place to discuss further the intellectual ferment of the post-Stalin era, described elsewhere in this volume.[3] Suffice it to say, that in its initial phases de-Staliniza-

[2] It is difficult to find an analogy in any other nation at any time for so close an interdependence of history and politics as that which exists in the U.S.S.R. at present. The controversies of Soviet historians which preceded the 20th Congress foreshadowed Khrushchev's and Mikoyan's revelations at the Congress; and it was no matter of chance that even before Khrushchev, at the Congress itself, Professor Pankratova, an historian, made one of the most startling pronouncements. Since then the historians' disputes have gone on almost uninterruptedly.

[3] See the essay "Post-Stalinist Ferment of Ideas," p. 52.

tion has been or was primarily the work of the intelligentsia. Writers, artists, scientists, and historians have been its pioneers. Their demands have coincided, at least in part, with the needs and wishes of the managerial groups and of influential circles in the party leadership. This accounts for the peculiarly limited, administrative-ideological character of the reforms carried out. Yet, as at the turn of the century, the intelligentsia has acted once again as the *burevestnik*, the storm finch. Its restlessness augurs the approach of an upheaval in which much wider social forces are likely to come into play.

2

The new working class which has emerged from the melting-pot of forced industrialization is potentially a political power of a magnitude hitherto unknown in Russian history. There are now in the U.S.S.R. four to five times as many industrial workers as there were before the revolution and even in the late 1920's. Large scale industry then employed not much more than three million wage laborers. It now employs at least fifteen million (not counting transport workers, state farm laborers, the medium and higher technical personnel, etc.). The working class has not only grown in size; its structure and outlook, too, have changed. These are not the old Russian workers who combined exceptional political *élan* with technological backwardness and semi-illiteracy. This, in its main sections, is a highly advanced working class which avidly assimilates skills and absorbs general knowledge. Among the young who now enter industry many have gone through secondary education. The change may be illustrated by the following comparison: about a quarter of a century ago as many as 75 per cent of the workers employed in engineering were classed as unskilled and only 25 per cent as skilled. In 1955 the proportion was exactly reversed: 75 per cent were skilled men and only 25 per cent remained unskilled. The relation is certainly not the same in other industries: engineering represents the most progressive sector of the economy. But the situation in this sector is highly significant, if only because engineering employs about one-third of the industrial manpower and accounts for about one-half of the total gross industrial output of the U.S.S.R.

The power of the Soviet bureaucracy was originally rooted in the weakness of the working class. The Russian proletariat was strong enough to carry out a social revolution in 1917, to overthrow the bourgeois regime, to lift the Bolsheviks to power, and to fight the civil wars to a victorious conclusion. But it was not strong enough to exercise actual proletarian dictatorship, to control those whom it had lifted to power, and to defend its own freedom against them. Here is indeed the key to the subsequent evolution or "degeneration" of the Soviet regime. By 1920-1921 the small working class which had made the revolution shrank to nearly half its size. (Not more than 1½ to 2 million men remained then in industrial employment.) Of the rest many had perished in the civil wars; others had become commissars or civil servants; and still others had been driven by famine from town to country and never returned. Most factories were idle. Their workers, unable to earn a living by productive work, traded in black markets, stole goods from the factories, and became *déclassés*. As the old landlord class and the bourgeoisie had been crushed, as the peasantry was inherently incapable of assuming national leadership, and as the industrial working class was half dispersed and half demoralized, a social vacuum arose in which the new bureaucracy was the only active, organized, and organizing element. It filled the political vacuum and established its own preponderance.

Then, in the course of the 1920's, the working class was reassembled and reconstituted; and in the 1930's, the years of forced industrialization, its numbers grew rapidly. By now, however, the workers were powerless against the new Leviathan state. The bureaucracy was firmly entrenched in its positions, it accumulated power and privileges and held the nation by the throat. The working class could not at first derive strength from its own growth in numbers. That growth became, on the contrary, a new source of weakness. Most of the new workers were peasants, forcibly uprooted from the country, bewildered, lacking habits of industrial life, capacity for organization, political tradition, and self-confidence. In the turmoil of the Second World War and of its aftermath, society was once again thrown out of balance. It is only in this decade, in the 1950's, that the vastly expanded working class has been taking shape and consolidating as a modern social force, acquiring an urban industrial tradition, becoming aware of itself, and gaining confidence.

This new working class has so far lagged behind the intelligentsia in the political drive against Stalinism, although it has certainly had every sympathy with the intelligentsia's demand for freedom. However, the workers cannot possibly remain content with the administrative-ideological limitations of the post-Stalinist reform. They are certain to go eventually beyond the intelligentsia's demands and to give a distinctive proletarian meaning and content to the current ideas and slogans of democratization. Their thoughts and political passions are concentrating increasingly on the contradiction between their nominal and their actual position in society. Nominally, the workers are the ruling power in the nation. In the course of forty years this idea has been ceaselessly and persistently instilled into their minds. They could not help feeling edified, elevated, and even flattered by it. They cannot help feeling that they should, that they ought, and that they must be the ruling power. Yet, everyday experience tells them that the ruling power is the bureaucracy, not they. The bureaucracy's strong arm has imposed on them the Stalinist labor discipline. The bureaucracy alone has determined the trend of economic policy, the targets for the Five-Year Plans, the balance between producer and consumer goods, and the distribution of the national income.

The bureaucracy alone has fixed the differential wage scales and wage rates creating a gulf between the upper and the lower strata. The bureaucracy has pulled the wires behind the Stakhanovite campaigns and, under the pretext of socialist emulation, set worker against worker and destroyed their solidarity. And, under Stalin's orders, it was the bureaucracy, aided by the labor aristocracy, that conducted a frenzied and relentless crusade against the instinctive egalitarianism of the masses.

Until recently the bureaucracy itself was subject to Stalin's whimsical terror and suffered from it even more than the working class did. This veiled, up to a point, the contrast between the theoretical notion of the proletarian dictatorship and the practice of bureaucratic rule. In their prostration before the Leader, worker and bureaucrat seemed to be equals. All the stronger did the beginning of de-Stalinization expose the contrast in their real positions. De-Stalinization was, at first, an act of the bureaucracy's self-determination. The civil servant and the manager were its first beneficiaries: freed from the Leader's despotic tutelage they began to breathe freely. This made the workers acutely aware of their own inferiority. However, the bureaucracy could not for any length of time reserve the benefits of de-Stalinization exclusively for itself. Having emancipated itself from the old terror, it willy-nilly relieved of it society as a whole. The workers too ceased to be haunted by the fear of the slave labor camp. Since that fear had been an essential ingredient of the Stalinist labor discipline, its disappearance entailed the end of that discipline. Malenkov's government proclaimed the obsolescence of the Stalinist labor code. That Draconic code had played its part in breaking the masses of the proletarianized peasantry to regular habits of industrial work; and only to those masses, bewildered and helpless, could it be applied. Vis-à-vis the new working class it was becoming increasingly useless and ineffective. A freer climate at the factory bench had indeed become the prerequisite for a steady rise in labor productivity and higher industrial efficiency.

Nor could the worker remain content merely with the relaxation of factory discipline. He began to use his freshly won freedom to protest against the pre-eminence of the managerial groups and of the bureaucracy. By far the most important phenomenon of the post-Stalin era is the evident revival of the long-suppressed egalitarian aspirations of the working class.

From this point the workers' approach to de-Stalinization begins to diverge from that of the intelligentsia. The men of the intelligentsia have been intensely interested in the political "liberalization," but socially they are conservative. It is they who have benefited from the inequalities of the Stalin era. Apart from individuals and small groups, who may rise intellectually above their own privileged position and sectional viewpoint, they can hardly wish to put an end to those inequalities and to upset the existing relationship between various groups and classes of Soviet society. They are inclined to preserve the social *status quo*. For the mass of the workers, on the other hand, the break with Stalinism implies in the first instance a break with the inequalities fostered by Stalinism.

It should not be imagined that the renascent egalitarianism of the masses is politically articulate. It has not yet found any clear and definite expression on the national scale. We know of no resolutions adopted by trade unions or by workers' meetings protesting against privilege and calling for equality. The workers have not yet been free enough to voice such demands or to make their voices heard. They may not even have been capable of formulating demands as people accustomed to autonomous trade-union and political activity would do. It is more than thirty years since they had ceased to form and formulate opinions, to put them forward at meetings, to stand up for them, to oppose the views of others, to vote, to carry the day, or to find themselves outvoted. It is more than thirty years since as a class they had ceased to have any real political life of their own. They could hardly recreate it overnight, even if those in power had put no obstacles in their way. Consequently the new egalitarianism expresses itself only locally, fitfully, and incoherently. It is only semiarticulate. It works through exercising pressure at the factory level. Its manifestations are fragmentary and scattered. Yet it makes itself felt as the social undertone to de-Stalinization, an undertone growing in volume and power.

Many recent acts of official policy have clearly reflected this egalitarian pressure from below. For the first time since 1931 the government has tackled a basic reform of wages; and although the reform has not yet taken final shape, the reversal of the antiegalitarian trend is already clearly discernible. Hitherto the piece rate has formed the basis of the whole wages system: at least 75 per cent of all industrial wages were, until quite recently, made up of piece rates, because these lend themselves much more easily than time rates to extreme differentiation. Within this system the so-called progressive piece rate was favored most of all, a method of payment under which the Stakhanovite producing 20, 30, and 40 per cent above the norm of output earned not just 20, 30, and 40 per cent more than the basic pay, but 30, 50, 80 per cent or even more. This method of payment, glorified in Stalin's days, as the supreme achievement of socialism, has now been declared as harmful to the interests of industry and workers alike. The grossly overadvertised Stakhanovite "movement" has been given a quiet burial. The time wage has again become the basic form of payment. It would be preposterous to see in this a triumph of socialism. Both the piece wage and the time wage—but the former much more than the latter—are essentially capitalist forms of payment; and it is only a measure of the retrograde character of some aspects of Stalin's labor policy that the return to the time wage should be regarded as progress. Yet progress it marks. It shows that workers no longer respond to the crude Stalinist appeal to their individual acquisitiveness which disrupted their class solidarity and that the government has been obliged to take note of this.

The year 1956 brought two further significant acts of labor policy: a rise by about one third in the lower categories of salaries and wages; and a new pension scheme with rates of pensions drastically revised in favor of workers and employees with low earnings. While in the Stalin era the purpose of almost every government decree in this field was to increase and widen the discrepancies between lower and higher earnings, the purpose of the recent decrease has been to reduce such discrepancies.

The reawakening egalitarianism has likewise affected the government's educational policy. Beginning with the school year 1956-1957, all tuition fees have been abolished. It should be recalled that these had first been abolished early in the revolution, when Lenin's government pledged itself to secure free education for all. Poverty, cultural backwardness, and extreme scarcity of educational facilities made universal free education unattainable. The pledge remained nevertheless an important declaration of purpose. Stalin then reintroduced fees for secondary and academic education. Only the bureaucracy and the labor aristocracy could afford paying; and so education was almost defiantly reserved as a privilege for the children of the privileged. The tuition fee extended to the ranks of the young generation the social differences which Stalin's labor policy fostered among their parents. It tended to perpetuate and deepen the new stratification of society. On this ground Stalin's Communist critics, especially Trotsky, charged him with paving the way for a new bourgeoisie. All the more significant is the present abolition of all fees. This renewed pledge of universal free education, given by Stalin's successors, is of far greater practical value than was Lenin's pledge, because it is backed up by a tremendously expanded and still expanding school system. Even so,

Soviet society has still a long way to go before it achieves genuine equality in education. Only in the towns are there enough secondary schools to take in all children—in the country there will not be enough of them before 1960 at the earliest. Universal academic education is *Zukunftsmusik*. All the same, the abolition of school fees is the rulers' tribute to the new egalitarianism.

Odd episodes from everyday life and street scenes described in the Soviet press allow sometimes even the outsider to watch this new mood as it surges momentarily, in quite unexpected ways, to the surface.

Recently, for instance, *Trud* related an incident that occurred at the Red Square in Moscow. A worker accosted a member of the Supreme Soviet and rudely chided him for "wearing such fine clothes" as no worker could afford. "I can see at once," the worker said, "that never in your life have you done a day's work at the factory bench." *Trud*, indignant at this example of "hooliganism," tells its readers that the member of the Supreme Soviet had in fact been a factory worker most of his life; and that the man who accosted him behaved cowardly for he withdrew and disappeared in the crowd before his identity could be established.

There is hardly a detail in this seemingly irrelevant episode which does not have almost symbolic eloquence. It was unthinkable in Stalin's days that a worker should dare to accost a member of the Supreme Soviet; and that he should do so at the Red Square of all places, just outside the Kremlin wall. This used to be the most heavily guarded spot in the whole of the Soviet Union—it swarmed with police agents and was usually shunned by the ordinary citizen who had no business to be there. But the worker's new daring still has its well-defined limits. Having chided the dignitary, he prefers to keep his anonymity, to withdraw, and to plunge into the crowd. Times have changed, but not enough for a worker to believe that he may vent with impunity his feelings at "their" fine clothes and "their" privileges. That many of "them" had risen from the working class is true, of course; but this does not make the underdog feel less of an underdog. The peculiar form of protest he chose may have flavored of "hooliganism." But, as a rule, men express their feelings in this way when they cannot easily express them in more legitimate forms. Yet, how much resentment at inequality must have been pent up in the man, and how bitter must it have been, to explode in this way!

Among his workmates the protester certainly feels on much safer ground than at the Red Square; and there, at the factory bench or at the canteen, the privileges of the bureaucracy and of the labor aristocracy have become the recurrent theme of daily conversation. It is the oldest of themes; yet how novel it is after the long and sullen silence of the Stalin era. There, among themselves, the workers are pondering anew their position forty years after the revolution and groping for new collective action. The day may not be far off when the anonymous man returns to the Red Square but not to accost a bigwig and vent resentment furtively. He will come back, head uplifted, and surrounded by multitudes, to utter anew the old and great cry for equality.

3

Of Stalin it has been said that like Peter the Great he used barbarous means to drive barbarism out of Russia. Of Stalin's successors it may be said that they drive Stalinism out of Russia by Stalinist methods.

The procedures of de-Stalinization are characterized by ambiguity, tortuousness, and prevarication. At first it was allegedly only a matter of doing away with the "cult of the individual," the grotesque adulation of the Leader. When the issue was first posed, in the spring of 1953, even the name of the "individual" who had been the object of the cult was not mentioned; and up to the Twentieth Congress, up to February 1956, the press still extolled the great Apostolic succession of "Marx-Engels-Lenin-Stalin." The cult was abandoned, yet it was kept up. But having made this first step, Stalin's successors could not help making the next one as well. They had to denounce the Leader's "abuses of power." They denounced them piecemeal and shrunk from saying frankly that these were Stalin's abuses. They found a scapegoat for him. As Beria had for fourteen years been Stalin's police chief, the responsibility for many of Stalin's misdeeds could conveniently be placed on him.

For a time this particular scapegoat was constantly held before the eyes of Russia and the world—until it refused to do service. For one thing, Stalin could not be dissociated from the man who had for so long been his police chief. For another, many of the worst "abuses," to mention only the Great Purges of 1936-1938, had occurred before Beria took office in Moscow. The denunciation of Beria implied the denunciation of Stalin himself; and it led directly to it. It was as if the scapegoat had returned from the wilderness to drag the real and the chief sinner down the steep slope. It threatened to drag others as well. Malenkov, Khrushchev, Kaganovich, Molotov, Voroshilov, had all been Beria's close colleagues and associates. The more they revealed of the horrors of the past, the stronger grew their urge to exonerate themselves and to find a new scapegoat—this time for themselves. That new scapegoat was none other than Stalin. "It was all his fault, not ours" was the *leitmotif* of Khrushchev's secret speech at the Twentieth Congress. "It was all his fault," *Pravda* then repeated a hundred times, "but nothing has ever been wrong with our leading cadres and with the working of our political institutions."

It was a most hazardous venture for Stalin's ex-associates to try and acquit themselves at his expense. This scapegoat too—and what a giant of a scapegoat it is!—is returning from the wilderness to drag them down. And so they are driven to try to re-exonerate Stalin, at least in part, in order to exonerate themselves.

Such attempts at "tricking history" and playing blindman's buff with it are all in good Stalinist style. In effect, Stalin's successors avoid telling the truth even when, on the face of it, truth should reflect credit on them. Their first move on their assumption of power was to repudiate the "doctors' plot." Yet, to this day they have not told the real story of that last great scandal of the Stalin era. What was hidden behind it? Who, apart from Stalin, staged it? And—for what purpose? Khrushchev's "secret" speech has not yet been published in the Soviet Union, a year after it was made; and this despite the fact that its contents have in the meantime been shouted from the housetops outside the Soviet Union. Special commissions have been at work to review the many purges and trials and to rehabilitate and set free innocent victims. But their work has remained a secret. Not even a summary account of it has been published to explain officially the background, the motives, the dimensions, and the consequences of the purges. Masses of slave laborers have been released from concentration camps; and many prisoners have regained freedom under a series of amnesties. Yet, not a single announcement has been made to say how many convicts have benefited from the amnesties and how many have left the concentration camps. The present rulers are so afraid of revealing the real magnitude of the wrongs of the Stalin era, that they dare not even claim credit for righting the wrongs. They must behave like that "honest thief" who cannot return stolen goods to their owner otherwise than stealthily and under the cover of night.

How many of the "stolen goods" have in fact been returned?

The break with Stalinism was initiated under the slogan of a return to the "Leninist norms of inner party democracy." The Twentieth Congress was supposed to have brought about the practical restitution of those norms. Yet to anyone familiar with Bolshevik history it is obvious that this was far from being true. The Congress adopted all its resolutions by unanimous vote, in accordance with the best Stalinist custom. No *open* controversy or *direct* clash of opinion disturbed the smooth flow of its monolithic "debates." Not one in a hundred or so speakers dared to criticize Krushchev or any other leader on any single point. Not a single major issue of national or international policy was in fact placed under discussion.

The change in the inner party regime has so far consisted in this: major decisions of policy are taken not by Khrushchev alone and not even by the eleven members of the Presidium but by the Central Committee which consists of 125 members (or 225 if alternate members are included). Inside that body free debate has apparently been restored; and differences of opinion have been resolved by majority vote. Only to this extent have "Leninist norms" been re-established. But under Lenin the differences in the Central Committee were, as a rule, not kept secret from the party or even from the nation at large; and the rank and file freely expressed their own views on them. The post-Stalinist Central Committee has never yet aired its differences in the hearing of the whole party. Thus, only the upper hierarchy appears to be managed more or less in the Leninist way. The lower ranks are still ruled in the Stalinist manner, although far less harshly. In the long run the party cannot remain half free and half slave. Eventually the higher ranks will either share their newly won freedom with the lower ranks, or else they themselves must lose it.

4

Within the Soviet Union de-Stalinization has so far been carried out as a reform *from above,* a limited change initiated and controlled at every stage by those in power. This state of affairs has not been accidental. It has reflected the condition of Soviet society both "*above*" and "*below*," in the first years after Stalin.

Above—powerful interests have obstructed reform, striving to restrict it to the narrowest possible limits, and insisting that the ruling group should in all circumstances hold the initiative firmly and not allow its hands to be forced by popular pressure. The attitude of the bureaucracy is by its very nature contradictory. The need to rationalize the working of the state machine and to free social relations from anachronistic encumbrances has induced the bureaucracy to favor reform. Yet, at the same time the bureaucracy has been increasingly afraid that this may imperil its social and political preponderance. The labor aristocracy has been troubled by a similar dilemma: It has been not less than the rest of the workers interested in doing away with the old terroristic labor discipline; but it cannot help viewing with apprehension the growing force of the egalitarian mood; and it resents the changes in labor policy which benefit the lower-paid workers without bringing compensatory advantages to the higher-paid. The various managerial groups and the military officers' corps are guided by analogous considerations; and they are, above all, anxious to maintain their authority. The attitude of these groups may be summed up thus: Reform from above? Yes, by all means. A revival of spontaneous movements from below? No, a thousand times no!

Below—everything has so far also favored reform from above. Toward the end of the Stalin era the mass of the people craved for a change but could do nothing to achieve it. They were not merely paralyzed by terror. Their political energy was hamstrung. No nation-wide, spontaneous yet articulate movements rose from below to confront the rulers with demands, to wrest concessions, to throw up new programs and new leaders, and to alter the balance of political forces. In 1953-1955 political prisoners and deportees struck in the remoteness of subpolar concentration camps, and these strikes led to the eventual dissolution of the camps. This was a struggle on the submerged fringe of the national life; but whoever has any sense of Russian history must have felt that when political prisoners were in a position to resume, after so long an interval, the struggle for their rights, Russia was on the move. Then the year 1956 brought much agitation to the universities of Leningrad, Moscow, and other cities. However, these and similar stirrings, symptomatic though they were, did not as yet add up to any real revival of the political energies in the depth of society.

It is not only that the working class had lost the habits of independent organization and spontaneous action. Stalinism had left a gap in the nation's political consciousness. It takes time to fill such a gap. It should be added that the gap is only relative. It is not by any means a vacuum. By spreading education, by arousing the people's intellectual curiosity, and by keeping alive the socialist tradition of the revolution, be it in a distorted and ecclesiastically dogmatic version, Stalinism has in fact accumulated many of the elements that should eventually go into the making of an extraordinarily high political consciousness. But Stalinism also forcibly prevented these elements from coalescing and cohering into an active social awareness and positive political thought. It increased enormously the potential political capacities of the people and systematically prevented the potential from becoming actual. Stalinist orthodoxy surrounded the nation's enriched and invigorated mind with the barbed wire of its canons. It inhibited people from observing realities, comparing them, and drawing conclusions. It intercepted inside their brains, as it were, every reflex of critical thought. It made impossible the communication of ideas and genuine political intercourse between individuals and groups. De-Stalinization has given scope to these constrained and arrested reflexes and has opened for them some channels of communication.

This does not alter the fact that the people entered the new era in a state of political disability, confusion and inaction; and that any immediate change in the regime, or even in the political climate, could come only through reform from above.

Reform from above could be the work of Stalinists only. Had any of the old-Bolshevik oppositions—Trotskyist, Zinovievist, and Bukharinist—survived till this day, Khrushchev, Bulganin, Voroshilov & Company would surely have long since been removed from power and influence; and anti-Stalinists would have carried out de-Stalinization wholeheartedly and consistently. But the old oppositions had been exterminated; and new ones could not form themselves and grow under Stalinist rule. Yet the break with Stalinism had become a social and political necessity for the Soviet Union; and necessity works through such human material as it finds available. Thus, the job which it should have been the historic right and privilege of authentic anti-Stalinists to tackle has fallen to the Stalinists themselves, who cannot tackle it otherwise than halfheartedly and hypocritically. They have to undo much of their life's work in such a way as not to bring about their own undoing. Paradoxically, circumstances have forced Malenkov and Khrushchev to act, *up to a point*, as the executors of Trotsky's political testament. Their de-Stalinization is like the "dog's walking on his hinder legs." It is not done well; but the wonder is that it is done at all! [4]

[4] History knows quite a few instances in which necessity worked through the most unsuitable human material when none other was available. Of course, whenever conservative rulers had to carry out progressive reforms, their work was self-contradictory and patchy; and it accumulated difficulties for the future. In my *Russia: What Next?* (1953), analyzing the social circumstances which would drive Stalin's successors to break with Stalinism, I compared their position with that of Czar Alexander II, the First Landlord of All the Russias, who, in conflict with the feudal landlord class and with himself, emancipated Russia's peasants from serfdom. Another example is Bismarck, the leader of the Junker class who transformed and adapted feudal Germany to the needs of bourgeois development. One might go much further back into the past and compare de-Stalinization to the reform which, early in the XVI century, was carried out in the Church of Rome as

5

Leon Trotsky once made the prediction that Stalinism *in extremis* would place Russia before the danger of a "Thermidorian counter-revolution." It will be remembered that in France the *coup d'état* of 9 Thermidor (July 27, 1794) brought about the downfall of Robespierre, the collapse of the Jacobin Party, the transfer of government from the Convention to the Directory, and the final ascendancy of the wealthy bourgeoisie over the revolutionary plebs. Although the *coup* looked at first like an episode in the internal struggles of the Jacobin Party, it did not, as its initiators had hoped, merely replace in government one set of Jacobins by another; it entailed a fundamental change in the balance of social forces and spelled the doom of Jacobinism. Trotsky was convinced that Stalinism would lead toward a similar crisis in consequence of which a struggle beginning inside the Bolshevik Party might transcend its initial limits and,

---

a prelude to the Counter-Reformation. The Church had been left by the Borgia Popes in a state of utter corruption and discredit; and it was by cardinals who had themselves been the Borgias' servants that it was reformed and raised up. The reformers first of all restricted the "cult of the individual" in the Vatican and limited the Pope's powers. Then they revealed to the faithful the crimes the Borgias had committed. Cardinal Gaspar Contarini, one of the most famous reformers, wrote to Alexander Farnese, Pope Paul III: "Can that be called a government whose rule is the will of one man, by nature prone to evil? . . . A Pope ought to know that those over whom he exercises power are free men." Counsels in the Vatican were divided on this issue as much as they have been in the Kremlin of our days. Some prelates objected to de-Borgiazation fearing that discredit thrown on the memory of the deceased Pontiff would rebound upon the Church and sap its authority. Cardinal Contarini met their objections with this argument: "How? Shall we trouble ourselves so much about the reputation of two or three Popes and not rather try to restore what has been defaced, and to secure a good name for ourselves?" The words might have been uttered by Khrushchev himself before he proceeded to unmask Stalin at the Twentieth Congress. However, in playing with such analogies one must not forget about the decisive differences in the character of rulers, in institutions, and in social backgrounds. The Church of Rome was not in charge of the affairs, and did not plan and manage the publicly owned economy, of a modern and expanding industrial society.

after the bourgeoisie and the *kulaks* had intervened in it, end in the restoration of the bourgeois order.

The notion of the "Soviet Thermidor" was not one of Trotsky's most lucid ideas—he himself was aware of this and repeatedly revised and modified it.[5] However, in the 1920's, when he first expounded the idea, the N.E.P. bourgeoisie and the *kulaks* still existed in Russia; and they had to be reckoned with as inherently counterrevolutionary forces capable of arousing the mass of the small-holding peasantry against Bolshevism and the weak "socialist sector" of the economy. Thirty years later the possibility of a Soviet Thermidor, as Trotsky first visualized it, appears to be very remote or altogether unreal. The N.E.P. bourgeoisie has disappeared; and it is difficult to see how the collectivized peasantry can ever gain ascendancy over the urban proletariat and restore the bourgeois order. Not only the old possessing classes have vanished. The political parties of the old Russia are also dead and beyond resurrection. It is nearly forty years—and what years!—since they were driven from the political stage. They have since been uprooted from the nation's memory. What is even more important, their programs and ideas have lost all relevance to the new structure and problems of Soviet society. The few émigré Mohicans—Monarchists, Cadets, Social Revolutionaries, and Mensheviks—if they returned to Russia, would appear incomparably more archaic to the present generation than the returning Bourbons appeared to the French or the restored

[5] Trotsky made the original predictions in 1926-1929. In the 1930's he redefined Thermidor as being not a counterrevolution proper but a "reaction within the revolution" and argued that Stalin had accomplished his Thermidor as early as 1923. A critical survey of this problem will be found in *The Prophet Unarmed*, the forthcoming and concluding volume of my biography of Trotsky. In this essay the term "Thermidor" is used as Trotsky used it at first to signify a veiled counterrevolution, the originators of which belong to the party of the revolution and are unaware of the consequences of their action. Although Trotsky's historical analogy is partly erroneous, the idea itself offers a clue to some recent events.

Stuarts to the English; they would seem as ancient as the phantoms of the Wars of the Roses were to the England of the machine age. Any new political movements which may spring into being can hardly be of a "Thermidorian" character. They are bound to seek to achieve their aims within the framework of the institutions created by the October Revolution and falsified by Stalinism.

However, if the Soviet Union need no longer be afraid of the specter that once haunted Trotsky, in Eastern Europe the chances of a "Thermidorian counter-revolution" are very real indeed. The Communist regime there is not even ten years old. Its foundations are not consolidated. The *kulaks* and even the urban bourgeoisie are still there. The peasantry as a whole has preserved private property and clings to it tooth and nail. The traditions of the old anti-Communist parties are still alive and potent. Some of the old cadres of those parties are still there and have not by any means lost contact with the masses. The masses have not lost their capacity for spontaneous political action. Moreover, in most of these countries Communist rule has been associated with Russian conquest and domination; and outraged national dignity and the longing for independence turn automatically against communism as well as Russia.

Consequently, the break with Stalinism has had a very different impact on Eastern Europe than on the Soviet Union. A momentous conflict has, in fact, arisen, between the logic of de-Stalinization in the U.S.S.R. and its logic in Poland, Hungary, and Eastern Germany. In the latter countries de-Stalinization is no longer the carefully calculated reform from above controlled at every stage by those in power. There, on the contrary, the explosive anti-Stalinism of the masses has tended to control those in power. Reform from above has led to the revival of movements from below. No sooner had Moscow begun to move away from the Stalin cult, in the spring of 1953, than Berlin rose in revolt. After the Twentieth Congress Poznan and Warsaw rose, and

Budapest took to arms. All over Eastern Europe the Communist parties have been torn between Stalinists and anti-Stalinists; and everywhere social and political forces have been present, ready to intervene in the internecine Communist struggle and to turn it into a Thermidor, a Thermidor which in appearance is also, or even primarily, a war of national liberation.

In the aftermath of the Second World War Stalin exported revolution to Eastern Europe on the point of bayonets. He then used the hidden but all-pervading police terror to keep that revolution in being. Now, when his police terror has gone or has ceased to terrorize, the great question has arisen whether a revolution begotten by foreign conquest can ever acquire an independent existence of its own and redeem itself. Can it ever be accepted by the people on the spot and gain their wholehearted support and devotion? Or must such a revolution collapse the moment the conqueror has withdrawn his bayonets?

There is perhaps no single answer to these questions. At any rate, the October upheavals in Poland and Hungary gave two different answers, perhaps none of them final. Poland rebelled against Russia but remained Communist. She retained the revolution and rejected the bayonets. Moreover, something like a proletarian revolution from below developed there, which adopted the Communist regime in order to free it from the Stalinist stigma, to transform it, and to shape it in its own political image. It was this proletarian movement from below which kept the Thermidorian forces at bay in October. In Hungary the position was different. There too the insurrection was at first Communist-inspired in its anti-Stalinism and sought to regenerate the revolution, not to overthrow it. Then Hungarian Stalinist provocation and Soviet armed intervention infuriated the insurgents, drove them to despair, and enabled anti-Communist forces to gain the initiative. Thus a Thermidorian situation arose: What had begun as an internecine Communist conflict and looked at first only like a shift from one Communist faction to another, from Gerö to Nagy, developed into a fully-fledged struggle between communism and anticommunism.[6] Hungary, in effect, rejected Russian bayonets together with the revolution which was originally brought to that country on those bayonets. This was not a counterrevolution carried out by a hated and isolated possessing class defending its dominant position against the masses. It was, on the contrary, the ardent work of a whole insurgent people. It may be said that in October-November, the people of Hungary in a heroic frenzy tried unwittingly to put the clock back, while Moscow sought once again to wind up with the bayonet, or rather with the tank, the broken clock of the Hungarian Communist revolution. It is difficult to say who it was who acted the more tragic, and the more futile or hopeless role.

It may not be out of place to recall here that thirty-five years before these events Trotsky warned the Russian Communist Party against the monstrosity of a Communist rule imposed upon a foreign people by force of arms. "He who wants to carry revolution abroad on the point of bayonets," Trotsky then said, "it were better for him that a millstone were hanged about his neck, and he cast into the sea." Stalin did not heed the warning, and he bequeathed the millstone to his successors. Ever since his death, the millstone has been "hanging about their necks."

6

De-Stalinization in Russia had provided the decisive impulse for the upheavals in Poland and Hungary; and now these upheavals inevitably sent their tremors into Russia. At once all the dilemmas inherent in de-Stalinization were aggravated to the utmost. The threat to Russia's strategic interests and her international position was obvious. The die-hards of

---

[6] Nagy and his faction played the role which Trotsky at one time assumed Bukharin and Rykov would play in Russia but which they did not play.

Stalinism could not but blame the reformers for provoking it by the encouragement they had given to "Titoism" and every variety of anti-Stalinism. The reformers replied that it was precisely the sluggish tempo of de-Stalinization that had driven Poland and Hungary to revolt. However, the first reaction of the Soviet ruling group in the face of peril was to close their ranks and to call a halt to de-Stalinization. Yet, they could not make any serious attempt to resuscitate the old orthodoxy. Twice such attempts had been made, first after the Berlin rising in June 1953, at the time of Beria's fall; and then at the beginning of 1955, when Malenkov was dismissed from the post of Prime Minister. Both attempts failed and only served to stimulate the reformist trend. A new attempt could have no other result—it could only intensify the disintegration of Stalinism. The desecration of the old orthodoxy had made too deep an impression on the mind of the people to be effaced. It was too late to put the broken idols together again.

More important than the effect of the crisis on the ruling group was its impact on the Soviet masses. The predicament in which Soviet policy found itself could not be concealed from them. Voices of Communist critics abroad could not be silenced. The Soviet press had to reproduce wholly or in parts the arguments of Tito, Kardelj, Togliatti, Gomulka, and others. The Polish press, which was now in the vanguard of anti-Stalinism, was avidly read in Russia; and it played its part in stimulating "ideological revision." The ferment reached a new pitch of intensity; and this time it spread from the intelligentsia to the working class. The rulers unwittingly helped to spread it. Khrushchev publicly threatened to expel from universities the most vocal of the "heretical" students and to send them, as a punishment, to work at the factory bench. The expelled students could only carry the germs of the heresies to the factories and infect the workers. (It is strange that this should not have occurred to Khruschchev: the Czars used similarly to punish rebellious students: they drafted them into the army as privates, with the result that the regiments where the students served became centers of revolt.)

The Polish-Hungarian drama has thus opened a new phase in the internal development of the U.S.S.R. If until now the pressure which on the factory level the workers exercised against the bureaucracy was "economist" in character, and if they were not animated by any clear political idea, the development now probably reached a point at which the intelligentsia, or rather its ideologues and theorists, began to politicize the consciousness of the working class and to inject into it their own ideas—just as sixty years earlier Social Democratic intellectuals had carried the notions of political socialism "from the outside" into the spontaneous movement of the workers. At any rate, the first stirrings made themselves felt of a movement from below; and this may bring to a close that chapter of history in which de-Stalinization was a matter exclusively of reform from above.

At present, at the beginning of the year 1957, two distinct yet interconnected processes seem to be developing: the formation of a new political consciousness; and the inception or regeneration of a spontaneous mass movement. It is a question fateful for Russia's and the world's future at what pace these two processes will evolve and how they will react upon one another. It is possible for a spontaneous mass movement to acquire suddenly a very stormy momentum and to outstrip the growth of political consciousness. Such a movement may well upset the nation's political balances before it has itself acquired a clear awareness of aims, a positive political program, and a firm and confident leadership. Such a movement may be guided only by its own impetus and express only the pent-up resentments of the workers (and/or the peasants). It may, in particular, raise the cry for equality in an extreme, uncompromising and Utopian manner while the nation's economic resources are insufficient for the extreme egalitarian demands to be met even half way, especially after a long period during which consumer industries were underdeveloped. Should such a disproportion arise between consciousness and spontaneity, and should it become very acute, then the revived mass movement may well suffer shipwreck. Instead of achieving genuine and lasting democratization it may become a factor of social disruption and chaos. The present rulers would probably try to deal with the situation by means of a combination of concessions and repression. But they would hardly go far enough in meeting popular demands. Nor would they be in a position to use the Stalinist organs of suppression against the bursting energy of the masses: they could hardly bring back to the scene the political police in the full panoply of Stalinist "efficiency." Their last resort would be to appeal for help to the army, as they did in Berlin in June 1953 and in Budapest in October-November 1956.

The assumption by the Soviet marshals and generals of the role of the guardians of "order" not only in satellite countries but within the Soviet Union itself would create a new situation. It should be remarked that Stalin never had the need to use his marshals and generals in this way—he did not send his armored divisions to crush popular uprisings—because he could rely on his infallible, invisible, and all-pervading police terror. This enabled him to keep the army leaders in a politically subordinate position. But should the latter, under Stalin's successors, come to act regularly as the guardians of order, an important shift of power would necessarily follow. Sooner or later, the army leaders would say to themselves that instead of guarding order on account of and for the benefit of the party leaders, they could as well do it on their own account and for their own benefit. In other words, the strains and stresses caused by a stormy revival of mass movements lacking leadership and clear political purpose, may lead to the establishment of a military dictatorship of the Bonapartist type. All the more so as the military could hardly view with indifference a situation in which they must see a threat to Russia's positions of power and to all the strategic gains she won in the last world war.

What Karl Marx wrote in *The 18th Brumaire* about how the various factions of the French bourgeoisie by calling repeatedly on the army to "save society" set the stage for military dictatorship is well worth quoting here, for despite all the differences of time and place (and despite Marx's somewhat old-fashioned imagery), his words may still apply:

> When barrack and bivouac were periodically thrown upon the head of French society to oppress its brain and keep it quiescent; when sword and musket periodically functioned as judge, administrator, guardian and censor, gendarme and nightwatchman; when military moustache and tunic were periodically acclaimed as the tutelary deities of society—was it not inevitable that it should eventually occur to barrack and bivouac, sword and musket, moustache and tunic, to save society once for all on their own initiative, by declaring their own rule supreme and by saving . . . society the trouble of self-government? . . . Barrack and bivouac, sword and musket, moustache and tunic would be only more apt to hit upon this idea, seeing that they might then expect higher pay for more exalted service.

Fortunately, "military moustache and tunic" have not yet been periodically acclaimed as the tutelary deities of the Soviet Union—although they may still gain that acclaim. Nor is it inevitable or even probable that the formation of a new political consciousness should lag so dangerously behind the revival of mass movements. The gap in consciousness created by Stalinism, it should be repeated, is relative only. Most of the elements needed to fill it are there. Under the shocks of the Twentieth Congress and of the events in Poland and Hungary, and amid an intense moral-political ferment, it may be filled much more rapidly than it would be otherwise. The great heart-searching and transvaluation of values, of which the Soviet press offers only minute and purely negative reflections, is going on. The Soviet peoples take the measure of their problems, view critically themselves and the world around them, and are getting ready for another world-shaking historic experience.

A society which has gone through as much as Soviet society has gone through, which has achieved so much and suffered so much, which has seen, within the lifetime of one generation, its whole existence repeatedly shattered, remade, and transformed to its very foundations, and which has again and again ascended the highest peaks of hope and heroism and descended to the lowest depths of misery and despair—such a society cannot fail drawing from its rich and uniquely great experience equally great generalizing ideas and practical conclusions and embodying these in a program of action worthy of itself. Nor can it fail to produce sooner or later the men and women strong enough in mind and character—a new "phalanx of heroes reared on the milk of the wild beast"—to transform ideas into deeds.

No one, however, can foresee the actual rhythm of historic developments. In moments of great crises spontaneous mass movements *do* run ahead of all political groups, even the most radical ones, and of their programs and methods of action. So it was in Russia in February 1917. The workers then found in the Soviets, the Councils of *their* deputies, the institutions within which they learned to harmonize impulse and thought, to test conflicting programs, and to choose leaders. Of those institutions Stalinist Russia preserved no more than the name and the dead shells. Yet in the memory of the working class the Soviets have survived as *the* instruments of socialist government and self-government, *the* organs of a "workers' state." Even in Hungary, amid all the confusion of revolution and counterrevolution, the insurgent workers hastily formed their Councils. Any political revival in the working class of the U.S.S.R. is almost certain to lead to a revival of the Soviets which will once again become the testing ground of political programs, groups, and leaders, and the meeting place of spontaneous movements and political consciousness.

Whatever the future holds in store, a whole epoch is coming to a close—the epoch in the course of which the stupendous industrial and educational advance of the U.S.S.R. was accompanied by deep political lethargy and torpor in the masses. Stalinism did not and could not create that state of torpor; it spawned on it and sought to perpetuate it but was essentially its product. Basically, the apathy of the masses resulted from the extraordinary expenditure of all their energies in the great battles of the revolution. The aftermath of the French revolution was likewise one of a deadening lassitude in which the people "unlearned freedom," as Babeuf, who was so close to the masses, put it. Christian Rakovsky, recalling in his exile at Astrakhan in 1928, Babeuf's remark, added that it took the French forty years to relearn freedom. It has taken the Soviet people not less time—but there is no doubt that they are at last relearning freedom.

2. Khrushchev on Stalin [1]

No one who has seen and heard N. S. Khrushchev speaking on a platform or arguing with people will doubt the authenticity of the text, published by the State Department of his secret speech at the Twentieth Congress of the Soviet Communist Party. The text probably has its gaps, and here and there the transcript or the translation may not be quite accurate. Nevertheless this is the real stuff—genuine Khrushchev saying indirectly about himself almost as much as about Stalin.

The style, like the man himself, is untutored, impulsive, discursive, almost chaotic; yet at the same time it is peculiarly dynamic and down-to-earth. This is no theorist or historian producing a Marxist explanation of the Stalin era or offering analytical ideas and generalizations. In this respect Khrushchev is immeasurably inferior to the great Bolshevik critics who have exposed Stalin before him, to Trotsky, Bukharin, or Rakovsky. Yet he gives by far the most vivid image of the Stalin era, or, at any rate, of its final phase, and incidentally also of Stalin himself. He takes us into the dark corridors and galleries of Russia's recent past as a miner would take us, lamp in hand, down a coalpit; and with a miner's tough fist he puts dynamite under the rocks of Stalinism down below.

His performance must be something of a puzzle to the purveyors of clichés and simplifications about the Stalin era.

1 A shortened version of this essay appeared in *The Reporter*, July 12, 1956.

How is it, one must ask, that a man of so sturdy a character, of a mind so inherently independent, and of so eruptive and untamable a temper could at all survive under Stalin, and survive at the very top of the Stalinist hierarchy? How did Khrushchev manage to control himself, to keep his thoughts to himself, and to hide his burning hatred from Stalin? How did he behave under the dictator's scrutinizing gaze when the dictator snarled at him: "Why do your eyes look so shifty to-day?"

This is not the place to analyze the working of the minds of men like Khrushchev during the Stalin era. I have attempted to do it elsewhere, for instance in my book *Russia: What Next?* (pp. 155-156, U.S. edition). But this much can be said here: in this miner and miner's son risen to his present position one can still feel something of that tenacious, patient, yet alert and shrewd spirit which once characterized the old Russian worker when from the underground he bored under the Czar's throne. To that spirit are now joined new mental horizons, a new capacity for organization, and an unwonted modernity. As one watches Khrushchev (even, as I have watched him, with a certain bias against him) one comes to think that he is probably still the Russian (or the Russo-Ukrainian) worker, writ large—the Russian worker who inwardly remained true to himself even in the Stalinist straitjacket, who has over the years gathered strength and grown in stature and grown out of the straitjacket. One might even say that through Khrushchev the old repressed socialist tradition of the Russian working class takes a long-delayed and sly revenge on Stalinism.

Yet, Khrushchev also makes the impression of an actor who, while he plays his own part with superb self-assurance, is only half aware of his own place in the great, complex, and somber drama in which he has been involved. His long, aggressive monologue is a cry from the heart, a cry about the tragedy of the Russian revolution and of the Bolshevik Party; but it is only a fragment of the tragedy. He himself did not expect to burst out with this cry. Only a few days before he made the secret speech, he did not know that he was going to make it; or, at any rate, he did not know what he was going to say. Even the composition of his speech shows that he spoke more or less impromptu: he dashes from topic to topic almost indiscriminately; he ventures spontaneously into side lines; and he seems to throw out reminiscences and confidences and asides as they occur to him. By its irregularity this speech, delivered at the closing session of the congress, on February 25, contrasts curiously with his own formal address delivered at the inaugural session ten days earlier. The two speeches form a striking contrast in content as well. In his inaugural address Khrushchev said, for instance:

"The unity of our party has formed itself in the course of years and tens of years. It has grown and become tempered in the struggle against many enemies. The Trotskyites, Bukharinites, bourgeois nationalists, and other most wicked *enemies of the people,* champions of a capitalist restoration, made desperate efforts to disrupt from the inside the Leninist unity of our party, and they all have smashed their heads against our unity."

The words might have come straight from Stalin's mouth. But ten days later Khrushchev argues thus:

"It is Stalin who originated the concept *'enemy of the people.'* This term automatically rendered it unnecessary that the ideological errors of a man, or men, engaged in a controversy be proven; this term made possible the usage of the most cruel repression . . . against anyone who in any way disagreed with Stalin. . . ."

Khrushchev then goes on to say that the Trotskyites, Bukharinites, and so-called bourgeois nationalists, whatever their faults, were not enemies of the people; that there was no need to annihilate them; and that they "smashed their heads" not against the party's "Leninist unity" but against Stalin's despotism.

The speaker to whom the congress listened on February 25 was a very different man from the one whom it heard ten days earlier. What happened during those ten days to change the man so radically? Clearly, some dramatic but as yet undisclosed event must have occurred in the meantime, an event which showed Khrushchev that it would not do to sit on the fence and that he had to come down on one side or the other in the conflict between Stalinism and anti-Stalinism. Did perhaps the small band of old Bolsheviks, wrecks from Stalin's concentration camps, who have been brought to the conference hall as guests of honor, stage some demonstration of protest which shook the assembly's conscience? Or were the young delegates, who had been brought up in the Stalin cult, so restive after Khrushchev's first ambiguous hints about Stalin (and even more so after Mikoyan's more outspoken remarks) that they forced him to come out into the open and take the bull by the horns?

Whatever happened, Khrushchev had to produce an answer on the spot; and the answer was an indictment of Stalin. To justify his new attitude he ordered, no doubt with the Presidium's approval,[2] that Lenin's testament be distributed among the delegates, that long-suppressed testament in which Lenin urged the party to remove Stalin from the post of General Secretary, the testament for the publication and execution of which the anti-Stalinist opposition once clamored for years and in vain.

To the student of Soviet affairs Khrushchev's disclosures bring little that is really new. A biographer of Stalin finds in them at the most a few more illustrations of familiar points. Khrushchev confirms in every detail the account of the relations between Lenin and Stalin toward the very end of Lenin's life which Trotsky gave. Stalin's old critics are also proved right in what they have said about his method

[2] Since these words were written I have learned that Khrushchev had for this the approval of the Central Committee, or rather of its majority—a large minority, consisting of Stalinist die-hards, was opposed to his coming out with the revelations.

of collectivization, about the purges, and about the Trotsky-
ite and Bukharinite "fifth columns," in the reality of which
not only Communists but conservatives, liberals, and socialists in the West once preferred to believe. Nor is there anything surprising to the historian in Khrushchev's revelations
about Stalin's role in the last war and about his miscalcula-
tions and mistakes.[3]

But it is not from the historian's viewpoint that Khrushchev's performance should be judged. He spoke not to
scholars, but to men and women of a new Communist
generation; and to them his words have come as a Titanic
shock, and as the beginning of a profound mental—and
moral—upheaval.

Consider only how Khrushchev's character sketch of Stalin,
drawn haphazardly yet extremely vividly, must affect Communists brought up in the Stalin cult. There they see him
now, the "Father of the Peoples," immured as he was in the
Kremlin, refusing over the last twenty-five years of his life
to have a look at a Soviet village—at the new collectivized
village; refusing to step down into a factory and face workers; refusing even to cast a glance at the army of which he
was the Generalissimo, let alone to visit the front; spending
his life in a half-real and half-fictitious world of statistics and
mendacious propaganda films; planning unleviable taxes;
tracing front-lines and lines of offensives on a globe on his
desk; seeing enemies creeping at him from every nook and
cranny; treating the members of his own Politbureau as his
contemptible lackeys, denying a Voroshilov admission to
sessions, slamming the door in Andreyev's face, or upbraid-
ing Molotov and Mikoyan; "choking" his interlocutors
"morally and physically"; pulling the wires behind the great
purge trials; personally checking and signing 383 black lists
with the names of thousands of doomed party members; or-
dering judges and N.K.V.D. men to torture the victims of
the purges and to extract confessions; "planning" the de-

[3] See, for instance, my *Stalin*, pp. 453–459.

portations of entire peoples and raging impotently at the size of the Ukrainian people too large to be deported; growing sick with envy at Zhukov's military fame; "shaking his little finger" at Tito and waiting for Tito's imminent fall; surrounded by dense clouds of incense and, like an opium eater, craving for more; inserting in his own hand passages of praise to his own "genius"—and to his own modesty!— into his official adulatory biography and into history textbooks; himself designing huge, monstrously ugly, elephantine monuments to himself; and himself writing his own name into the new national anthem which was to replace the Internationale. Thus did Khrushchev expose before his party the huge, grim, whimsical, morbid, human monster before whom the Communist world lay prostrate in the course of a quarter of a century.

And yet Khrushchev adds that "Stalin was convinced that all this was necessary for the defence of the interests of the working class against the plotting of the enemies and against the attack of the imperialist camp." When he surmised that even those who stood closest to him did not share his phobias and suspicions, Stalin wrung his hands in despair: "What will you do without me?" he growled. "You are all blind like chicken!" "He saw this," Khrushchev assures the congress again, "from the position of the interest of the working class . . . of socialism and communism. We cannot say that these were the deeds of a giddy despot. . . . In this lies the whole tragedy!"

Yet the mainspring of the tragedy remains hidden from Khrushchev. His whole speech is full of the denunciation of the hero cult; yet it is nothing but inverted hero cult. Its one and only theme is the power, the superhuman power, of the usurper who "placed himself above the party and above the masses." In passage after passage Khrushchev argues that all the evil from which the Communist Party, the Soviet people, and the international labor movement have suffered for so long sprang from this one "individual." And then he tells us in quite as many passages that it is utterly wrong to imagine that one man could exercise so much influence on history, for the real makers of Soviet history have been the masses, the people, and the "militant Bolshevik Party" bred and inspired by Lenin.

Where then was that "militant party" when Stalin "placed himself above it"? Where was its militancy and its Leninist spirit? Why and how could the despot impose his will on the masses? And why did "our heroic people" submit so passively?

All these questions, which have so close a bearing on the Marxist *Weltanschauung*, Khrushchev leaves unanswered. Yet, if one agrees that history is made not by demigods but by masses and special classes one has still to explain the rise of this particular demigod; and one can explain it only from the condition of Soviet society, the interests of the Bolshevik Party, and the state of mind of its leadership. But no sooner have we descended with Khrushchev to this depth of recent Soviet history than his lamp is blown out, and we are once again enveloped by dark and impenetrable fumes.

The political evolution of the Soviet regime falls broadly into three chapters. In the first the Bolsheviks under Lenin established their monopoly of power, the single-party system, in which they saw the only way to preserve their government and to safeguard the October Revolution against domestic and foreign foes. But having suppressed all other parties, the Bolshevik Party itself split into several factions which confronted one another in utter hostility. The single-party system turned out to be a contradiction in terms: the single party was breaking up into at least three parties.

In the second chapter the rule of the single party was replaced by the rule of a single Bolshevik faction, the one led by Stalin. The principle of the "monolithic" party was proclaimed. Only a party which does not permit diverse currents of opinion to emerge in its midst, Stalin argued, can safeguard its monopoly of power. However, the rule of the single faction also proved to be chimerical. Once it had gained complete mastery, the victorious faction, like the victorious party before it, was torn by internal rivalries and divisions.

In the third and final chapter the rule of the single faction gives way to the rule of the single leader, who by the nature of the whole process had to be intolerant of any potential challenge to his authority, constantly on his guard, constantly suspicious, and constantly bent on enforcing his will. The monopoly of power reached its culmination.

The Bolshevik Party, while it was suppressing all other parties, up to the year 1921, was still innerly free and democratically ruled. But having deprived others of freedom, it could not help losing its own freedom. The same then happens to the Stalinist faction. Between 1923 and 1930 it destroyed "inner party democracy" for its opponents; but it was itself still more or less democratically ruled. In the end, however, it had to surrender all its freedom to its own leader.

From stage to stage the monopoly of power grew ever narrower. The narrower it was, the more fiercely and the more unscrupulously it had to be defended, and the fewer and the weaker were the inhibitions and restraining influences. The early Bolsheviks cherished controversy in their own ranks too much to be able to enforce the ban on controversy outside their ranks by anything like the Stalinist violence. Even the Stalinist faction, before it succumbed to Stalin, only expelled its opponents and exiled them; it could not even contemplate the bloody *dénouement* of the great purge trials. Stalin had to suppress his own faction before he could stage the holocaust.

Each phase of this evolution followed inexorably from the preceding one: the rule of the single leader from that of the single faction, and the rule of the single faction from that of the single party. What gave to the whole development its momentum and its convulsive and cruel character were the

social tensions in a nation which was first ruined and fam-
ished after seven years of war, revolution, and civil war, and
which was then rushed through forced industrialization and
collectivization and drawn into devastating war and armament races, all calling for heavy sacrifice, rigid discipline,
and massive coercion, and all providing Stalin with the justifications and pretexts for his use and abuse of the monopoly
of power.

Stalin did not, thus, appear as a *diabolus ex machina*. Yet
it is as a *diabolus ex machina* that Khrushchev presents him.
It is not difficult to grasp why he views Stalin in this way.
Khrushchev and his colleagues represent the Stalinist faction, or, rather, what has remained of it more than twenty
years after its suppression. This is a different faction from
that of twenty years ago. It rules a different country—the
world's second industrial power. It leads a different "socialist camp"—a camp containing one-third of mankind. It is
richer in experience and in dearly bought insights. It is
anxious to understand what has happened to it, and it
is probing restlessly into its own mysterious past. But this
is still the Stalinist faction, trying to grind its old ax and
caught up in the tangle of its own experiences and of its
traditional but now untenable viewpoints.

Khrushchev has described how the members of the Presidium, the men who rule the Soviet Union and manage its
vast, nationalized economy (the world's greatest single industrial concern!) spend their days and weeks poring over
the archives of the N.K.V.D., questioning the officials, who
once conducted purges and extracted confessions, and re-
living in their thoughts the long nightmare of the past. Yet
the understanding of which the members of this Presidium,
especially the older ones, are capable, has its historically
formed limitations, which they cannot easily transcend. They
cannot see where and why things had "gone wrong." They
would like to cross out, if this were possible, the last chapter
of their story, the one in which Stalin oppressed and "be-

trayed" his own followers. They would still like to think that what was done in the earlier chapters was justified and beneficial and need not have led to the final debacle and shame.

They denounce after the event the rule of the single leader but see nothing wrong in the rule of the single faction, which in its turn was rooted in the rule of the single party. They would like to remain Stalinists without and against Stalin, and to recapture the spirit of the "sane" and "innocent" Stalinism of the 1920's, of that Stalinism which had not yet soaked its hands in the blood of the Old Bolshevik Guard and in the blood of masses of peasants and workers. They do not realize that the latter-day "insane" Stalinism had sprung from the earlier "sane" Stalinism; and that it was not only Stalin's whimsical and cruel character that was responsible for it.

This approach governs all of Khrushchev's reasoning. It dictates the range and the nature of his disclosures. Because Khrushchev pleads the case of the old Stalinist faction "betrayed" by Stalin, his evidence against Stalin shows huge gaps and is all too often ambiguous, despite the bluntness of the language he uses and the shocking character of the facts he relates.

Khrushchev builds his case against Stalin on three sets of facts: on Lenin's denunciation, in his testament, of Stalin's "rudeness and disloyalty"; on Stalin's role in the purges; and on the faults of Stalin's leadership in the war. Under each count of the indictment he treats the facts selectively so as to turn the evidence against Stalin rather than against the Stalinist faction.

He conjures up Lenin's ghost, because only with this ally at his side can he, after thirty years of Stalin worship, hope to lay Stalin's ghost. He quotes from Lenin's testament the passages aimed directly against Stalin, but he passes over in silence all that Lenin said in favor of Trotsky and Bukharin. He assures us that he now views "objectively and with de-

tachment" the old party feuds, but he still labels Trotsky and
Bukharin "enemies of Leninism," although they are no
longer "enemies of the people." In the light of Lenin's testament, Trotskyism and Bukharinism may be seen as offsprings
of Leninism at least as legitimate as even the early Stalinism.
The testament was therefore at first not published in Russia
—it was only distributed to the delegates at the Twentieth
Congress.[4] And even in his secret speech Khrushchev is
afraid of making too extensive use of it.

Even more eloquent are the gaps in Khrushchev's story of
the purges. He begins with dark hints about the assassination of Kirov in 1934, the event which set in motion the
avalanche of the terror. He alludes to Stalin's connivance at
the crime but adds that nothing is certain; and he leaves the
mystery as deep as ever. Then he gives a more or less detailed and horrifying account of the secret purges of Eikhe,
Postyshev, Kossior, Chubar, Mezhlauk, and Rudzutak, who
perished between 1937 and 1940, and of the purge of
Voznessensky in 1951. But he has nothing explicit to say
about the purge trials of 1936-1938, which shocked the
world and in which the defendants were men of world fame,
the recognized leaders of Bolshevism, of the Red Army, of
Soviet diplomacy, and of the Communist International. He
reveals nothing of the inner story of the purges of Zinoviev,
Kamenev, Bukharin, Radek, Rakovsky, Pyatakov, Tukhachevsky. He is silent on Trotsky's assassination which was
instigated by Stalin and Beria. Eikhe, Postyshev, and Chubar were by comparison insignificant figures: their names
meant little or nothing not only to the outside world, but
even to the young Soviet generation. But they were men
of the Stalinist faction; and through Khrushchev the faction
honors in them its martyrs.

That the Stalinist faction should rehabilitate its men,
that it should pay tribute to its martyrs and that it should
show up the cup of misery which its own leader made it

---

[4] It has since been published in *Komunist*.

drain is understandable. Only the meanest of its enemies can give themselves to *Schadenfreude* over this spectacle, or make light of the tragic note which reverberates through Khrushchev's speech. Khrushchev has revealed the enormity of the pogrom which Stalin inflicted on his own followers. Not for nothing did he dwell so much on the fortunes of the delegates to the Seventeenth Congress, which was held in 1934.] At that assembly the Stalinist faction celebrated its final triumph over all its adversaries, and in party annals the congress is referred to as the "Victors' Congress." Of nearly 2,000 of those "victors," delegates present at the congress, about 60 per cent were, according to Khrushchev, "arrested on charges of counterrevolutionary crimes (mostly in 1937-38)." Of the 139 members of the Central Committee then elected "98 persons, i.e. 70 per cent, were arrested and shot (mostly in 1937-38)." Thus, in those years alone Stalin annihilated 60 per cent to 70 per cent of the leading cadres of his own faction; and there were uncounted victims among the rank and file.

Public opinion outside Russia has in recent years been aware of the fate of the anti-Stalinist victims of the terror. It is only right that it should also be aware of the fate of the Stalinist victims. But do not Khrushchev and his associates feel the indecency of their exclusive concentration on their own Stalinist martyrs? Do they really think that a Trotsky, a Zinoviev, a Bukharin, a Tukhachevsky, or a Rakovsky, not to speak of others, will be forgotten while an Eikhe and a Postyshev are not?

Throughout Khrushchev's indictment of Stalin runs the motif of self-exculpation. We feel as if we had sat in court and listened to a counsel for the prosecution who, while heaping accusations on the man in the dock, must remember all the time that he has also to prove that he, the prosecutor, and his friends, have had no share in the defendant's crimes. We readily believe in the defendant's guilt, but we wonder whether the prosecutor has not gone too far in self-exculpation. We even feel a sneaking suspicion that in order to exonerate himself he may have painted, here and there, the defendant's character just a shade too black.

"Everything depended on the wilfulness of one man," Khrushchev repeats again and again. But if so, "comrades may ask us: where were the members of the Political Bureau . . . ? Why did they not assert themselves . . . why is this being done only now?" These Whys buzz in Khrushchev's ear like hateful wasps, and somewhat angrily he tries to chase them away. Unwittingly he only demonstrates that much more was at play than the "wilfulness of one man." Stalin had so much scope for his willfulness only because Khrushchev and his like acknowledged him as their leader and accepted his will.

Khrushchev recalls how at first they all trusted Stalin and zealously followed him in the struggle against the other Bolshevik factions until they made him so powerful that they themselves became powerless. He shows that even when they might have been able to act against him they did not wish to act. He relates that in 1941, when the Red Army reeled under Hitler's first onslaught, Stalin's nerve snapped; he was despondent and sulked in his tent. It might seem that this was an opportunity for the party leaders to get rid of him. Instead they sent a deputation to Stalin to beg him to seize the reins again; and so they condemned themselves and the country to another twelve years of terror and degradation. None of them had the confidence and courage of Trotsky, who as early as 1927 foresaw such a turn of events and said (in his famous "Clemenceau Thesis") that in such a crisis it would be the duty of party leaders to overthrow Stalin in order to wage war more efficiently and to a victorious conclusion.

The Politbureau of 1941 was afraid that a change of leadership in the middle of war would produce too dangerous a shock to morale; and it rallied to its oppressor. It should be noted that this was not the first situation of this kind. In exactly the same way the Politbureau had hoisted a dejected and sulking Stalin back into the saddle nine years earlier, at the height of collectivization. In every major emergency the Politbureau felt the need of the "strong arm," and it turned to Stalin only to groan under his strong arm years thereafter. They had puffed up his authority sky high and so in a crisis they felt that they had not enough authority to take his place. As the history of the Soviet Union was one sequence of emergencies and crises, the Stalinist faction was all the time in an impasse, from which it was unable to get out even if for so many of its leaders and members the impasse was the grave.

The question inevitably arises whether during all those years no members of the ruling group made any attempt to destroy the incubus. It would have been unnatural if no plots at all had been hatched against Stalin in his own entourage. If Khrushchev and his colleagues really thought that "it all depended on the wilfulness of one man" (which Trotsky, Zinoviev, and Kamenev never thought), might not some of them have concluded that the way out was to eliminate that one man? Khrushchev tells us that Postyshev, Rudzutak, and other leading Stalinists did indeed come into opposition to Stalin. But here, too, he leaves many things unsaid; and so the full story of the Stalinist opposition to Stalin remains to be disclosed.

The historian finds a further contradiction in Khrushchev's testimony, one which it has in common with Trotsky's appraisal of Stalin, although in Khrushchev the contradiction is, of course, far cruder. Khrushchev stresses the achievements as well as the failures of the Stalin era. For the achievements—industrial advance, educational progress, planned economy, victory in war—he praises the masses, the people, the party, the Leninist doctrine, and even the Central Committee, the cowed and docile Central Committee of the Stalin era! For the failures he blames Stalin alone. This distribution of praise and blame is too neat to be convincing.

That Stalin's personal contribution to the black sides of Soviet life was exceptionally heavy goes without saying. But surely the backwardness and apathy of the masses and the stupidity and blindness in the party also had something to do with the failures?

If the qualities of one man were responsible, say, for the Soviet military disasters of 1941-1942, were they not also in some measure responsible for the victories of 1943-1945? If all major decisions on policy and strategy were taken by Stalin alone, as Khrushchev says, then it is at least illogical to deny Stalin all credit for the results.

At times Khrushchev's argument savored of Tolstoy: in *War and Peace* Tolstoy argues that all ideas, plans, and decisions conceived by emperors, generals, and "great men" are meaningless and worthless; and that only the innumerable, spontaneous, and uncoordinated actions of nameless masses of people shape history. But Tolstoy is consistent: he attributes to "great men" no special influence on history, for evil any more than for good, whereas the present Soviet ruling group seems to play heads-I-win-tails-you-lose with Stalin's ghost.

As a reaction against the Stalin cult this is inevitable and perhaps even healthy. Not the first time in history is an orgy of iconolatry followed by a bout of iconoclasm. In a sense the man who smashes his idol stands above the one who prostrates himself before it; his understanding comes closer to truth. Yet his is still only a negative and limited understanding. The higher comprehension of her past which post-Stalinist Russia has yet to reach will surely transcend both iconolatry and iconoclasm.

No matter how vigorously Khrushchev pleads the alibi for himself and the present ruling group, he proves a semi-alibi only. This particular prosecutor cannot convince us that he has not been the defendant's accomplice—at best he persuades us that he was an accomplice under duress. He

speaks of Beria as that "villain who climbed up the government ladder over an untold number of corpses." How true!
But was Beria alone? Who of those who mounted the ladder
of government under Stalin did not climb over his comrades'
corpses? One wonders whether Beria, if he had been given
the benefit of a public trial, would not have used in self-de-
fense the same arguments that Khrushchev uses. Did he not
use them at the secret trial?

However, we need not go so far. Khrushchev describes
with horror the character of a former official who took part in
preparing the purges of 1937-1938 and in extracting confessions—the official was brought before the Presidium and
questioned. He is, says Khrushchev, "a vile person, with
the brain of a bird, and morally completely degenerate."
Again, we need not doubt the truth of the description: the
man's qualities evidently suited his function. But what does
this repulsive character claim in his defense? His plea, as
reported by Khrushchev, is that he acted on higher orders
which he understood it to be his duty as a party member to
carry out; and that he could do nothing else. Khrushchev
indignantly rejects this apology as worthless. Yet almost in
the same breath he uses the same apology for himself and
the other members of the Politbureau: Under Stalin, he
says, "no one could express his will."

The tragedy of contemporary Russia is that the whole
"elite" of the nation, its intelligentsia, its civil service, and
all its politically minded elements share in one degree or another in Stalin's guilt. Probably no one in Moscow who
would set himself up today as Stalin's accuser and judge
could prove his own alibi. Stalin made of the whole nation,
at any rate of all its educated and active elements, his accomplices. Those who refused to do his bidding perished, with
very, very few exceptions, long ago.

This is the unpropitious background against which de-
Stalinization is now carried out. That it is being carried out
at all shows to what extent it has become a national necessity

for the Soviet Union. But the initiators and the agents of de-Stalinization are themselves inevitably tainted with Stalinism—no other human material is or can immediately be available. To paraphrase a famous Bolshevik saying, the edifice of post-Stalinist society has to be built with the bricks left over from Stalinist Russia.

Whatever is said against Khrushchev and his associates, the blow he has struck against Stalinism is much more than a tactical maneuver, and much more than the move of a dictator anxious to elevate himself at his predecessor's expense. Khrushchev has exposed not only Stalin but Stalinism, not only the man but his method of government; and this renders the continuation or revival of the method nearly impossible. He set out to state only the case of the Stalinist faction against Stalin; and he has destroyed the case of the Stalinist faction. He has, after all, been unable to confine himself to the rehabilitation of the Stalinists only. The logic of his argument led him to rehabilitate, reluctantly and half-heartedly, the martyrs of anti-Stalinism as well. He read out Lenin's and Krupskaya's letters from which the party learned that not Stalin and Molotov but Kamenev and Zinoviev (whom Khrushchev himself had described as "enemies of the people" only a few days earlier) were the men who had stood closest to the founder of Bolshevism. He added that if the party had managed its affairs in the Leninist and not in the Stalinist manner, it would have worked tolerantly with those "enemies of the people," even if it disagreed with them.

These were not just bygones. Nor was Khrushchev merely crying over spilled blood. Willy-nilly, he has exploded the idea of the monolithic party and of the monolithic state in which all must think alike. In terms of a historical revision he has proclaimed a new principle legalizing a plurality of views, differences of opinion, and controversy. He further justified and enhanced this new attitude by rejecting emphatically Stalin's theory which had served as the

moral excuse for government by terror, the theory that as
Russia advances along the road to socialism class conflicts
grow sharper and "class enemies" become more dangerous.
Against this, Khrushchev insisted that the class conflicts
grow milder, and the class enemies become fewer, less malignant, and less offensive; and that there was no need therefore to fight them in the manner in which they have been
fought hitherto.

In acclaiming this view the Twentieth Congress has shattered the system of terroristic rule bequeathed by Stalin. It
has also given a new impulse to the reversal of the trend
that had led from the single party to the single leader, and
from the monopoly of power to the monopoly of thought.

Having produced the shock, Khrushchev is anxious to
soften its impact. "We cannot let this matter get out of the
party, especially not to the press," he warned his listeners.
"It is for this reason that we are considering it here at a
closed Congress session. We should know the limits; we
should not give ammunition to the enemy; we should not
wash our dirty linen before their eyes."

It was, however, hardly of the anti-Communist world, the
"enemy," that Khrushchev and the other party leaders were
afraid in this case. One may even suspect that the indiscre-
tion which has allowed the State Department to act as
Khrushchev's first publisher, was not unwelcome to Moscow.
It is from the mass of the Soviet people that his speech has
been kept secret so far. To them the truth is conveyed only
in carefully weighed and carefully graded doses.

It may be that the Soviet people would have reacted
nervously or even morbidly to this awakening from the Stalin
era, if it had been too rude. But it is just as possible that they
would have shown the gratitude which people usually feel
when they are awakened from a nightmare—and the ruder
the awakening from a nightmare the better. However, an
outsider cannot easily appraise the position in the Soviet
Union. It may be that those in charge of this difficult

and salutary operation judge the psychology of their own people correctly.

All the same, the "washing of the dirty linen" can hardly be carried on behind the back of the Soviet people much longer. It will presently have to be done in front of them and in broad daylight. It is, after all, in their sweat and blood that the "dirty linen" was soaked. And the washing, which will take a long time, will perhaps be brought to an end by hands other than those that have begun it—by younger and cleaner hands.

3. Post-Stalinist Ferment of Ideas [1]

The ferment of ideas in Russia which has come to the surface since Stalin's death continues to develop. For more than a year the Russian intelligentsia have been plunged in a controversy, the like of which they had not known for nearly a quarter of a century. Scientists, men of letters, artists, educationists, all have argued the issues which preoccupy them; and they have sometimes done this with a zest which shows them to be, after all, the descendants of the old Russian revolutionary intelligentsia. Behind the controversy there have been attempts, some audacious and others timid, at a "transvaluation of the values" inherited from the Stalin era.

It is in this triumph, be it even temporary, of controversy over conformity that Russia's break with the Stalin era may be seen most clearly at present. This is no more a matter of calculated mechanical moves made by party bosses, politicians, and diplomats, moves of which it may still be said that they point to no significant change in the political framework or the social background of the Soviet Union. When some of the accepted standards of thought and behavior and some of the sacrosanct axioms of Stalinism are emphatically and even vehemently questioned by scientists, authors, artists, and even party spokesmen, when the whole of the Russian intelligentsia are engaged in restless and dangerous

[1] A shortened version of this essay appeared in *The London Times* in November 1954 and gave rise to a considerable controversy in its correspondence columns.

heart-searching, it is no longer possible to doubt that the urge for change and reform is strongly at work; and only those who know little about Russia's history can still argue that the intellectual ferment has little or no bearing on Russia's practical politics.

What could be heard in all the recent debates has been a protest of the Soviet intelligentsia against the mental sterility and mediocrity to which Stalinism has condemned them. Economists have vented their resentment at an orthodoxy under which they were reduced to the role of Stalin's gramophone records. Biologists have reacted against the humiliation they had suffered at Lysenko's hands. Physicists have declared that they have had enough of the chauvinistic Great Russian swank, which was *en vogue* until recently, and of isolation from Western science. Painters and sculptors have revolted against that "socialist realism" which has compelled them to dress, in shoddy style, Stalin and his entourage as demigods. Novelists and poets have expressed disgust at the patterns into which thought control had sought to constrict their creative imagination, at the compulsion to produce dramas without real conflict, novels without living people, and lyrical poetry without genuine feeling. "We have had enough of your Stalin Prizes and of the fantastic fees and of privileges corrupting us and our minds," some of them have cried out publicly. The youth of Russia, the students of the universities of Moscow, Leningrad, and Kiev, have rebelled against the hypocrisy and rigid formalism of the Stalin cult. Two generations have joined hands in this movement: old people who have borne the burden of Stalinist orthodoxy in fear and meekness during the greater part of their lives; and the young ones who are straining to throw off that burden at the threshold of adult life. Even in the concentration camps in the polar regions, if recent ex-inmates are to be believed, the deportees have formed themselves into distinct groups, produced their political programs and blueprints for the future, and argued among themselves, something they had not done in the course of about twenty years.

The attitude of Stalin's successors towards these developments is equivocal. Two souls seem to dwell in the breast of the Malenkov government. It was that government itself which initiated the present heart-searching when it buried the Stalin cult together with Stalin, when it ordered party propagandists to launch the attack against the "un-Marxist cult of the single leader," when it intimated to the people that the time had come to do away with the totems and taboos of the Stalin era, when it threw into dramatic relief Stalin's failures in various fields of policy, and when it thrust open the heavy gates of the Kremlin to the man in the street and to the youth of Russia. The intelligentsia have taken all these gestures and hints as a promise of a new era, an encouragement and a challenge to their thought, courage, and dignity. Not for nothing did Ilya Ehrenburg call his new and controversial novel *The Thaw*.

Stalin's closest associates and successors were indeed the first to break the ice. But soon they began to wonder in perplexity whither the drifting floes might not carry them. They had done away with the Stalin cult, by which they themselves had been oppressed, with a sigh of relief but also with mental reservations. Malenkov, Khrushchev, and Molotov, not to speak of Beria, had owed their positions of power to Stalin. In varying degrees they had all been his accomplices. A frank and a radical disavowal of Stalinism would threaten to bring discredit upon their own heads. They cannot allow the Soviet people to know the full truth about the Stalin era. They cannot drag the corpse of their Master through the mud and at the same time save their own faces. Having at first quietly abandoned the cult, they could not then but seek to salve its wreckage. Having sneaked away from Stalinist orthodoxy, they cannot but try to sneak back to it.

Their dilemma is not, however, determined by these considerations alone. There are in the Stalinist heritage important elements which no Communist government could renounce, not even one consisting of men altogether untainted by Stalinism, if such a government were possible. Moreover, no anti-Communist government could renounce them either. None could dismantle the planned economy set up under Stalin, or allow the peasants to leave *en masse* the collective farms and restore smallholdings, without condemning Russia to chaos, misery, and famine (as this writer has argued in greater detail in one of his recent books). Stalin's successors are, of course, explicitly committed to preserve and develop these elements of the Stalinist heritage.

Here is the deeper source of most of their dilemmas. The present social structure of the Soviet Union is already established too firmly to be undone, but not yet firmly enough to function altogether of its own accord, without coercion from above. It no longer needs for its survival all the totalitarian discipline by which it was set up, but it cannot altogether dispense with that discipline. Malenkov's government has tried to find, by trial and error, a new balance between coercion and persuasion. It has relaxed the Stalinist discipline, but it watches anxiously to see whether the discontents and ferments released thereby are not growing into a menace to both the structure of society and the position of the ruling group. The controversy in the ranks of the intelligentsia and the official reactions to it are symptomatic of this complex situation.

The road back to Stalinist orthodoxy and discipline is barred, because that orthodoxy and discipline belong to an epoch which has come to a close. They fitted an essentially primitive, preindustrial society engaged in feverish industrialization and collectivization. They resulted from the attempt to impose on the Russia of *muzhiks* an ideal and a way of life for which that Russia was not prepared, either materially or mentally. The primitive magic of Stalinism, the deification of the Leader, and the bizarre and elaborate ritu-

als of Stalinism had all sprung from Russian backwardness
and all served to tame that backwardness. Since the vast and
swift transformation of the whole social outlook of Russia,
undertaken by Stalin, was not based on the will and understanding of the people, its origin had to be traced to the superhuman wisdom and will of the Leader. Opposition was
branded as the Devil's work, especially when it was inspired
by the Marxist tradition which was irreconcilable with the
cult of the Leader and the primitive magic. Throughout the
Stalin era the rulers, the ideologists, and the policemen, too,
were constantly engaged in turning the modern conceptions
of Marxism into the idiom of primitive magic and in trans-
lating the do's and don't's of that magic into the vocabulary
of Marxism.

After decades of this ideological diet, the Soviet intelligentsia are visibly suffering from moral nausea. This is a
very different intelligentsia from that which witnessed Stalin's ascendancy. Their background is not the inert and helpless Russia of the *muzhik* but the second industrial power
of the world which has reached the threshold of the atomic
age almost simultaneously with the United States. To be
sure, much of the old primitivism and barbarism remains
embedded in Russian life. But while the old intelligentsia
suffered acutely from the discrepancy between their own
intellectual progress and the nation's poverty and backwardness, the present generation of the intelligentsia suffers even
more acutely from the contrast between the nation's material
progress and the backwardness of its spiritual climate.

This state of affairs concerns Soviet society as a whole, not
merely the intelligentsia. The working of the national economy, the functioning of social institutions, and the efficiency
of administration are affected by it no less than academic
life, literature, and the arts. The monolithic thought-
control, which Stalinism had used to force through industrialization and collectivization and to make Soviet society
accept all the attendant miseries, has now become a formida-

ble obstacle to further progress in technology, government, and social organization. Having for decades lived under its own (triumphant!) brand of McCarthyism with its loyalty tests, charges of un-Bolshevik activities, witch hunts and purges, terroristic suspicion and suspicious terrorism, Soviet society is now driven by self-preservation to try to regain initiative and freedom of decision and action. Too many of its public men, civil servants, scientists, intellectuals, and workers have become cowed and intimidated creatures devoid of creative aspiration and ambition. What is surprising under the circumstances is not Russia's failures but Russia's achievements in so many fields. It is a fact that not long ago some of Russia's best aircraft constructors, for instance, designed their best engines in prison cells and places of exile; and their lot was almost symbolical for the condition under which Russia's creative energies sought to assert themselves under Stalinism.

But a modern industrial nation cannot allow its creative energies to be so constricted, unless it is prepared to pay the penalty of ultimate stagnation. The more a nation is technologically advanced the greater is the danger, because its very existence depends on the freedom of its technologists and administrators to exercise their abilities and judgment. The needs of Russia's development are now in a much more direct and dramatic conflict with the Stalinist magic than ever before. The aircraft designers must be let out of the prisons, literally and metaphorically, if Russian aircraft design is to meet the demands which the international armament race, to mention only this, makes on it. The biologists have to be allowed freedom of research if farming is to make good its long lag behind the rest of the economy. Industrial managers must be released from the fetters of that Stalinist supercentralism which was still tolerable on a lower and less complex level of industrialization, when the Politbureau could still have some insight into the affairs of every major industrial concern and settle them by its fiat.

Nor can the mass of skilled industrial workers be kept in a condition of semiserfdom if the efficiency of their labor is to rise. And, last but not least, authors, artists, and journalists must be unmuzzled if the moral gulf between the rulers and the ruled is to be bridged or narrowed. This is why Stalin's successors cannot easily go on enforcing the old discipline, no matter how much they may be afraid of the consequences of relaxation.

The twists and turns of their policy are reflected in the recent fortunes of the Stalin cult. For months after Stalin had died his name was not mentioned publicly. The silence about him could not have been deeper if he had died a hundred years earlier; and its meaning was underlined by the emphatic denunciations of the "un-Marxist cult of the single leader."

But there was something unreal and awkward in that silence. There was in it a sense of tension and embarrassment which came from the fact that the new skeleton in the Soviet cupboard was the omnipresent deity of yesterday. After a lapse of time Stalin began to be mentioned once again, as if casually, by the propagandists. Discreet reminders followed of his merits so quickly forgotten. Then he was stealthily half-restored to the apostolic succession of Marx-Engels-Lenin. Even now, however, the place accorded to him in the historical retrospects, which are constantly drawn and redrawn and retouched, is not more than a modest footnote to the epic story of Lenin, the revolution, and the Soviet State. Salvaged from the refuse heap, soiled and defaced, Stalin's figure has been granted a new but rather meager allowance of ideological respectability. These posthumous vicissitudes of the Stalin cult, so comic to the outsider, are gravely portentous to the Soviet citizen to whom they indicate how far he is, or is not, allowed to drift away from the old orthodoxy and discipline.[2]

2 Readers will remember that this was written in 1954, three years before Khrushchev's denunciation and subsequent "rehabilitation" of Stalin. The

The debunking of Stalinism is now evidently under a ban. But quietly the departure from Stalinism continues in many fields. Where orthodoxy hampers technological progress and economic efficiency, the canons of Stalinism are being jettisoned without much ado. At the same time the reaction against Stalinism is being curbed and discouraged in those fields where it may directly impinge upon the political stability of the regime. But it is not easy to draw a line between social efficiency and political expediency, because often their requirements conflict with one another.

Perhaps the most important reform has just been decreed in education. Not only has the Stalin cult, which has clogged all processes of education, been played down. The educational system is in addition being freed from the grip of authoritarianism, and pedagogy is encouraged to take up again those experimental and more libertarian conceptions which animated the Soviet school in the early years of the Soviet regime. Under Stalin the educational system gave the pupil, apart from technical training and *Politgramota* ("political literacy") the habits of unquestioning obedience. The relation of teacher to pupil was one of old-fashioned paternalism, a reflection of Stalin's own paternalistic attitude towards "his" people. Austere classroom discipline, obligatory uniforms, a multiplicity of severe and highly formal examinations had made the Stalinist school almost indistinguishable, in the manner and style of the teaching, from the school and seminary of the Czarist era. Coeducation was, of course, frowned upon and eventually forbidden. The ghost of Pobedonostsev, the famous reactionary ideologue, seemed to stalk the schoolrooms and smile with malignant contentment.

Under the new reform coeducation has been rehabilitated and reintroduced. The curriculum has been broadened and made less rigid. The number of examinations is substan-

pattern has remained the same; but it is more distinct in 1957 than it was in 1954.

tially reduced, and school discipline is to be less formal. The paternalistic system is giving place to one in which more emphasis is placed on the formation in the pupil of an independent mind and character. And, after an interval of nearly a quarter of a century, the Soviet school is now resuming the experiment in "polytechnical education," which aims at bringing the classroom close to the industrial workshop and the farm, and at combining brainwork with manual labor. When the experiment was tried out in the early years of the Soviet regime it failed in part because "polytechnical" education requires for its success a highly modern industrial background and environment which was still lacking. In addition Stalin viewed the polytechnical school with suspicion and hostility because of its modernistic and antiauthoritarian outlook. Post-Stalin Russia needs an educational system more modern and free than that bequeathed by Stalinism; and even though such a system may become the breeding ground of political ferment, the dictates of efficiency seem to have prevailed in this case over those of political expediency.

Changes are also introduced in "inner party education," that is in the methods by which the collective mind of the party is shaped. Stalinist techniques of indoctrination are being partly abandoned in favor of a more sober and open-minded propagation of pristine Marxism-Leninism, as Stalin's successors understand it. To people in the West, inclined to lump together all these *isms*, the difference may seem too subtle to be of practical political significance. To Soviet citizens, however, the idea of a restoration of original Marxism-Leninism has a peculiar appeal, comparable perhaps to that which the Protestant rediscovery of the Bible once had to Western Europeans surfeited with the scholasticism of medieval theology. During the Stalin era an "exaggerated" devotion to Marx and Lenin tended to mark a party member as a heretic. The Marxist classics were read, as a rule, in predigested excerpts and under the guidance of official commentators. During the great purges of the 1930's Stalin even issued a formal ban on the "individual" study of Marx by party members. The reading of Marx's works was allowed only within the party's study circles; and attendance at those circles was compulsory for party members. Stalin felt that the individual study of Marxist classics induced in the student an attitude of independent inquiry critical of accepted truths; and he devised rules of party indoctrination which left the member with no time and opportunity for brooding over the texts and drawing his own conclusions. Marx had "sown dragons"; and Stalin needed sheep.

Stalin's successors can hardly wish to raise a new breed of dragons; but they have not much use for the Stalinist sheep either. Compulsory indoctrination through party cells and study circles is abolished—attendance at those circles is henceforth optional. Party members are allowed and encouraged to study Marxist literature and party history in private. An all-round attempt is made to free "ideological training" from canonical rigidity and to impart to it a somewhat more modern and businesslike style, although it is extremely difficult to eradicate from the party's mind (including the mind of its instructors) the ecclesiastical stamp which Stalinism had left on it.

The new outlook has been most remarkable in academic life, especially in those branches of science the teaching of which has the most direct bearing on economic efficiency. Already the appointment last year of G. Alexandrov to the post of Minister of Culture augured a new departure. At the height of the Zhdanov period Alexandrov had been dismissed from his post as the chief officer for ideological instruction and he remained eclipsed till the end of the Stalin era. In his *History of Philosophy* he had allegedly sinned with "objectivism" and "kowtowing" before Western philosophy. In truth, his *History* was written well within the party tradition, but as an academic textbook it baldly but objectively, without the admixture of much polemical invective, outlined the main trends of classical and modern philosophy. This was an unpardonable offense only a short time ago. Alexandrov's appointment to the Ministry of Culture foreshadowed therefore encouragement for conscientious academic inquiry, a break with the glorification of all things Russian, and also a sound reappraisal of the achievements of Western science.

The reappraisal has since found its expression in a series of debates on the fundamentals of philosophy and science which are still in progress in all Soviet seats of learning, and in the scholarly periodicals, from where the controversy has overspilled into the national press. Recently, for instance, an eminent academician, Professor S. L. Sobolev, surveyed in *Pravda* the problems of Russian academic life in terms which amounted to a severe indictment of the Stalin era and to a fervent plea for the restoration of intellectual integrity. The glorification of all things Russian and the drive against "kowtowing before the West" had, according to Sobolev, led Soviet academic bodies to "ignore the new physics" developed in the West. Sobolev castigated the obscurantist attitude prevalent until recently toward the work of Einstein, for which Lenin had shown high respect and intense interest, regardless of Einstein's "naïvety in matters of pure philosophy." Ridiculing the attempts to "annihilate the theory of relativity" Sobolev writes: "To us are dear also the names of the scientists of all countries. . . ." "The most interesting discoveries . . . are always connected with the renunciation of pre-conceived ideas and with the audacious breaking of old norms and notions." "The clash of opinions and freedom of criticism are the most important pre-requisites of scientific progress." "The dogmatic attitude, which substitutes fixed propositions for genuine research is the mortal enemy. . . . Our academic circles are still far from having lived down that attitude. . . . Some trends and works are given testimonials of political loyalty. Others . . . get the standard labels 'reactionary' or 'idealistic.' " This is only one of the very many voices which could be heard recently pleading for the abandonment of the black-and-white approach and for the revival of the art of fair and dispassionate debate.

In the course of this controversy more problems may well arise than its initiators had intended to pose. When *Pravda* readers are told that the "clash of opinions and the freedom of criticism are the most important prerequisites of the development of science" they may well reflect whether this applies to social and political sciences as well, and to politics itself. In those fields there has been almost no sign of any "clash of opinions" or freedom of criticism. True, the political outlook, too, is more sober and rational than it was in Stalin's days, but it continues to be "monolithic." Stalin's successors are evidently determined to keep politics insulated from the ferment of ideas. They appeal to the party to exercise its "collective judgment," to rely on no single leader, and to revive "inner party democracy." But, like some of the characters in Tolstoy's *War and Peace* who, criticizing the Czar's policy, always instinctively stopped just at the point where they might seem to reflect on the Czar himself and on autocracy, so the party spokesmen always stop at the point where the logic of their own arguments might lead them to plead for the right of the rank and file to dissent from the policies of the leaders and to seek a change in the party leadership.

The politically minded citizen finds, however, a sort of a substitute for political controversy in recent literary debates. Something like an explosion of discontent occurred in literary circles soon after Stalin's death. The distance between literature and politics is, and has always been, extremely short in Russia, where art for art's sake has never found much response. Russians have always expected their novelists, and poets, and literary critics to act as their social conscience and to produce the political message of their time.

Only very few of the great writers have failed to meet that expectation. Pushkin, Tolstoy, Dostoevsky, Gorky, not to speak of such writers as Byelinsky or Chernyshevsky, each was something of a political institution in his days. On the other hand, many of the leaders of the revolutionary movements were men of letters. When Trotsky was once asked why Soviet Russia had no literary critic of the caliber of a Byelinsky, he answered that the new Byelinskys sat on the Politbureau and had not enough time for literary pursuits. Stalin expelled the Byelinskys from the Politbureau and from literature; and he exterminated them. But Trotsky's observation was essentially correct: the Russian man of letters is potentially a political spokesman; and any ferment of ideas in literature affects contagiously the political atmosphere in the country.

Let us now survey briefly the issues that have stood in the center of the literary debates and consider their significance.

To outsiders it may appear odd that the debates reached the highest pitch of political passion when one literary critic, V. Pomerantsev, published an essay saying that the test by which a work of literature must be judged is whether it expresses a *sincere* emotion or not. To treat sincerity as the criterion of artistic value is hardly a new or a very sophisticated idea. An essay like Pomerantsev's would scarcely have given rise to a *cause célèbre* outside Russia. But in Russia this exaltation of sincerity has had the effect of a bombshell. After the terrified hush-hush of so many years, Russia's political acoustics have become very sensitive, so that now even fairly innocent words may sound like a call to revolt. Implicitly, Pomerantsev has denounced the literary output of the Stalin era as a product of hypocrisy, and this alone would have been enough to set against him multitudes of ax grinders. He has also tried to substitute the test of sincerity for the accepted tests of ideological reliability and political loyalty. Unwittingly perhaps, he suggested that for a Soviet writer to be loyal meant to be hypocritical, or, at any rate, that disloyalty may be redeemed if there is a sincere emotion behind it. This is how the party leaders have understood him, and how the reading public, too, was bound to understand him.

Pomerantsev has been silenced and denounced, although the denunciation has been couched in terms far less severe than those that were customary in Stalin's days. The party spokesmen have argued that the need for sincerity is taken for granted but that it is intolerable that the test of sincerity should be set against the tests of truth and devotion to the Communist cause. And hosts of propagandists and writers are engaged in a drive against "Pomerantsevism." Nobody who does not wish to forfeit respectability will now come out to defend that old frail lady, sincerity.

But before the drive against Pomerantsev had begun sincerity was by no means defenseless. To her rescue rushed enthusiastically the undergraduates of the universities of Moscow and the *Komsomoltsy*. They swamped the desk of the editor of the *Komsomolskaya Pravda* with letters ardently supporting Pomerantsev's "thesis"; and some of the letters got printed. For weeks the lecture halls of the universities and the clubs and locals of the *Komsomol* resounded with passionate pleas for Pomerantsev.

This seems to have been the critical point of the story. The *Komsomoltsy* protested not only against the stereotypes of the Soviet novel, its lifeless heroes, its unconvincing plots, and its "ideologically correct" happy endings. By allusion, or perhaps even directly, they also criticized the accepted conventions of political life, conventions equally artificial and equally "lacking in sincerity." They blamed the literary mirror and also the political reality it mirrored. Older people had taken the new promise of a freer era with a dose of incredulity and caution: they had burnt their fingers before. The teen-agers, on the contrary, reacted with an ardor and flamboyance by which the party leaders were taken aback. Official spokesmen have, in fact, declared that the last occasion when a similar outburst of youthful rebelliousness was witnessed in Moscow was thirty years ago when—oh, horror! —Moscow's undergraduates acclaimed Trotsky's tirades against the "degenerate" party bureaucracy. Unfortunate boys and girls! After the intellectual slump of the Stalin era a Pomerantsev was enough to kindle their enthusiasm! Yet despite its crudity, this adolescent riot will probably be remembered as a blow struck by Russia's youth at the Byzantine hypocrisy bequeathed by Stalinism.

The next controversial issue, which may also seem odd to outsiders, ostensibly concerns only the theater. Even in Stalin's day the public, the critics, the actors, and the producers had already grumbled about "the lack of real conflict" in the contemporary Soviet drama; and this lack has since come to be recognized as the main fault of the contemporary Soviet play. In the Russian theater the performance of a classical play is usually a sublime artistic festival. But the same theater is transformed into a pit of boredom the moment a contemporary play is put on the stage. Now the audience has as if risen to boo and to hiss; and the booing and hissing are echoed by the literary and theatrical periodicals.

Here again a political issue looms in the background. The theater pays the penalty of monolithic politics. No real contemporary conflict can be acted on the stage when no such conflict is permitted or admitted in life. Rather unfairly, the playwright is asked to solve a problem the solution of which lies ultimately in the hands of political leaders. The official view is still that there cannot and does not exist any antagonism between the various classes and groups of this allegedly classless society, between worker and peasant, manager and bureaucrat, party man and nonparty man, or between ruler and ruled, and young and old, not to speak of any conflict between the sexes. The monolithic regime has been designed precisely to veil and to suppress existing social antagonisms, and to keep them below the surface of the national mind. Society is not allowed to become aware of the nature of its inner conflicts, to let those conflicts run their course, or to seek consciously a solution to them. Soviet drama has thus been denied its nourishment and lifeblood, and, not surprisingly, it has been withering from pernicious anemia.

From this point the literary debate has shifted to the problem of the "positive hero" and the villain in current literature. Here again the literary debate touches the very springs of Soviet morale. Whether a literature succeeds in producing "a positive hero" and whether that hero evokes response depends, apart from the writer's power of artistic presentation, on whether the ideals and virtues embodied in the hero carry conviction with a given environment, and whether they correspond with its mood. Under dictation the literature of the Stalin era tried to portray the ruling group as the paragon of virtue; and so its characters could not be animated by genuine emotion or invested with psychological truth: they had always to move and speak and behave in accordance with the latest party resolution or government decree. As Pomerantsev put it, readers of the Soviet novel "have been deafened by the triumphant roar of tractors"; and in this roar were drowned the cries, the groans, the sighs, and the rejoicings of the human being. The "positive hero" has been an automaton driven by a false official optimism; and the present demand for a hero with genuine emotional experience is part of a revulsion against the crudity of that "optimism."

An official spokesman and laureate, Konstantin Simonov, writes in *Pravda:* "We have often shown our positive heroes in a vacuum. We have laid out with carpets the road on which they were to walk, and with our own hands we have removed from it all obstacles and have evened out all the humps and bumps. Sometimes we have taken the villains by their hands and led them off the broad road on which our positive hero was about to march. Thus we have done away with the genuine difficulties which are encountered in any struggle against evil and backwardness." The novelistic

"heroes" were, of course, modeled on the bureaucratic leaders of the Stalin era who also "moved in a vacuum," making
sure that no hurdles and no humps and bumps of opposition
were in the way.

Reacting against this, Soviet writers have recently produced a crop of novels and dramas with villains as their chief
characters. As was to be expected, the reaction took an extreme and crude form, and it has been all the more revealing
for that. As a rule, the villain is only yesterday's hero turned
inside out. More often than not he is a member of the dominant and privileged social group shown as corrupt, opportunist, and cynical. Even official critics have sometimes admitted
that the villain appears more alive and psychologically convincing than the "positive hero." Yet there is still no sign of
any "real conflict," for the villain finds no worthy antagonist
in any positive character. In a few cases the only positive
type is a survivor of the Old Guard of the revolution, once
the butt of the Stalinist satire, who is now portrayed wist-
fully as a character of moving if somewhat anachronistic
nobility and is poignantly contrasted with the young bureaucrat and careerist. This streak of nostalgia after the early
days of the revolution comes sometimes very clearly to the
surface. In one of the most hotly debated novels, *Seasons of
the Year* by V. Panova, the characters are full-blooded and
alive in the early days of the revolution, but become shadowy and fade as soon as they move into the Stalin era. A
Pravda critic remarks that the mere transfer from the one
era to the other seems to cast a blight on Panova's every
character; and that only the criminal types are an exception:
they flourish throughout. Consequently, he says, the moral
outlook of Soviet society "resembles the landscape of an
Arabian desert."

This revelation of the real temper of an important section
of writers and artists has caused alarm in the ruling group.
The well-known poets and novelists, Tvardovsky and Pan-
ferov, who edited *Novyi Mir* and *Oktyabr,* leading monthlies

which have been the mouthpieces of the literary opposition, have been dismissed from their posts. But the suppression has been halfhearted by Stalinist standards; and so far it has affected only the extreme manifestations of opposition. The debate still goes on between party spokesmen and those writers who have voiced discontent in a more moderate manner.

A most instructive exchange has taken place between Ilya Ehrenburg and Konstantin Simonov in connection with Ehrenburg's *The Thaw*. Ehrenburg's chief character is a painter, Vladimir Pukhov, who has wasted his artistic personality through the constant adaptation of his gift and craft to prevalent tastes and prejudices. Pukhov is painfully aware of his decline, and in Russian fashion he indulges in restless morbid self-exposure, which does not prevent him, however, from going on with his opportunistic pot-boiling. It is difficult to withstand the impression that Pukhov is a pathetic projection of Ehrenburg himself who was once a novelist of considerable talent. "In present circumstances," Pukhov-Ehrenburg holds, "it is nonsensical to speak of the love of art, and it is impossible to engage in genuine art." Ehrenburg produces a whole gallery of frustrated and embittered artists, and the situations he depicts are reminiscent of older novels describing the tragedy of the artist in Victorian society. "All here are tacking about and dodging and telling lies, some cleverly, others stupidly." "They do not pay for ideas—if you have any ideas you can only break your neck." "The injured are not liked by us—we trust only the successful," these are some of the epigrams of the disillusioned Pukhov-Ehrenburg.

The official critics have not denied the truth of Ehrenburg's picture as far as it goes. Simonov writes: "It is also true that in our visual arts we have had and still have too much official pomposity. . . . We have seen too many idealized portraits, too many medals, uniforms, gala dresses, and too little thought and human warmth on faces . . . too

little of the life of ordinary people, of their workaday experience, love, and friendship." What Simonov reproaches
Ehrenburg with is that he treats Pukhov with too much
sympathy, as a victim of Soviet society, not one of its drones;
and that by failing to bring to life a single positive character,
Ehrenburg has overdrawn the picture in a hue of unrelieved
gloom. Finally, Simonov hints that the emotional exaggera-
tions of the literary opposition strengthen only the hands of
the defenders of the Stalinist *status quo.*

The cry for "real conflict" and for genuine heroes and
villains will not die down soon. It has its origin in an urge
felt by the intelligentsia, and far beyond the intelligentsia's
ranks, for a revision and redefinition of the accepted ideals
and values. The cry testifies to the restless search of post-
Stalin society for its own moral, political, and cultural
identity. This is a difficult and in part a tragic search which
is likely to go on for years. What it does demonstrate is that
the society which is emerging from three decades of Stalinism has little resemblance to that of Orwell's *1984.* Its creative impulses and longings have not been destroyed under
the crushing pressure of thought control. Flattened and
cramped, they are nevertheless throbbing and stirring.

4. The New Five-Year Plan, (1956-1960)

1

A leading Soviet economist, Professor A. Notkin, wrote recently: "Before the second world war the volume of the industrial output of the U.S.S.R. was only slightly larger than that of Germany *or* of Great Britain. It is now larger than the combined output of both Great Britain and Western Germany; and it approximates the pre-war output of the United States." This sums up the results of a quarter of a century of Soviet industrialization. Last year[1] the U.S.S.R. produced 45 million tons of crude steel, while the combined output of Western Germany and Great Britain was 41 million tons. Soviet coal mines turned out 390 million tons against 360 million tons mined in Britain and the Federal Republic. The U.S.S.R. generated 166 billion kilowatt-hours of electricity compared with 155 billion produced by the two most highly industrialized nations of Western Europe. American production shortly before the Second World War was only slightly above the present Soviet level: 444 million tons of coal, 51 million tons of steel, and 146 billion kilowatt-hours of electricity in 1937. The pride which Soviet economists take in this achievement is understandable.

"We are entering upon a stubborn struggle," Professor Notkin continues, "in which our objective is to surpass the industrial output of the United States." The new phase of the industrial race is opened with the inauguration of the

[1] In 1955.

sixth Five-Year Plan, which covers the years 1956-1960 and has been adopted at the Twentieth Congress of the Soviet Communist Party.

The Plan anticipates a rise in real national income by about 60 per cent and a growth of industrial output by 65 per cent (70 per cent in producer goods and 60 per cent in consumer goods). The number of people employed in industry and in the administration (excluding collective farming) is to rise from 48 million to 55 million. The output of coal and steel is to be increased by about 50 per cent, coal up to nearly 600 million tons and steel up to nearly 70 million tons a year. The extraction of oil is to be nearly doubled, increased to 135 million tons; and so is the generation of electricity which is to reach 320 billion kilowatt-hours. Finally, the engineering industries are expected to double the volume of production.

How are these indexes and targets related to Soviet grand strategy; and how are they going to affect the balance of economic power between the Soviet Union and the United States?

It is not easy to give a plain answer to this question. A glance at the latest American production figures shows that if the chief Soviet targets are attained, as they are likely to be, the output of the Soviet basic industries will in 1960 still be considerably below American output in 1955. True, Russia is almost certain to become, within two or three years, the world's largest coal producer. This in itself is an important historic development—twenty-five years ago Russia produced not more than 35 million tons of coal per year! But the planned production of electricity will still be only a little more than half the American output, and Soviet steel mills will turn out "only" two-thirds of America's 1955 output. Where the rival powers will stand in relation to each other by 1960 depends also on the trend of American business. If American industry continues to expand, Russia's lag will be quite long; but a recession or a slump might enable Russia to catch up with the United States earlier than can now be expected.

However, it would be a mistake to measure the relative économic strength of the two powers only by the output of their basic industries. The great differences in the structure and balance of the two economies should not be overlooked, differences which are thrown into relief by the continued Soviet emphasis on heavy industry and neglect of light industry.

It is no paradox to say that for industrial purposes one American ton of steel does *not* equal one Soviet ton. A much smaller proportion of each Soviet ton goes to meet consumer needs, to build private cars, refrigerators, houses, etc., and a much greater proportion is used in engineering plants. Russia has built a disproportionately vast engineering industry on a relatively narrow basis of steel output. The United States probably needs an annual output of 65 million to 70 million tons of steel to support an engineering industry comparable in size and weight to that which the Soviet Union is basing on an output of 45 million tons. (It is only with the backing of so vast an engineering industry that the Soviet Union could make within so short a time the tremendous advance it has made in the field of atomic and hydrogen weapons, and that it can now plan to develop its atomic power stations on a scale larger than anything contemplated in the West.)

The structural disproportions of Soviet industry remain of great importance. While one sector of Soviet industry, engineering, a sector which accounts for 50 per cent of Soviet industrial output, is already so advanced as to be within sight of the American level, the other sectors remain backward in various degrees, below and sometimes far below Western European standards. Thus manifests itself that "law of combined development"—the expression is Trotsky's—which has governed Russia's industrial history. Since Stalin's death Soviet economists have come to face this problem frankly and soberly, insisting that progress should be measured not merely by figures of total output but primarily by output per head of population. By this test Russia's progress appears, because of her vast poulation, far less impressive. Russia still produces per head only about half the steel that Western Europe produces and only a quarter of the American output; the target is to reach by 1960 the present Western European standard.

The same applies to electricity. Impressive schemes for electrification are a prominent feature of the new Plan. A single grid is to be established for the whole of European Russia. Giant power plants, some with a capacity of more than 3 million kilowatts, are to be erected in Soviet Asia. But when these schemes have been carried out the supply of electricity per head will be 1400 kilowatts, as much as it is in Western Europe now, and less than half of the American supply.

The development of transport does not keep pace with the general industrial progress; and here may well be the Achilles heel of the new Plan. Many new railway lines are to be laid; old lines are to be modernized and electrified; and the steam engine is to go out of production as obsolete. Even so, the railway network will remain far too small in relation to area and population. With regard to motor traffic, the Soviet Union still remains a primitive country, with very few cars and very few modern roads.

The preparation of the Plan was accompanied by a violent attack on planners with a pro-consumer bias; and so light industry takes a secondary place in the whole scheme. The anticonsumer bias is evident in the Plan; but it is less marked than might have been expected. It would be an exaggeration to describe the Plan as a genuine compromise between the "productionist" and the "consumptionist" viewpoints; but the Plan does offer a few concessions to the consumer. The most important of these concerns the housing program. It is on this that the controversy was centered, because housing,

more than any other consumer industry, competes heavily
with producer industries for building materials and labor.

Under the Plan 200 million square meters of new urban
housing space is to be provided, twice as much as was built
in the years 1950-1955. This, however, will not solve the
disastrous and chronic housing crisis which has accompanied the whole course of the Soviet industrial revolution.
Between 1930 and 1960 the urban population of the Soviet
Union will have grown by over 65 million souls—it has so
far grown by some 60 million, mostly peasants transferred
from the country. The new housing space provided in the
course of those thirty years will amount altogether to 600
million square meters. Much of this goes to make good the
appalling destruction of urban dwellings in the last war.

Housing space in the cities and towns is now at the most
7 square meters per person—which means that many
workers must be herded in barracks. It should be 9
square meters by 1960. The miseries of such overcrowding
will continue to plague the Soviet town-dweller until the
government decides to tackle this problem in all seriousness.
Then it will take at least ten years of intensive slum-clearing
and of building on a scale ten times larger than the present
before housing attains standards worthy of a modern industrial nation. In the meantime Soviet workers will probably continue to dwell in slums until the Soviet industrial
potential has been developed to an American level.[2]

2

The Plan foreshadows a general rise in the output of consumer goods by 60 per cent. This general figure conceals
wide discrepancies between various categories of consumer

[2] In February 1957 the target for the year was revised upwards so that the
building of houses should exceed the original plan by 30 per cent. The revision was advertised as an important concession to consumer interests. Our
calculation underlines its paltriness.

goods; and it does not accord with the planned increase in real wages and salaries by only 30 per cent and of peasant incomes by 40 per cent. The government probably assumes that the rise in incomes may be higher or that light industry may, as so often before, fail to achieve its targets. By planning a steeper rise in the supply of consumer goods than in incomes, the government also aims at creating a safety margin against the inflationary trend of recent years, when too much money has purchased too few goods.

The increase in supply is to come mainly from those consumer industries that can expand with only a minimum of investment and that do not compete with heavy industry for materials. In those consumer industries where higher production would require much new plant and would absorb much steel progress will be negligible. In other words, a marked improvement is planned in food and clothing, but not in the so-called durable consumer goods.

By 1960 only 650,000 motor cars are to be produced annually. Of these only 100,000 to 150,000 will be passenger cars, the rest will be lorries. Thus only 3 to 4 per cent of Soviet people will possess private cars. The output of refrigerators is to be increased four times; even so, only one family in a thousand will be able to install a refrigerator in its kitchen. Six times as many washing machines are to be produced in 1960 as in 1955. Yet not even one housewife in a thousand will have the chance of obtaining a machine.

Against this must be set the very considerable improvement planned in food and clothing. This is indeed the first decade in which the standard of living of the Soviet working class has been rising steeply, the first after the frightful depression which lasted nearly twenty years, from 1930 till 1950, when the Soviet worker bore the brunt of industrialization, armament, and war. The new Five-Year Plan aims at bringing the standards of popular feeding and clothing up to a Western European level, which is, of course, well below the American level.

The consumption of meat in Soviet towns (rural consumption is not assessed statistically) is to be about one pound and a half per person per week—it was only about half a pound five years ago and is a little above one pound at present. It remains to be seen how the agricultural schemes launched in recent years work out in the end, whether the virgin soils plowed up in the East yield the expected crops, whether the *kolkhozes* really take to the cultivation of maize advocated by Khrushchev, and whether cattle stocks grow sufficiently to support higher nutritional standards. But it seems that the government is anxious to honor this promise to the consumer even in case of a partial failure in farming. The Soviet Ministry of Foreign Trade has in recent years become the world's largest importer of meat; and if, as it expects, there is a glut in the world's meat markets and a drop in prices it may be able to step up greatly its purchases.

The supply of cotton goods, which was only 20 yards per person in 1950 and about 25 yards in 1955 is to reach about 32 yards in 1960, approximately the British standard. Consumption of woolen fabrics will remain far below the British and American levels but not below the French or the German. The output of shoes, which is at present one pair and a half per person per year, is to rise to more than two pairs, which is roughly the British proportion. This is a remarkable achievement for a nation which was traditionally barefoot and which some twenty years ago produced annually not more than one pair of shoes per three or four persons.

There is thus an extremely unequal tempo in the development of the various items which make up the standard of living of a modern nation. There is to be a relative abundance of first essentials, except for housing; and there is a continued scarcity of the modern amenities of life. On the whole, the second strongest industrial nation of the world is still living a Spartan life, without the luxuries, and most of the semiluxuries of an industrial civilization. However, a people with a strong and still fresh peasant background is sure to exult in the marked improvement of its feeding and clothing and may not even notice that it is still destitute of the more technical refinements of life. The new plan, when it was announced, undoubtedly gave the Soviet people the exhilarating sense of a tremendous social advance.

Nowhere is this advance as striking as in the new educational program. In the course of the next five years obligatory secondary education is to become nearly universal, in the country as well as in the town. The number of schools to be built is twice as large as that built in the years 1950-1955, and nearly four times as large as in 1945-1950, although educational building enjoyed a very high priority even then. More important still, fees for higher secondary and academic education are abolished. This is a sensational reversal of the policy of Stalin. It will be remembered that the revolution of 1917 had promised free education for all and had abolished school fees. But the Bolshevik government was not able to keep that promise. There were not enough schools, not enough teachers, not enough textbooks, not enough educational equipment. About twenty years ago Stalin reintroduced school fees. His critics then denounced the act as a betrayal of the revolution and a measure designed to perpetuate the privileges of a minority which alone could afford to give its children higher education. The abolition of fees is therefore a landmark in the social evolution of post-Stalin Russia. Higher education ceases to be a privilege for the few; and the social-educational barrier between bureaucracy, labor aristocracy, and the mass of workers and peasants is largely falling to the ground.

This expansion of the educational system, which has no parallel in the West, serves primarily the needs of Russia's industrial ascendancy. The bias of education is predominantly technological. The secondary school is reverting to the classical Marxian conception of "polytechnical" education and seeks to combine instruction, scientific training, and training in labor skills. The number of specialists that are to graduate from secondary and academic schools is to be nearly doubled. In this field the U.S.S.R. has indeed left the West far behind. As Sir Francis Simon, Oxford Professor of Thermodynamics, has declared recently, the number of students entering Soviet technical schools is greater "than in the whole non-Communist world." Facilities for adult education are similarly extensive, for it is [the purpose of Soviet labor policy to transform the bulk of the working class into skilled laborers.

This policy is dictated, apart from "ideological" considerations, by the state of Soviet manpower and by technological needs. The U.S.S.R. has not yet recovered from the losses in manpower it suffered in the Second World War. The wartime fall in the birth rate will soon make itself felt and will be reflected in a decreasing influx of fresh labor to industry. The late 1950's and early 1960's will in this respect be critical years. The deficit can be made good only by increasing the efficiency of the existing labor force. The fear of a shortage of manpower acts as a strong stimulus for laborsaving and in particular for the automation of industry.

[The average productivity of the Soviet worker is still greatly inferior to American productivity,[3] but Soviet industry evidently hopes to bridge this gap by pressing ahead with automation.

In this it enjoys one decisive advantage: Soviet workers, unlike Western workers, are not afraid of the unemployment which may result from radical laborsaving operations; and Soviet trade unions are eager to co-operate with management in speeding up automation.

Automation, however, demands an industrial labor force of superior technical knowledge and efficiency; and it threatens to make of many unskilled and semiskilled work-

[3] From statistical data which Malenkov gave at the congress it appears that the *average* Soviet productivity per manhour is 40 per cent of the American —it was 10 per cent in the 1920's. (The average British and French productivity index is around 35.)

ers sad survivals of a bygone era. Any nation that fails to gear its educational system and industrial training schemes to the new structure of industry, which is now beginning to take shape, is in danger of falling by the roadside in the economic race. This idea obviously inspires the Soviet educational program which forms an integral part of the whole Five-Year Plan.

In addition, [Soviet schools and universities are training the technicians who are to carry the industrial revolution not only to the remotest corners of Soviet Asia, but to Manchuria, to Sinkiang, beyond the Yangtse, and also to Eastern Europe. The broader and unmistakable purpose of the Plan is to enhance enormously the Soviet Union's position as the industrial workshop—and the arsenal—of the entire Soviet bloc.]

postscript

The modifications in the Five Year Plan, which were announced in February 1957, give as yet no ground for a revision of this appraisal of Soviet economic policy, even though they neglect a growing pressure of consumer interests, and underline further the disproportion between heavy and light industries. The recent revision of the Plan aims principally at a concentration of investment which should prevent the dispersal and freezing of too much capital in too many construction projects. It remains to be seen whether *in the long run* this results in a slackening of the tempo of industrial development. It goes without saying that such a slackening may result from a consumers' revolt against the neglect of their needs, especially in housing, and from subsequent political interest.

Part Two

THE CLOSE
OF THE STALIN ERA

1. Mid-Century Russia *

1

It is more than a hundred years since Alexander Herzen, the great Russian rebel and exile, wrote in his "Open Letter to Michelet" that "Russia is quite a new State—an unfinished building in which everything smells of new plaster, in which everything is at work and being worked out, in which nothing has yet attained its object, in which everything is changing, often for the worse, but anyway changing. . . ."

On another occasion Herzen contrasted the outlook of the Russians with that of the Poles. The latter, he said, cultivated a romanticism utterly alien to the Russians. They lived in their national past while the Russians, finding in their past and present little that was worthy of attachment, fixed their gaze exclusively on the future. The thoughts and emotions of the Poles hovered mournfully over ancestral graves, while Russia was full of "empty cradles waiting for children to be born."

Herzen's reflections must have sounded topical to many Russians even in the middle of this century. Since his days revolutions had followed one another; whole classes of Russian society had disappeared or had been liquidated; new classes had grown up or had been forcibly brought into existence by government decree; national institutions, beliefs,

---

* This essay is based on a series of my articles which appeared in *The Reporter* (New York) in the summer and autumn of 1951.

ideas, and illusions had been destroyed and manufactured wholesale; and the whole social and moral climate of the country had changed so much that it seemed that even the old character and temperament of Russia had suffered complete extinction or complete transformation. And yet mid-century Russia was still the "unfinished building smelling of new plaster"—and of—smoldering ruins. Nothing in it "had yet attained its object, and everything was changing, often for the worse, but anyway changing."

When one thinks how many generations of Russians have consoled themselves with the thought that their national existence was "an unfinished building" one may, at moments, feel with a shudder that a Sisyphean curse hangs over Russia's labors. This must have been the feeling with which, in 1945-1946, many millions of demobilized soldiers and wartime evacuees were returning to their homes in western Russia and in the Ukraine. They found their native towns and villages razed to the ground. They found that the coal mines, the steel mills, and the engineering plants they had built, amid blood and tears, under the prewar Five-Year Plans, were flooded, demolished or dismantled and carried away. The western provinces of the Soviet Union, where so many gigantic battles had been fought, were heaps of ruins; and the tools were lacking with which to clear the ruins away. Twenty-five million people lived in mud huts and dugouts. And, in 1946, as if to fill the cup of bitterness which victorious Russia was draining, a calamitous drought, the worst within living memory, scorched the fields and blighted the crops. Bled white, half-crazy with suffering, hungry, half-naked and barefoot, Russia began to build anew.

A few statistical indications will show that this is not an overdramatized description of the condition in which Russia emerged from the war. When the last shots were fired, Soviet industry produced less than two-thirds of its prewar output; and, of course, the bulk of its produce consisted of munitions. The annual output of steel was down to about 12 million tons, only a little more than half the prewar output. The factories were turning out about 40 per cent of the clothing and footwear they used to produce, and most of it went to the armed forces. Even before the drought, the sugar plantations yielded less than a fourth of their normal crop. The Soviet consumer could not get more than one-fourth or one-fifth of the meager rations of meat, fat, and milk he consumed before the war. Apathy and weariness threatened to thwart recovery. The Politbureau strove to stir and shake up the working class with exhortation, threat, and promise; and a note of genuine alarm sounded in all its appeals for higher production.

Yet five years after the surrender of Hitler's armies Russia's recovery was well under way. The momentum of that recovery was the most important development of the first postwar decade. In 1945 Russia still ranked as only the fourth or fifth among the industrial powers of the world; in 1950-1952 she was indisputably second only to the United States. Her steel output, approaching 40 million tons per year, was three to four times as large as it was toward the end of the war and more than twice as large as in 1940. It was this recovery which enabled Russia to consolidate and expand the positions of power which she had precariously acquired through military victory.

2

How can a nation achieve so startling an advance within so short a time?

This is not the first time in history that a nation has found its economic ascendancy stimulated and speeded up by military victory. The Franco-Prussian War of 1870, for instance, led not only to the unification of the German States under Prussia's leadership but also to the rapid rise of Germany's modern industry. The contribution which Bismarck levied on defeated France amounted to a transfusion of economic power from the Third Republic to the Hohenzollern Reich. The French contribution payments fed the orgies of financial and industrial speculation which were characteristic for the *Gruender-periode* of the 1870's and 1880's. Up to 1870 France had been the leading industrial nation on the Continent. She lost that position to Germany never to recover it.

Stalin's reparation policy resulted in a similar transfusion of economic power. The dismantling and confiscation of industrial plant in defeated countries, the reparations from current production, the mixed joint stock companies set up, under Russian management, in Eastern and Central Europe, all served to transfer wealth from at least eight countries to the Soviet Union. This policy could not but rekindle the hatred of Russia among her neighbors; and it piled up before the Russian government dangerous problems and difficulties which were to outlast Stalin. But it cannot be doubted that the policy was a powerful catalyst of Russia's economic growth. It deprived Germany of the rank of the leading industrial power on the Continent with the same finality with which Germany had deprived France of that rank after 1870.

However, important though this transfusion of economic power was, it was not decisive for Russia's ascendancy. Turning from war to peace, the Soviet Union found a firm and solid basis for its recovery in those industries which it had built up in its eastern provinces, in the Urals and beyond, in the 1930's and which it had feverishly expanded during the war. The east had fed with munitions the retreating and advancing Soviet armies; and now it supplied the sinews of reconstruction to the western provinces. No wonder that the Soviet east loomed very large in the mind of mid-century Russia. Even after the rehabilitation of the western lands, it was in the east that the pulse of the Soviet economy beat more strongly. More than half of the industrial plant remained in the Urals and beyond.

The tempo of postwar industrialization represented a triumph of Soviet planning. After the economic setback of the war, it was even more important than before that the nation's resources should be marshaled, allocated, and used in accordance with a single national plan enforcing a severe economy of scarce materials and tools and a strict labor discipline. The techniques of planning, which had first been developed awkwardly and with many costly and even tragic mistakes in the 1930's, were now brought up to a relatively high standard of efficiency, even though they were hampered by bureaucratic rigidity. The theory of planning was one of those very few fields in which the general intellectual depression of the Stalin era did not prevent the achievement of definite progress. The planners had at their disposal an amazingly effective "secret weapon": the famous theorems of "simple and expanding reproduction" which Karl Marx had developed in the second volume of *Das Kapital*. Those theorems, modeled on Quesnay's *Tableaux Economiques*, describe the composition and circulation of a nation's productive resources under capitalism. Adapted by Soviet planners to a publicly owned economy and further developed, they helped to produce results which future historians may well describe as the most momentous feat in social technology achieved in this generation.

But the planners with their theorems would have been suspended in a vacuum without the sustained daily labor of the many millions of workers, skilled and unskilled, and of the technicians and managers. Many of the workers and managers did their work willingly and even enthusiastically, bringing into it something of that spirit of devotion and sacrifice which had enabled Russia to win the war. Few blamed Stalin's government for the ruins and for the miseries which attended Russia's victory—these were seen as the work of Hitler, not of Stalin. But there was also in the Soviet people much despondency and plain demoralization, against which the government proceeded to use the well-tested instruments of totalitarian terror. This bred new grievances and new resentments all the more poignant because the terror was applied to people whose self-confidence had been heightened through victory and who had been sustained in the ordeals of battle by the hope that postwar Russia would be a freer and better country than the Russia of the 1930's with her cruel labor codes, purges, and concentration camps. The rulers resolved to nip in the bud any incipient opposition. They resorted once again to the tightest thought-control. Once again Zhdanov came forward as the intellectual Inquisitor of the day.

3

Thus, feats of planning, enthusiasm for reconstruction and a most severe and comprehensive discipline combined to enable Russia to make the new stupendous jump ahead.

To accumulate wealth, the maximum of wealth in a minimum of time, was the overriding purpose of Stalin's policy in his last years. More coal, more steel, more machine tools! More oil wells, more railway lines, more waterways, more power stations, more atomic piles! Mid-century Russia was worked up into a frenzy of accumulation. Implacably the employer-State kept down the wages of workers, grabbed the earnings of peasants, and feverishly plowed back its fabulous profits into the national economy.

Mid-century Russia was nearly completing "Primitive Socialist Accumulation." Nobody dared to utter these words, because the man who had first put forward the formula, Eugene Preobrazhensky, had been denounced and purged as a traitor and an enemy of the people. An old Bolshevik and an original theorist and economist, Preobrazhensky had, even in Lenin's last years, opposed the party's drift toward the totalitarian State, and later he joined hands with Trotsky. But, paradoxically, it was he who supplied in advance the text for Stalin's work, without suspecting for a moment to what ruthless use his theory would be put.

Marx describes as "primitive accumulation" the ways and means by which the early middle-classes accumulated wealth in the sixteenth, seventeenth, and eighteenth centuries when modern industry was still too small and too feebly developed to expand on its own, "legitimate" profits. The main sources of early capitalist wealth, Marx argued, were the dispossession of the yeoman-peasantry, colonial plunder, piracy, and later also the underpayment of wages. Only with the growth of industry and its productive power did the normal profits of the capitalist entrepreneur become substantial enough to serve as the main source for the further, normal accumulation of wealth. It was only then that a respectable and civilized capitalism could expand without necessarily robbing workers of their wages and plundering other classes of society.

Before the Russian revolution it had never occurred to Marxists that "socialism," too, might pass through a phase of Primitive Accumulation. They had always assumed that the already accumulated bourgeois wealth, when nationalized, would serve as the basis for socialism. But there was not enough of that wealth in old Russia; and still less of it was left by the time the Bolsheviks had won the civil war and began to look to the future. When in the early 1920's Preobrazhensky expounded the idea of Primitive Socialist Accumulation he caused an uproar of Bolshevik indignation: it was still blasphemous to suggest that socialism could be built by methods comparable to those employed by early capitalism. Yet, the whole social history of Stalinism, right up to the middle of the century, was nothing but the massive and awe-inspiring epic of Primitive Socialist Accumulation. As its promoter, Stalin expropriated the private farmers, confiscated the produce of the collective farms, and kept the industrial working class, ever swelling in numbers, on a bare subsistence level.

But towards the end of his life the great pirate of socialism had done his job. Russia's new wealth had grown so enormous that it could now begin to expand rapidly from the surplus of its own produce, by means of normal accumulation rather than by means of plundering the working classes and the peasantry. But Stalinism could not free itself from all the habits and the powerful inertia of Primitive Accumulation; and it resisted mentally the demands of a new time which called for a transition to normal accumulation.

The wealth of the nation stood in the sharpest contrast to the poverty of the people. In its main branches Soviet industry was now producing per head of the population as much as was produced, say, in France, though still less than in Britain and the United States. To see the advance in the proper perspective it is well to remember that twenty to twenty-five years earlier Russia was still much nearer in this respect to the level of India and China than to that of France. This is not to say, however, that the Soviet people enjoyed anything like French living standards. The industrial wealth of the nation consisted primarily of producer goods which were used to turn out more producer goods, and only a minimum of articles of consumption. In its frenzy of accumulation Stalinism seemed spellbound by that "production for production's sake" in which Marx had seen the lunacy of capitalism. Under nearly all the Five-Year Plans the consumer industries had failed to reach the very modest targets set to them. By 1950 there was little or no starvation; but Russia's staple diet was still bread, potato, and cabbage. The city dweller consumed hardly more than half a pound of meat in a week, one-sixth of the American consumption; and not more than a pound of fats of all sorts in a month. For clothing he had to do with about 20 yards of cotton fabric per year, while the American had 60 yards and the Briton 35; and the Soviet citizen could obtain almost no woolen fabrics, no rayon, and no nylon. Statistically he was able to buy one pair of shoes per year, while the average American bought three, and the average Briton at least two pairs.

Worst of all was the housing situation which resembled

the dismal picture of the slums of early Victorian England described by the young Engels. During a quarter of a century, between 1925 and 1950, the urban population of the Soviet Union grew by about 50 million people, as much as the whole population of the British Isles, the vast majority of the newcomers being peasants shifted from the countryside. The cities and towns had not been prepared for so formidable an influx. The housing programs were absurdly inadequate. Stalin's upstart bureaucracy and he himself were more interested in erecting grandiose public edifices and monuments, unsurpassed in respectable banality, than in building dwellings for human beings. Under the first postwar Five-Year Plan 100 million square meters of housing space was provided; but this was too little to make good even the wartime destruction of housing. The average space for every homeless or virtually homeless town-dweller amounted at the most to four square yards, less than any decent farmer would allow his beast of burden. Lack of accommodation for workers threatened at times to disrupt the industrial plans. In Stalin's last years the few startling cases in which Soviet citizens dared openly to critize Ministers were those connected with the housing scandal.

4

While, despite all her miseries, urban and industrial Russia was forging ahead with mighty vitality, rural Russia sluggishly lagged behind. The war had robbed the farms of manpower, tractors, horses, and cattle. Yet the structure of collective farming did not collapse—it was only weakened. Much as the peasant originally resented collectivization, he now knew that there was no way back from it. The old private smallholding had been inseparable from the horse, its chief traction power. But the horse had since been disappearing from the countryside; and its place on the fields had been taken by columns of huge tractors operated by the

State-owned Machine Tractor Stations and suited for work only on large-scale farms. The first thing the government did after the war was to restore and re-equip the Machine Tractor Stations, which formed the most massive links between town and country and the instruments of the town's economic predominance. The peasant knew that he could not do without the help of the Machine Tractor Station and that he could benefit from it only as a collective farmer. But not all the economic energy of the peasantry was directed into collected channels. The *kolkhoz* remained an economic hybrid, semicollective and semiprivate. Beside the commonly owned fields there were still the residual tiny smallholdings privately owned by members of the *kolkhoz*. The peasant tenaciously clung to his smallholding, and often tried to develop it at the expense of the collective economy. He had to divide his time between the collective field and his own plot which competed intensely for his labor.

The still smoldering resentments of the peasantry and the cleavage inside every farm between its collective and its private elements accounted for agriculture's lagging behind industry. This was the most important domestic issue which preoccupied Stalin's Politbureau in its last years. If industry was to grow, farming had to feed the continuously expanding urban population; and the growth of agriculture had to be stimulated especially in the east where there were too few settled farming communities around the new industrial centers. Otherwise the whole convoy of the Soviet economy would in the end be compelled to move at a pace dictated by its slowest sector.

In 1950 rural Russia was once again in the throes of an upheaval which affected the lives of a hundred million people. In the spring of that year the government decreed a merger of farms throughout the Soviet Union. This was the most sweeping change since the initial collectivization of the early 1930's—a supplementary collectivization. At the beginning of 1950 there existed in the Soviet Union 250,-

ooo collective farms, each with an average acreage of about
1,000 acres. By the end of the year there were only 120,000
farming units, each covering about 2,500 acres. The reform
aimed at weakening or destroying what had survived of the
old individualistic village. The pre-1950 collective farm was
fitted into the framework of the old rural community: in
most cases the peasants of one village had been organized in
one collective farm. Under the supplementary collectivization not only farms but entire communities were merged.
The Politbureau hoped that the enlarged farms would be
more efficient and easier to control and manage.

The peasantry accepted the merger with reluctance, but
without any of that desperate resistance with which it had
fought against the initial collectivization. It mattered little
to the peasant, at least immediately, whether the collective
fields he tilled belonged to a smaller or a larger *kolkhoz*. And
the memories of the pitiless suppression of the rebellion of
the early 1930's were still alive and discouraged new acts of
resistance.

The supplementary collectivization, however, could not
lead to a rapid and massive rise in agricultural efficiency.
The Stalinist Politbureau was divided over policy toward
the peasantry and decreed the merger of farms as a pallia-
tive. So many years after the liquidation of the various Trotskyist and Bukharinist oppositions the ghosts of the old controversy still haunted the Kremlin. Some members of the
Politbureau argued that in order to obtain higher crop
production and a bigger output of meat and dairy produce,
it was necessary to give more scope to the peasantry's repressed but still surviving individualism. This meant lower
agricultural taxation, payment of higher prices for food to
the peasants, and a more abundant supply of cheap industrial goods to the countryside. Other members of the Politbureau held, on the contrary, that the peasant's individualism should be curbed and suppressed even more severely
than hitherto, and that collectivization should be carried

to its extreme conclusion. The country had a glimpse of the controversy when N. Khrushchev, then leader of the Moscow branch of the party, proposed in public that the merger of the collective farms should be accompanied by a resettlement of the rural population. The farmers, he urged, should be shifted from their houses and huts to special settlements, Agrotowns, which were to be built in the center of the new enlarged *kolkhoz;* and the *kolkhoz* should take possession of the privately owned plots of land which usually adjoined the farmer's old dwelling. Khrushchev's scheme was supported by other party dignitaries, but it was emphatically disowned by the Politbureau. Stalin was afraid, not without reason, that so drastic a policy would plunge the countryside into bloody turmoil; and in his old age, beset by grave international problems, he was not prepared to start another collectivist crusade. Nor was he willing to adopt the alternative policy of concessions to the peasantry. True to himself to the end, he played for time and meanwhile he attempted to strike a balance between conflicting policies. He was to leave his successors to grapple with the unresolved crisis in agriculture.

5

With all her unresolved problems mid-century Russia was the prodigy of modern history. An incredulous world witnessed her breaking the American monopoly of atomic energy: in 1949 it learned about the event from an official announcement put out by the White House, not by the Kremlin. More than anything else that event drove home to the West the meaning of the transformation that Russia had undergone under Stalin. Who would have believed it possible that "backward, inefficient, semi-Asiatic" Russia should be able to overtake so rapidly the old industrial nations of Western Europe and to reach the threshold of the atomic age second only to the United States?

In 1945 it was still possible to wonder just how enduring would prove Russia's military ascendancy over Europe. It was still plausible to see in Stalin merely a modern successor to Peter the Great who had also worked ruthlessly to modernize Russia, to teach her the crafts of more advanced countries, to build up her military power, and to extend her influence abroad, but whose achievement had, on the whole, not outlasted his own reign. The flow and ebb of Russian power was familiar in a later age, too. The armies of Alexander I had marched triumphantly into Paris as Stalin's soldiers marched into Berlin. Nicholas I, the gendarme of the counterrevolution, had dictated his will to Russia's small neighbors and had treated Prussia as his vassal. But then Russia's power slumped; her armies returned home; and her influence abroad shrunk because her internal structure was too weak and obsolete to back it up. Whatever some of the Tsars had done to modernize Russia, their achievement was superficial and ephemeral: economically Russia remained the least developed of the great European powers. It was from her fitful attempts to emerge from backwardness and from her equally fitful relapses that the feeling sprang, so aptly expressed by Herzen, that Russia was for ever the "still unfinished building," rising and crumbling and rising again and always as far from completion as ever.

At the end of the Stalin era, however, for the first time in history Russia's power rested on solid and stable industrial foundations. Stalin's achievement therefore was different in kind from that of Peter the Great. Peter the Great broke open a "window to Europe," but he left the entire edifice of Russia rickety and backward. Stalin, on the contrary, slammed, blocked up, and blacked out all of Russia's windows to the outside world; but he rebuilt the whole edifice to its foundations, and modernized and expanded it beyond recognition. The black-out was designed to keep out all external influences that might have interfered with the work of construction inside, and it prevented the builders from

comparing their own existence with what was going on outside.

Russia's hermetic isolation from the world was a precondition of Primitive Socialist Accumulation. But it was carried
to the most grotesque excess when Primitive Socialist Accumulation was already far advanced. Mentally trapped
behind the slammed doors and windows, Russia was taught
to distrust and despise the world outside, to glory in nothing
but her own genius, to care for nothing but her own self-
centered greatness, to rely on nothing but her own selfish-
ness, and to look forward to nothing but the triumphs of her
own power. Stalinism tried to annex to Great Russia all the
feats that the genius of other nations had created. It declared
it to be a crime for the Russian to entertain any thoughts
about the greatness, past or present, of any other nation—to
"kowtow to Western civilization"—and a crime for the
Ukrainian, the Georgian, and the Uzbek not to kowtow to
Great Russia. Stalin himself, the clumsy and inarticulate yet
awe-inspiring deity of mid-century Moscow, stood as the
embodiment of that Great Russia, of her history, power, and
genius.

6

There can be no doubt that the enlightened elements among
the Soviet people felt oppressed by the mental isolation from
the world, to which Stalinism subjected them; and some of
them reacted with acute claustrophobia. In fact Russia's
isolation was receding into the past, and this made the self-
centeredness of Stalinism all the more unbearable. In the era
of Socialism In One Country nothing was more natural for
the Russian communist than to cling desperately to his soli-
tary "rampart of socialism." But several smaller "outposts of
socialism" had since risen in Eastern and Central Europe;
and the Chinese revolution was just erecting another gigantic
rampart in Asia. The feeling of isolation could not but begin

to dissolve in Russia. Yet to the end Stalinism went on to fan it, to exacerbate it, and to exploit it to the utmost.

The victory of Chinese communism did not at once make its full impact on Russia. For years Soviet citizens had read in their newspapers about obscure guerrilla fighting in various parts of China. But these stirrings of a remotely creeping revolution did not in their eyes change the picture of the world to which they had become accustomed. And when as if suddenly the Chinese revolution ceased to creep and rose for its Marathon race, and when the old order of China came down with a crash, the event was so unexpected in its magnitude as to appear almost incomprehensible and unreal.

Before the Chinese revolution most of Russia's wartime and postwar acquisitions were still tenuous. The new Communist regimes in Eastern Europe were only limited and local gains; and each of those regimes might have turned out a broken reed. With Warsaw and Budapest and even Prague in Communist hands, Socialism In One Country and its mentality had not yet outlived their day. But the Chinese revolution shook the world as it had not been shaken since 1917. It brought a supreme triumph to Stalinism. Yet in the cup of victory, mixed with the wine there were a few drops of poison. The rise of Chinese communism rendered ridiculous some of the Stalinist habits of mind, especially its self-centeredness and self-adulation. China suddenly reopened the vistas of international revolution which had inspired Bolshevism in its early, Leninist days and which later seemed to have hopelessly faded. It was as if the ghost of early Bolshevism mocked the aging Stalin. He shrunk convulsively and tried to pull his party even deeper into its Russian shell, into its spurious Great Russian pride and xenophobia. For a few years the deafening din of an official chauvinistic-Great Russian propaganda was the only sound that came out of Russia. The mental horizon of Stalinism contracted most pathetically just when communism was achieving undreamt-of material expansion.

In a way the last years of Stalinism were as nightmarish as were its middle years. True enough, there were none of the volcanic outbursts of terror which occurred in the 1930's. On the contrary, the terror seemed to have spent much of its impetus. Up to the time of the scandal with the Kremlin doctors, that is up to 1953, there was no unearthing of sinister conspiracies in Moscow, no hectic search for traitors and enemies of the people, no witches' Sabbath comparable to that of 1936-1938. During the whole closing phase of the Stalin era only one member of the Politbureau, N. Voznessensky, the head of the State Planning Commission, was purged; he disappeared suddenly and noiselessly, without being called upon to prostrate himself and confess his crimes in public. Other party members charged with heresy or deviation suffered mild demotion but escaped the extreme forms of punishment. Yet the outward surface of Soviet life was more monotonous and more deadly uniform than ever before; and it was this unrelieved monotony that was almost as excruciating as were the bloody spasms and convulsions of the 1930's. With the Stalin cult at its dizzy height, with all thought stagnant and congealed, it looked as if Russian history had come to an uncanny standstill. This was, of course, an optical illusion: the appearance of stagnation concealed an intense movement.

7

Late in the last century Frederick Engels wrote about the United States:

> *The Americans may strain and struggle as much as they like, but they cannot discount their future—colossally great as it is —all at once like a bill of exchange: they must wait for the date on which it falls due; and just because their future is so great, their present must occupy itself mainly with preparatory work for the future, and this work, as in every young country, is of a*

predominantly material nature and involves a certain back-
wardness of thought. . . .

Engels' words could *a fortiori* be applied to Russia at the
middle of this century. The contrast between her material
progress and the backwardness of her thought was her most
striking characteristic. Yet the most idealistic elements of
Soviet society could not but "strain and struggle" in mute-
ness, and try to "discount" their "colossally great" future.
Once again they fixed their gaze on the vision of that future,
on those "empty cradles waiting for children to be born"
which Herzen had seen.

The only relatively free debate which occurred in mid-
century Russia was concerned with the "transition from socialism to communism." To outsiders this was bizarre scholastic quibbling over esoteric dogma; and this in part it
was. But to those engaged in it the dispute offered an occasion for dreaming aloud, dreaming about the day when
the nightmares of the present would dissolve, when the
State with its all too familiar terrors would wither away,
after all, when the social inequalities of the Stalin era would
be overcome, and when the mastery of man over man would
become a memory of the past.

No other modern nation has been as creative and as tragically wasteful of energies, men, ideas, and dreams as contemporary Russia. At mid-century her birth rate was probably higher than that of almost all other Western nations; so
was her mortality. Even before the war, for every child born
in New York more than two were born in Moscow. But for
every funeral in New York there were nearly two funerals in
Moscow. The Russians were consequently an astonishingly
young nation. But throughout the Stalin era, the young people had little time to enjoy the taste of youth; very early they
had to shoulder the burden of grim maturity, and they grew
old with frightening rapidity.

This was symbolic of the Stalinist way of life and of the production of material and spiritual wealth. The government had made the people build thousands of factories and mines under a single Five-Year Plan. Then thousands of factories were destroyed or burnt down through war, hundreds of mines were flooded, scores of cities were razed, and flourishing lands were turned into deserts. Thousands of new schools and scores of universities were opened under each Five-Year Plan; and, at great expense to society, a generation of educated and intelligent people was brought up, of which the most civilized nation would be proud. Yet a terribly high proportion of that new intelligentsia was swallowed by concentration camps opened simultaneously with the universities. The brains of those who escaped this lot were flattened and stultified by the bureaucratic machine which absorbed them. At mid-century 37 million people were being educated at Soviet schools of various grades. This achievement did the greatest credit to a people many of whom had lived in illiteracy until recently; and in any case it was an encouraging promise for the future. But how many of those who received their education could be confident that they would be allowed truly to serve society with their brains?

No nation in the last century was as productive as Russia of epoch-making ideas, world-embracing Utopias, and momentous revolutions. Yet nowhere were ideas, Utopias, and revolutions as cruelly perverted. But the fertility of the Russian mind was by no means exhausted. In ideas, as in population, the balance of the high birthrate and the high mortality remained unknown.

And there were a multitude of empty cradles all over the place.

2. "Socialist Competition" [1]

1

The economists and theorists of all socialist schools of thought agree in the denunciation of capitalist competition and of its laissez-faire apologists. But behind this unanimity in denunciation can be discerned wide differences in approach and argument, differences which finally come into the open when any socialist school tries to look beyond capitalist society and to answer the question whether socialism itself is compatible with any form of competition. The different answers given to this question reflect broader differences between the various visions and conceptions of socialism.

Perhaps the most crucial theoretical controversy over this subject took place between Marx and Proudhon more than a century ago. Proudhon saw socialism essentially as a "free association" of small property owners, of independent producers owning their means of production. It was natural for him to envisage the economic activity of such a society in terms of competition. The evil of capitalism, Proudhon argued, was that it gave the banker and the industrialist a monopoly on the means of production and thus degraded the small artisan and peasant into wage slaves. Under such conditions, "genuine" competition, which presupposed the equality and the freedom of those taking part in it, was impossible. The form which competition had taken under capitalism was therefore the Hegelian antithesis of free associa-

[1] *Foreign Affairs,* April 1952.

tion and co-operation. Socialism would break the capitalist monopoly on the means of production; it would restore to the individual the tools of his labor; and thereby it would also restore competition to its proper role. From a factor of social disruption and disintegration, competition would become a factor of harmony; and socialism would represent the final synthesis between association and competition. "Competition," Proudhon wrote, "is as essential to labour as is division of labour . . . it is necessary for the advent of equality." It is inherent in human nature, and therefore "there can be no question of destroying competition, a thing as impossible to destroy as liberty; we have only to find its equilibrium. . . ."

Marx's approach was essentially historical. He replied to Proudhon's argument with the assertion that precapitalist society knew little or no competitive economic activity. The feudal landlords had been engaged in all sorts of political and military rivalry; but, as a rule, they had not confronted one another as economic competitors, buyers or sellers, because their economy had not developed in terms of market relationships. Nor had the peasant serfs (or the slaves in economies based on slave labor) competed with one another as laborers. Only as market relationships had spread and become universal, i.e. under capitalism, did every form of economic activity assume a competitive aspect. Even capitalism was not always competitive. In its mercantilistic beginnings it was monopolistic. Only with its growth and consolidation, and with the development of modern industry, did monopoly give place to free trade and competition. But then free competition itself, progressively concentrating wealth in the hands of the few, tended toward monopoly. Competitive economic activity was thus characteristic only for a relatively short period in man's history; and from that period Proudhon mistakenly projected it into the past and the future.

Marx did not question the assumption that the urge for emulation was inherent in human nature. He merely insisted that this urge ought not to be confused, let alone identified, with economic competitiveness. "Competition is emulation for profit." Since, in contrast to Proudhon, he saw socialism as the abolition of property, not a new redistribution of it, and as a free association of producers collectively owning their means of production, not as an association of small property owners, Marx could see in socialism no room for profit and, consequently, no room for "emulation for profit." "Socialist competition" was to him a contradiction in terms; and he ridiculed Proudhon's view about "the eternal necessity of competition."

Of special relevance to the subject of this article is Marx's view of competition as it affects the working class, that is, of competition among the workers themselves. In one of his earliest works, *The German Ideology,* he wrote: "Competition makes individuals, not only the bourgeois but *still more so the workers,* mutually hostile, in spite of the fact that it brings them together. It takes therefore a long time before these individuals can unite." The worker appears on the market to sell his labor force, which has become a commodity. On the labor market he competes against members of his class; and this competition is governed by the law of supply and demand. When the market is against him, the worker cuts the price of his peculiar commodity, agrees to work for lower wages and longer hours, and compels other workers to do likewise. The competition rages inside the factory and workshop as well—competition in intensity and productivity of labor; and at the bench as on the labor market the brutality of the competition depends on the size of the "reserve army of unemployed." Through trade-unionism the workers may restrain and curb their own competition, but they cannot abolish it. The whole social and political development of the industrial working class is nothing but a constant struggle of that class to keep down the economic individualism of its members and to impose on them solidarity vis-à-vis the employers.

"The separate individuals form a class," continues Marx, "only in so far as they have to wage a common battle against another class; otherwise they are on hostile terms with each other as competitors." Only in so far as the workers overcome their own competitiveness and grow aware of their deeper and broader antagonism to the capitalist class do they begin to act as *eine Klasse für sich,* a class for itself. Nevertheless, under capitalism they can never quite escape the curse of competition. No matter how strong their trade-union, every slump tends to destroy or to weaken their hard-won solidarity. And throughout all the phases of the trade cycle competition goes on inside the factory and the workshop; and each form of wages has a different effect on it. Time wages appear to be less detrimental to the workers' solidarity than piece wages, for although they may induce some men to work longer hours, they do not induce them to outdo their fellow workers by greater intensity of labor within any time limit. Piece wages, on the other hand, play much more strongly upon the worker's competitive instinct. "Since the quality and intensity of the work are here controlled by the form of the wage itself," Marx writes in *Das Kapital,* "the piece wage automatically registers the slightest difference in the quality and intensity of the work performed." It "tends to develop on the one hand the individuality of the worker and with it the sense of liberty, independence and self-control of the labourers, on the other—their competition with one another. Piece work has, therefore, a tendency, while raising individual wages above the average, to lower this average itself. . . . *Piece wages is the form of wages most in harmony with the capitalist mode of production.*" [2]

Neither Marx nor Engels, nor any of their eminent intel-

[2] The italics are those of the present writer. Incidentally, Marx carefully distinguished between "productivity" and "intensity" of labor. Higher productivity comes with improved machinery and better organization of labor; it may or it may not indicate increased exploitation. Higher intensity of labor comes from the greater physical exertion to which piece wages spur on the worker—it nearly always amounts to increased exploitation.

lectual disciples such as Kautsky, Plekhanov, or Lenin, has ever drawn any blueprints of the society of the future. At most they all deduced certain general features of socialism by inference from the opposite. They assumed, expressly or implicitly, that economic phenomena which they saw as being peculiar to capitalism would vanish with capitalism or would not, at any rate, survive into the age of fully-fledged socialism. Wages, profit, and rent represented such social relationships, peculiar to capitalism and unthinkable in socialism. The same was true of the modern division of labor, especially the separation of brainwork from manual labor; and, last but not least, of competition.

Marxist theory takes it for granted that the members of a socialist community will have to perform certain functions in many ways similar to those performed by their ancestors under capitalism or feudalism. In every social order men have to produce in order to live. In every economic system there must be some balance between production and consumption. Every society, if it is not to stagnate and decay, must produce a surplus of goods over and above the sum total of the goods necessary for the upkeep of the producers, the maintenance and replacement of productive equipment and so on. Yet the social relationships within which these functions are performed are so different in various systems that it is useless to search for common historical and sociological denominators for these functions. The surplus produce of a capitalist economy takes the form of rent, profit, and interest; and this determines the entire mode of life of the capitalist world. In socialism, the surplus produce, belonging to society as a whole, would cease to be profit. The function of that surplus and its impact upon social life would be altogether different from what it was under the old order, when the scale and the rhythm of any nation's productive activity were normally determined by whether that activity was or was not profitable to the capitalist class. In the same way, the emulation in which men would engage under socialism (or communism) would have little or nothing in common with their ancestors' competition. Under capitalism, men compete for profits or wages. Socialist emulation would be economically disinterested.

It is perhaps important to remember the major premise of this argument. In original Marxist theory, communism (or socialism) is associated with a development of mankind's productive resources and capacities superior to that achieved under capitalism at its peak. Marx and Engels held that man cannot make his leap "from necessity to freedom," from "pre-history into history," or for that matter from competition to emulation, as long as he has to devote the major part of his creative energy to the satisfaction of his material needs. Unlike some socialist sentimentalists, the founders of the Marxist school had no quarrel with the familiar view that the higher achievements of our culture and civilization have been essentially the work of the "leisured classes." But they believed that the time was not very far off when technological development would enable mankind as a whole to become a single "leisured class," as it were, provided mankind could in time achieve a new social organization. In Marx's age the average working day in industry was twelve hours; and Marx hailed the introduction of the ten-hour day in England as the first great victory of the socialist principle. To most of his contemporaries the idea of a six- or seven-hour day appeared as fantastic as that of a two- or three-hour day may appear now. Yet, some Americans at least will perhaps agree that if the United States were merely to maintain the rate of its technological progress (and on condition that this progress does not become a factor of destruction and self-destruction), the two- or three-hour day should come within the realm of the possible for the American people before this century is out.

What are the implications of such a hypothesis? What would a two- or three-hour working day mean to the American people? It would certainly revolutionize their way of life and their outlook to an almost unimaginable extent. It would in the first instance render obsolete the inherited division of labor, especially the separation of brainwork from manual labor. It would leave the physical worker with enough leisure for him to be free to acquire the education and to engage in the intellectual or artistic activity which under the present division of labor is open to the brainworker only. On the other hand, even the most specialized scientist and artist could easily perform physical labor for two or three hours, without thereby being diverted from his special intellectual pursuit.

It was some such society as this hypothetical American society of the end of the twentieth or the beginning of the twenty-first century that Marx and Engels had before their eyes when they discussed the various phases in the development of communism. Only in this light can one understand, for instance, the following passage, almost bursting with optimism, from Engels' *Anti-Dühring:*

"In making itself the master of all the means of production, in order to use them in accordance with a social plan, society puts an end to the former subjection of men to their own means of production. *It goes without saying that society cannot itself be free unless every individual is free.* The old mode of production must therefore be revolutionized from top to bottom, and in particular the former division of labour must disappear. Its place must be taken by an organization of production in which, on the one hand, no individual can put on to other persons his share in productive labour, this natural condition of human existence, and in which, on the other hand, productive labour, instead of being a means to the subjection of men, will become a means to their emancipation, by giving each individual the opportunity to develop and exercise all his faculties, physical and mental, in all directions; in which therefore *productive labour would become a pleasure instead of a burden.*" (Italics those of the present writer.)

Only in such a society, holding a modern industrial cornucopia, did Marx and Engels expect that productive labor could become a disinterested sportslike social activity and that competition could give place to emulation.

To most reform-minded socialists and trade-unionists these Marxist vistas of the future have always seemed either too unreal or too remote to be taken very seriously. The "romantic undertone" in Marxism has evoked a response in the revolutionaries, as Lenin's *State and Revolution* strikingly testifies. The reformists have tried more empirically to find a compromise between capitalism and socialism; and they have tended to project that compromise on to the future, at least on those rare occasions when they have not shied off from generalizations about the future. Thus, the English Fabians imagined that socialism would inherit most economic "categories" from capitalism and "remodel" rather than abolish them. They believed that workers' competition, i.e. their competition for material rewards, would be both useful and necessary to a socialist economy, as John Stuart Mill had pointed out even before the Fabians. But while Fabian ideologists were anxious theoretically to infuse competition into the future socialist order, the trade-unionists, who have directly or indirectly drawn inspiration from them, have been concerned mainly with eliminating or mitigating workers' competition under the existing order. The trade-unions of most countries have at one time or another bitterly opposed the advance of "scientific management and organization of labour" and the introduction in industry of such innovations as the stopwatch, the man-record chart, and so on. Before the First World War, the American Federation of Labor vehemently denounced the attempt of employers to drive the workers into scientifically organized, "suicidal" competition in the factory shop. The A. F. of L. then rallied its following to resist the onslaught on their class solidarity, the onslaught led by Frederick Winslow Taylor. American trade-unionism seems long since to have made its peace with "scientific management"; but the old battle cry of the A. F. of L. was taken up in Europe, and there it has resounded for decades. Throughout the 1920's and 1930's Taylor and Taylorism were to the European worker synonyms of the worst capitalist exploitation. In this opposition to "technical rationalization," the defense of the worker's interests and the fear that scientific organization of labor would result in an increase of redundant labor have inevitably been blended with an instinctively conservative attitude toward technological progress. The more limited a country's resources, and the fewer its chances for economic expansion and rapid absorption of redundant labor by new industries, the more acute has been the workers' fear of their own competitiveness.

2

Any labor party, Marxist or non-Marxist, social democratic or communist, revolutionary or reformist, finds this traditional attitude untenable as soon as it assumes office. In this one respect there is little difference between Lenin and Trotsky and Attlee and Cripps. Very soon after the Bolshevik revolution Lenin tried to impress his party with the crucial importance of industrial productivity and with the need to raise the discipline and efficiency of labor. Without hesitation he recommended to his followers "the adoption of much that is scientific and progressive in Taylor's system, the correlation of earnings and output." [3] He further urged his adherents to try out the effect of piece wages upon the workers and their productivity, although at the same time, in March 1918, he proposed that the new program of the party should provide for the "gradual levelling out of *all* wages and salaries in *all* occupations and categories." He encouraged

[3] Cf. *The Next Tasks of the Soviet Regime.* Lenin's Menshevik critics bitterly attacked him more than once for urging the Russian workers to imitate the evil methods of American capitalism.

the introduction of piecework and piece wages with some caution, as an experiment; and he went on to insist on the regime's basic commitment gradually to reduce the inequality of wage earners and salary earners. He also placed great emphasis on the value of emulation, which was to develop "in humane not in zoological forms." He interpreted emulation rather broadly:

"The problems on which emulation in the communes, associations of consumers and producers, and in the soviets ought to centre . . . are these: in which commune, in which part of a city, in which factory, in which village are there no hungry people, no unemployed ones, no rich idlers . . . where has more been done to raise the productivity of labour, to build new and good homes for the poor or to house them in the mansions of the rich? Where has most been done in order that every child in a poor family should get its bottle of milk?"

There was little emphasis in all this on competition between individual workers for higher output and higher wages. Lenin returned to the idea of emulation in 1919, when he wrote on the so-called *Subbotniki*, groups of workers, communist railwaymen, who, at the height of the civil war, volunteered to do special shifts of work during weekends in order to help to supply the Red Army. The *Subbotniki* started an "emulation"; and they received and expected no pay at all for their weekend shifts. Lenin extolled their enthusiasm and disinterestedness and remarked that the example given by them pointed by way of anticipation to the socialist emulation of the future. This was an incident in the building up of communist morale during the civil war rather than a pronouncement on economic policy; and the incident would not perhaps have been worth mentioning had it not been for the fact that Stalinist publicity for the latter-day brand of "socialist emulation" uses Lenin's words on the *Subbotniki* as its text. As we shall see later, the "socialist emulation" of the Stalinist era has little in common with its alleged precedent.

During the civil war (1918-1920) and in the years that followed, Lenin did not specifically resume his advocacy of "Soviet Taylorism"; and this was no matter of chance. Scientific management and organization of labor are meaningless unless they are applied to a more or less orderly economic environment, in which at least the even flow of raw materials and equipment to the worker is assured and the worker's basic needs are more or less satisfied. None of these conditions existed then. The Russian economy had utterly disintegrated; industry was cut off from raw materials; industrial plant was half destroyed or rotting; and the industrial population was starving—in Moscow and Petrograd the worker's daily food ration often consisted of one-eighth of a pound of bread and a few potatoes. It was an extraordinary achievement for the Soviets to wrest from this disintegrated economy the munitions, the food, and the clothing which the Red Army needed. The achievement was due to a set of emergency policies which came to be rationalized and idealized into the system of "war communism." There was no lack of emulation among groups of Bolshevik enthusiasts; but there was little talk as yet about *socialist* emulation. Despite all the familiar illusions of war communism, the Bolshevik leaders were aware that this idealistic emulation was not characteristic of the economic climate of the country. Amid the appalling poverty of those years, the prevalent form of "emulation," a form in which the vast majority of the people engaged, was black-market competition.

Only towards the end of the civil war, when the Soviet leaders began to prepare for the economic transition to peace, did they make a new attempt to tackle the problem; but the attempt was still made in terms of war communism. Trotsky, hesitantly supported by the Central Committee of the party, was the chief author of the economic policy of that period, a policy which consisted in militarization of labor, labor armies, and "socialist emulation." He submitted to the Ninth Congress of the party (1920) the following resolution which was adopted:

"Every social system . . . has its own methods and ways of labour compulsion and education for labour in the interest of the exploiting classes.

"The Soviet order is confronted with the task . . . of developing its own methods, designed to raise the intensity and efficiency of labour on the basis of a socialized economy and in the interests of the whole people.

"On a par with the propaganda of ideas, which should influence the mind of the toiling masses, and with repressive measures, to be used against deliberate idlers, drones and disorganizers, emulation is the most powerful means towards raising productivity of labour.

"In capitalist society emulation had the character of competition and led to the exploitation of man by man. In a society in which the means of production have been nationalized, emulation in labour ought, *without impinging upon the workers' solidarity*, only to raise the sum total of the products of labour.

"Emulation between factories, regions, shops, workshops, and individual workers should be the object of careful organization and attentive research on the part of the trade unions and the economic administration." (The italics are those of the present writer.)

To this day these words are quoted in the U.S.S.R., without their author ever being mentioned, as a sort of a Magna Carta of Stalinist "socialist emulation." Trotsky was aware of the dilemma implied in his appeal. He insisted that emulation should not "impinge upon the workers' solidarity," that it should not, in other words, "degenerate" into competition. But how was this to be achieved? In the hypothetical Communist society of the future the contradiction was to resolve itself automatically. Amid an unheard-of abundance of goods, collectively produced and owned, the producers' interest in the material rewards would gradually wither away. Men would no longer wrest from one another the necessities, and perhaps not even the luxuries, of life. Only then would emulation and solidarity become fully compatible. But how could they be made compatible at the early stages of the transition from capitalism to communism, in a country whose economic resources were then, and were to remain for decades, greatly underdeveloped? Trotsky placed qualified trust in the nationalization of the means of production as a safeguard against the recrudescence of the old competition among the workers. But was this an adequate safeguard? Years later, Trotsky himself remarked with disillusioned sarcasm that by itself "State ownership of the means of production does not turn manure into gold." Nor could it by itself transform competition into emulation.

In the last year of war communism, Trotsky in his turn appeared before the Russian workers as the chief advocate of Soviet Taylorism. He had to consider whether the Russian worker could be persuaded to accept Taylorism or whatever was to pass under that name, and not to expect special material rewards for individual efficiency. Could "scientific management and organization of labour" make progress, without using wages policy as its instrument? Trotsky hesitated. Alternately he advocated the adoption of incentive wages and the equalization of wages. Lenin was quick to point to Trotsky's inconsistency: "You cannot have emulation, i.e. inequality in production," he argued, "without admitting inequality in consumption." But "inequality in consumption"—differential wages—tended to undermine the workers' solidarity. The "gold" of socialist emulation was turning into the "manure" of bourgeois competition.

On the eve of N.E.P., Lenin, at any rate, was clear-sighted enough to see that the Russian economy could not be rebuilt, and that the next step toward socialism could not be made, without the reintroduction of a strong element of

ordinary bourgeois competition, including competition between workers. But as a Marxist theorist, Lenin was also
scrupulous enough not to label this "socialist emulation."
Thus he who early in 1918 had first sketched in public state-
ments and more extensively in private notes the prospects of
socialist emulation was in later years more reticent on this
subject than almost any Bolshevik leader.

After the introduction of N.E.P. in 1921 little or nothing
was heard about emulation during nearly a decade. During
the major part of this period the Soviet economy had to con-
tend with vast industrial unemployment; and neither the
workers nor the trade-unions nor even the party were in a
mood to work out the Soviet version of Taylorism.

Only in 1929, at the beginning of the first Five-Year Plan,
was the call for socialist emulation raised again. It was Stalin
himself who raised it; and he did so without any of the
theoretical or sociopolitical scruples that had inhibited the
leaders of the earlier period. He was embarking upon the
industrialization of the U.S.S.R. with the conviction that he
had to foster among the workers the most intense competition in productivity and that he had to offer them, together
with persuasion and coercion, the attraction of incentive
wages. He was determined to unleash "bourgeois" competition among the workers; but he was also bent on labeling
it "socialist emulation." With characteristic vigor and crudity
he stated in May 1929:

"Emulation is the communist method of constructing socialism on the basis of the utmost activity of millions of toil-
ers. . . . Socialist emulation and competition represent two
altogether different principles. The principle of competition
is defeat and death of some competitors, the victory and
domination of others. The principle of socialist emulation
is that the advanced workers should render comradely assistance to those who lag behind in order to advance together."

This oversimplification served a definite purpose. The
"principle" of competition is, of course, not "the defeat and

death of some and victory and domination of others," although this may be the result of competition. Its principle is, as Marx put it, emulation for material reward. Stalin banished this plain and incontrovertible definition from Soviet economic thinking in order that the new regime introduced in industry together with the Five-Year Plans—the regime of shock work, Stakhanovism, and of sharply differentiated incentive wages—could be invested with the halo of socialist emulation. At the Sixteenth Congress of the party (1930) Stalin went even further: "The most remarkable feature of emulation," he stated, "is that it brings about a basic change in people's views on labour, that it transforms labour from a drudgery and a heavy burden . . . into a matter of honour, a matter of glory, a matter of bravery and heroism." The more brutally he shifted his practical emphasis toward material rewards (and other methods in which there was neither honor nor glory nor heroism), the more did Stalin's "ideological" propaganda describe his labor policy in terms of the ultimate Communist ideal.[4]

Whatever the ideological embellishments, the "bourgeois" competition which Stalin fostered in the Soviet working class was to a large extent both necessary and useful to Soviet industry. This is not the place to try to summarize Soviet

---

[4] That Stalin and the Politbureau had their reasons for surrounding "Socialist competition" with ideological embellishments is understandable. This helped them to break down the original resistance to competition inside the party, in the trade-unions, and among rank-and-file workers. What is much more strange is the assiduous credulity with which the ideological embellishments were sometimes accepted at the face value by outsiders. The Webbs, for instance, devoted a whole chapter of their *Soviet Communism* to the reproduction of all the myths on Socialist emulation. They surpassed themselves, however, in the following incongruous passage:

"The pleasurable excitement of Socialist emulation was actually brought into play in 1931–33 among the tens of thousands of convicted criminals, 'politicals,' and *kulaks* employed, as we have already described, on the gigantic civil engineering works of the White Sea canal. Brigade competed with brigade as to which could shift the greatest amount of earth, lay the greatest length of rail or construct the greatest amount of embankment within the prescribed period—sometimes, it is recorded, refusing to stop work when the hour for cessation arrived, in order to complete some particular task."

labor policy under planned economy—I have recently attempted to do this in a monograph on the Soviet trade-unions. Suffice it to say here that in the last decade or so before the Second World War the industrial working class of the U.S.S.R. expanded so rapidly that it grew from about 10 to nearly 35 per cent of the Soviet population. This growth was interrupted by the war, but it has continued again since 1945-1946. The bulk of the new labor force—24 million people under the prewar Five-Year Plans—has been recruited from the rural population. It has had to be given some elementary, hasty industrial training; and a relatively numerous section of it has had to be trained into skilled and efficient workers. The government has had an obvious interest in gradually raising the efficiency of this vast and ceaselessly expanding mass. For this a comprehensive and elaborate system of incentive wages has been needed. Piece wages, that classical stimulant of workers' competition, became the dominant form of payment in Soviet industry. Already toward the end of the 1930's about 75 per cent of all Soviet workers were paid piece rates; and their proportion has grown since, while the rates have been ever more and more differentiated. This alone gives a measure of the competitive climate prevailing in the Soviet factory and work shop.

The "socialist emulation" of the 1930's and 1940's represented only a primitive though broad approach by Soviet industry toward Taylorism and kindred versions of scientific management and organization of labor. No doubt some technologically advanced concerns and establishments carried out complex experiments in this field throughout this period. But in most sectors of Soviet industry the rhythm of technological advance was at first too slow and then too uneven and jerky, the labor force too raw and management too much hampered by political and bureaucratic interference for any systematic scientific organization of labor to be practiced over most of these years. Only recently has there been evidence of a more genuine attempt to apply Soviet Taylorism more or less on a mass scale. Specialized Soviet periodicals discuss this attempt in a tone suggesting that Soviet management is breaking completely new ground. On closer analysis it seems that, despite all claims to originality, the U.S.S.R. is essentially still in the imitative period in this field, trying hard to adopt methods which have long been familiar elsewhere. The stopwatch and the man-record chart are still startling innovations. Undoubtedly, they do mark an important stage in the growth of Soviet industrial productivity.

It is only natural that Soviet conditions should impose modifications, which make the Soviet version of Taylorism in part less and in part more effective than its American original. By and large, Soviet workers still compete for the bare necessities of life. This in itself tends to make the competition much more brutal than that to which a working class living in a capitalist country but enjoying a higher standard of living would be willing to lend itself. The fact that the Soviet trade-unions, or the bodies that exist under that name, far from curbing the competition, do their utmost to spur it on, works in the same direction. Too fierce competition between workers is by no means conducive to scientific organization. Nor does the customary Soviet emphasis on quantity production, so often harmful to quality, agree with either scientific management or the rational planning of labor processes.

On the other hand, Soviet industry derives certain exceptional advantages from the circumstance that it is publicly owned and centralized. It is not encumbered by vested interests and restrictive practices. It is—or, at any rate, it should be—easy for any successful innovation in scientific organization of labor to spread, without undue friction or delay, over any sector of industry where it can be applied. Whatever other sorts of secrecy may be characteristic for the Soviets, internal commercial secrecy is not one of them. No Soviet concern or trust can have any solid motive for withholding its experience and achievements from other concerns; and the central pooling of technological and organizational experience is a decisive advantage.

In one further respect does the climate of Soviet industry favor Soviet Taylorism. The fear of unemployment never haunts the Soviet worker, whatever other fears may prey upon his mind. Restrictive craft practices are virtually unknown to him. Vertical mobility, to use the American term, is extremely high. In a society relentlessly forging ahead with its industrial revolution, to which it sets no limits, the chances of promotion open to workers are practically unlimited, or limited only by the fear of responsibility that goes with promotion. Nothing deters the skilled worker from imparting his skill to the novice and the junior at the bench; and there is much to induce and even to compel him to do so. It is one of the characteristic obligations which figure prominently in all the contracts for socialist emulation that experience in more efficient management and use of labor should be unstintingly turned into common property.

It is rather difficult to gauge the effect of the nonmaterial incentives and deterrents which are widely employed in "socialist competition." The rewards of the efficient worker include official decorations, flattering publicity, social standing. The inefficient finds his name on the blackboard over the bench. Whether favorable distinction or blacklisting has the intended effect depends largely on the morale of the environment in which the worker finds himself. Among a discontented or sullen factory crew, official praise and honors are most likely to isolate the Stakhanovite. But it is impossible to say what is the prevailing mood at the bottom of the industrial pyramid. As a rule, the moral prizes go to the Stakhanovite together with the material ones; and both mutually enhance their respective effectiveness.

Finally, one more aspect of this problem, a purely political one, should be considered. We have quoted Marx as saying that "competition makes individuals, not only the bourgeois, but even more so the workers, mutually hostile." Marx goes on to say: "Hence it is a long time before these individuals can unite. . . . Every organized power confronting these isolated individuals, who live in relationships daily reproducing their isolation, can be overcome only after long struggles. To demand the opposite would be tantamount to demanding that competition should not exist in this epoch of history, or that the individuals should banish from their minds relationships over which, in their isolation, they have no control." Competition, in other words, tends politically to atomize the working class and to prevent it from organizing and using its strength for its own ends. Here is perhaps a clue—to be sure, only one of many—to the political amorphousness of the Soviet working class in the last decades, an amorphousness contrasting sharply with the political initiative, vitality, and organizing ability of the Russian workers under Czardom. The new generation of Soviet workers has brought with it from the countryside a residual but still strong peasant individualism, upon which "socialist competition" superimposes a new brand of individualism. Because most often the Soviet worker must fiercely compete for the bare necessities of life, his competitive individualism has certainly assumed extreme forms, making it difficult for him to develop his own political personality. Primitive economic individualism in the worker is, paradoxically, one of the essential preconditions for Stalinist collectivest uniformity, as essential as political terror, if not more so. Socialist emulation, because it is only competition under a new name— the struggle of all against all—makes the workers mutually hostile and "isolated from one another." They live in relationships which daily reproduce their isolation. Their energy, politically shapeless and undifferentiated, is therefore easily made to flow into molds operated by a single party. They work and build new cities and open up deserts and fight world-shaking battles; but, like most of mankind,

they are still merely the object of history. They may become something more only after long struggles. "To demand
the opposite would be tantamount to demanding that competition should not exist in this epoch of history." Or, that
the Soviet workers should "banish from their minds relationships over which in their isolation they have no control."

3. Stalin's Last Word [1]

1

Shortly before his death, Stalin himself, in his *Economic Problems of Socialism in the U.S.S.R.*, offered a virtual survey of the social achievement of the U.S.S.R. in the Stalin era. In his own way he pointed not only to the grandeur but also to the contradictory nature of that achievement. His essay may now be read as his political testament. The following article, written and set before Stalin's death, analyzes some of his ideas. One need not be a devotee of the Stalin cult to recognize Stalin's last published work as a significant political document, despite its characteristically dogmatic and scholastic style.

The Economic Problems of Socialism in the U.S.S.R. contains three different lines of argument: a statement of dogma; a survey of crucial economic and social problems; and suggestions for practical policy. All these aspects are closely interconnected, and so the survey of current problems and the suggestions for future policy cannot be properly understood without some attention being paid to the dogmatic points.

Stalin wrote his article (and the accompanying letters to various Soviet economists) in connection with a discussion which took place, in November 1951, over the conspectus of a new textbook of political economy. His remarks are devoted mainly to the treatment accorded in the textbook to the "transition from socialism to communism." For some

[1] *Soviet Studies*, April 1953.

time past this "transition" has stood in the center of theoretical argument and of day-to-day propaganda. The slogan refers back to the familiar distinction, drawn by Marx in his *Critique of the Gotha Programme,* between the "two phases" of communism, the "lower" or the socialist and the "higher" or the Communist proper. For many years it has been a virtual canon of Stalinism that the Soviet Union has already completed the building of socialism. Thus the problem of the transition to communism has been posed almost automatically. Recently the discussion of the ways and means and of the tempo of the transition has tended to become specific; and differences of opinion have begun to appear. In what phase of the transition does the Soviet Union find itself at present? What are the immediate prospects? In what way can the transition be speeded up and facilitated? These have been the problems under debate.

Inevitably an air of unreality has enveloped much of the discussion, if only because its chief premise—the achievement of socialism—is itself utterly unreal. Stalin's Marxist critics have often asked how the Soviet economic system can be described as socialist when the standards of living of the Soviet peoples are notoriously low, much lower than those attained in Western capitalist countries. Is socialism compatible with growing economic inequality? Or with massive coercion by the State? Stalin has in the past done his best to evade some of these questions and to answer others in terms of the Marxist doctrine. He has argued that economic inequality is justified and unavoidable under socialism, as Marx clearly indicated when he drew the distinction between the two phases of communism. Stalin has further pointed out that the withering away of the State (that is of coercion by government), which the founders of Marxism expected, could occur only in an international socialist commonwealth, not in a single, isolated, socialist State. But Stalin and his followers have carefully avoided any realistic comparison between Soviet and foreign standards of living, because it has been politically impossible for them to admit that standards of living were and still are lower in the Soviet Union than in the capitalist West.

The claim that the Soviet Union has achieved socialism is based on the view that nationalization of the means of production and the prevalence of planned economy by themselves constitute socialism, regardless of how developed or underdeveloped are the economic resources of the country concerned, how high or low its standards of living and under what degree of State compulsion the country lives. Even in the light of this simplified definition, however, the socialist character of the Soviet economy must still appear doubtful. While Soviet industry may be said to conform to the definition, Soviet farming has, even after collectivization, represented a mixed type of economy. The land has, in strict law, been national property ever since 1917, although this legal fact has even now hardly become part and parcel of the peasantry's thinking and attitude towards the land. The Constitution and the Statues of the *kolkhoz* guarantee eternal use of the land to the collective farms and of small private plots to individual members. The Machine Tractor Stations are owned and operated by the State. Livestock, implements, buildings are corporate or private property. The *kolkhoz* owns its crops; and after having met its obligations toward the State, it is free to sell the crops. The individual *kolkhoz-nik* is free to take to the market the produce of his private plot and that part of the collective crop which is allocated to him. Collective farming thus represents at best a semiprivate and semisocialist sector of the economy. Officially, however, collective farming has been labeled socialist, in order to justifiy the claim that socialism had been established in the entire Soviet economy.

This misrepresentation of the social aspect of Soviet farming has produced a great deal of doctrinal equivocation and "double-talk." Stalin's article deals in fact with some of the effects of that equivocation. This is not merely a matter of dogma, for dogma impinges on practical policy and administrative experience. Since the canon about the achievement of socialism had been proclaimed, new cadres of economists, administrators, planners, and organizers have grown up. Some of them have received a thorough grounding in classical Marxist economic theory. In their minds the tenets of that theory often tend to clash with the Stalinist canon. These "young cadres" have the advantage over the Bolsheviks of an earlier generation that they have been plunged directly from school into a vast, complicated, and rapidly expanding planned economy, where they can test academically acquired notions of Marxist theory against facts of life. Sooner or later—perhaps later rather than sooner—they may be able to enrich the theory in the light of their unprecedented experience and thus to contribute toward overcoming the present stagnation and decadence of Marxist economic thought. For the time being, however, they themselves are the victims of the bureaucratic-ecclesiastical manipulation of economic theory. Stalin now tries to free them from some ill effects of that manipulation and in his turn exposes them to new manipulation.

The young economist or administrator who accepts the canon about the socialist character of the economy is inevitably puzzled and bewildered by many aspects of Soviet policy. He wonders, for instance, why "socialist" farms should trade their produce and why market relationships should persist under socialism? If he has read carefully the famous passage from Marx's *Critique of the Gotha Programme* (the passage so often referred to in which Marx drew the distinction between the two phases of communism), he must have noticed that Marx insists that even under the "lower phase of communism" "the producers do not exchange their produce" and that no class distinctions exist any longer "because everybody is only a worker." If the present Soviet system represents socialism then it follows that the distinction between the peasant and the worker should have become irrelevant and the member of the *kolkhoz* should be a worker *on a par* with the industrial producer. *Kolkhoz* trade and *kolkhoz* markets should then be relegated as anachronisms to a museum of antiquities. It is with such reasonings that Stalin deals in his article. A way out of the confusion would be to admit that the Soviet economy is still only a halfway house between capitalism and socialism, not devoid even of features of precapitalist relations. But Stalinist orthodoxy cannot afford such an admission.

On a more theoretical level the problem is formulated as follows: does the law of value, in the Marxist sense, operate under socialism? In Marxist theory the "law of value" is bound up exclusively and inseparably with the market economy in its precapitalist and capitalist varieties. The notion itself of value (i.e. exchange value as distinct from use value) does not exist outside production for the market, commodity exchange, and trade. By definition there is no room for it in a socialist economy, for under socialism the community is expected merely to distribute and allocate its social product—the members of the community are expected to produce for the common pool and to consume from the common pool, without exchanging their produce among themselves. There is no room for selling and buying or seller and buyer. In the Soviet Union a great deal of selling and buying is, of course, going on in various forms, including forms normally associated with a black market. The young Soviet economist remembers the fantastic inflation of prices on *kolkhoz* markets during the recent war and in the first postwar years. He remembers the depreciation of the ruble which compelled the government to carry out the drastic postwar currency reform. Marxist theory has explained to him money as the reflex or embodiment of pure value, springing into and fading out of existence together with the exchange of commodities. How then is the existence of money, not to speak of its irrational value movements, to be fitted into the picture of a socialist economy?

Stalin is trying to fit these phenomena into the theoretical picture. Since he must insist on the socialist character of the economy and at the same time on the Marxist orthodoxy of his views, he is compelled to produce an essay in squaring the circle. He tries to prove in terms of classical Marxist theory something which in those terms is an absurdity, namely that the law of value continues to operate under socialism. It is, of course, possible to hold such a view; and some socialist schools of thought have held it. But it is as little possible to argue it coherently in terms of Marx's theory as it would be to argue in terms of Copernican cosmology that the earth is flat.

2

Behind manufactured scholastic dogma loom serious practical problems. We have mentioned the new cadres of the economists and administrators whom Stalin addresses. This is how he himself sees those cadres:

"It might be said that all that has been stated here is correct and generally known but contains nothing new and that consequently there is no need to waste time on repetition of truisms. Of course, there is nothing new in all that, but it would be incorrect to think that it is not worth while to spend time on repeating some of the truths familiar to us. We, the leading nucleus, are joined every year by thousands of new young cadres, who burn with the desire to help us and to prove themselves but who do not have sufficient Marxist education and do not know many of the things familiar to us. . . . They are impressed and bewildered by the colossal achievements of Soviet power, they are made dizzy by the extraordinary successes of the Soviet regime, and they begin to imagine that Soviet power can 'do anything.' . . . Some comrades say that the party acted incorrectly when having seized power and nationalized the means of production in our country it preserved commodity production."

It may well be that Stalin crudely exaggerates the simple-mindedness of the "young cadres" and thus sets up imaginary whipping-boys whom it is easy to belabor in controversy. It is difficult to believe that the "young cadres" should be unaware of the experiment of war communism, which was nothing else but an abortive Bolshevik attempt to abolish the market economy. Whatever the truth, Stalin leaves no doubt that pressure for the abolition of market relationships has recently made itself felt in Soviet ruling groups. Since market relationships have had their main basis in the structure of farming, in its semiprivate character, the pressure has actually been for a further radical transformation of farming and its absorption in the nationalized economy.

The present structure of the *kolkhoz* system is, as we have seen, characterized by an elaborate and unstable balance between private and collective interests. The private interest has tended to expand beyond prescribed limits; and the government has striven to impose and maintain the priority of the corporate interest. In this tug-of-war the balance has swayed now in one and now in the other direction. During the last war, when the so-called millionaire-*kolkhoznik* was the hero of the day, private interests obviously gained much scope. The postwar currency reform, confiscating the "fortunes" made on *kolkhoz* markets, tilted the scales in favor of the collective interests. So did the recent merger of the *kolkhozy* into larger units. It is now clear that the merger had been decided upon after an acute controversy which had rent the last Politbureau since 1948-1949. Apparently more extreme measures for the suppression of the private interest were advocated. Khrushchev, we know, proposed the formation of Agrotowns; and the abolition of the residual private farming carried on within the *kolkhozy* was also contemplated. It is now vaguely suggested that Voznessensky, the former head of *Gosplan* and member of the Politbureau, stood for even more extreme ("adventurist") policies designed not merely to restrict the private interest within the collective farms but to carry farming as a whole from collectivization to "socialization." It is impossible to say whether this was really so, because only one party to the controversy has been allowed to air its views; and as Stalin and his associates have sometimes in the past shown themselves quite capable of stealing clothes from their bathing adversaries, it may even be that the policies now adopted are those originally expounded by the excommunicated Voznessensky. Whatever the truth, after a moment of apparent hesitation over the more extreme measures, the ruling group has rejected them, holding that a *bouleversement* of farming would produce more economic and political disruption than the Soviet Union could at present afford.

Nevertheless, the problem of the market economy, or more specifically of *kolkhoz* trade, remains. The market economy, as Stalin points out, tends to come into conflict with the needs of central planning. It introduces a huge element of "spontaneity" and unpredictability in a field which even without it would still remain relatively unpredictable. In the course of nearly a quarter of a century farming has eluded planning. Few of the targets set for the output of grain and for the breeding of livestock have been attained. That the contradiction between the elements of planning and those of a market economy constitute the greatest single cleavage within the Soviet economy no critically minded student could ever have doubted. Until recently Stalinist writers denied or explained away this contradiction. It is on it, however, that Stalin has now turned the limelight. In his letter to L. D. Yaroshenko he writes:

"It is therefore the task of the leading bodies to indicate in good time the growing contradictions and to take timely measures towards their overcoming. . . . This applies above all to such economic phenomena as the group property in collective farming and the circulation of commodities. Of course, at present we successfully utilize these for the development of the socialist economy. . . . They will undoubtedly be of benefit in the nearest future as well. But it would be unforgivable blindness not to see that at the same time these phenomena are already beginning to act as a brake on the powerful development of our productive forces, in so far as they hamper State planning in its striving to encompass the whole of the national economy, especially of the rural economy. There can be no doubt that the further we proceed the more will these phenomena act as a brake on the continued growth of our country's productive forces. Consequently, it is our task to liquidate these contradictions by way of a gradual transformation of *kolkhoz* property into national property and by way of a gradual substitution of the exchange of products for commodity circulation."

) It should be underlined that Stalin describes not merely the private interest of the *kolkhoznik* but even "group ownership" of the *kolkhoz* as a brake on planning. He forecasts that the "brake" is likely to act more powerfully in the future; and he sees the eventual solution in the complete assimilation of farming to socialized industry. If the present structure were to be left unchanged, he says, then the conflict between planning and market relationships would eventually assume critical forms. This diagnosis is undoubtedly realistic, and it would be a mistake to see in it a symptom of Soviet economic weakness. It is, on the contrary, only against the background of the stupendous growth of Soviet economic power in recent years that this diagnosis could be made and that the problem to which it points could arise.

Despite its enormous human and material *faux frais*, the Soviet planned economy has achieved a high degree of consolidation. Its basis and its volume have been growing with the continuous industrial revolution, with the expansion in productive capacities and in reserves of skilled manpower. Experience accumulated in a quarter of a century shows itself in improved techniques of planning. The firmer the foundations on which the planned economy rests and the greater its dynamic expansiveness, the earlier, however, must it hit the limits which market relationships impose on it, and the stronger must be its tendency to eliminate anarchical "spontaneity" from the whole system. This again is no matter of abstract economic principle only. The practical issue at stake is the adjustment of agriculture to industrial development. The supply of food to the rapidly growing industrial population and the geographic redistribution of food-producing centers to suit the changing industrial map of the country have proved chronically inadequate. These disproportions, if they were to persist, would slow down or even bring to a standstill industrial expansion. The stronger the Soviet economy is as a whole, especially its industrial sector, the more does the present condition of Soviet farming become a source of weakness.

This is the central issue behind Stalin's survey of the Soviet economy. But here again dogmatic considerations superimpose themselves on realistic analysis. What Stalin has described is, in Marxist terms, a "contradiction between productive forces and productive relationships," a contradiction inherent in all class society, including any society which may be in transition from capitalism to socialism. To the Marxist this contradiction is unthinkable under socialism. "Productive relationships" mean nothing else than the property relations prevailing in any given society and the corresponding mutual connections between social classes and groups. The "contradiction between productive forces and productive relationships" is, in other words, the conflict between the needs of economic development and established property relations. Under capitalism there is the constant, latent or open, conflict between private property in means of production and the social interdependence of the producers or, more generally, the social character of the productive process. Only social ownership of means of production can, in the Marxist view, resolve the conflict between productive forces and productive relationships. In so far as private (or "group") ownership predominates over a vast sector of the Soviet economy (farming) the conflict persists, albeit in new form.

This conflict once again defies the accepted picture of Soviet "socialism." Consequently, either that socialism is exposed as a myth; or else it must be declared that the contradiction between productive forces and relationships, far from being a characteristic of past society only, remains a feature of socialism as well. In deference to a canon of his own making, Stalin in fact argues that this contradiction will be inherent in human society for ever. One must assume that Stalin puts into these formulas some other meaning which has little in common with their accepted Marxist sense, for otherwise his conclusion would be that under socialism and communism the needs of economic development would continue to clash with the new forms of ownership, i.e. with social ownership. In such a view the "contradiction between productive forces and productive relationships" would be transformed into an eternal, metaphysical element of human history.

From Stalin's correspondence with the economists it appears that this point of his argument has caused bewilderment even among people accustomed to accept every word from his mouth with prescribed reverence. Marxism explains social revolutions as the violent processes through which productive relationships are brought in line with the development of productive forces. If Stalin's argument were to be taken at its face value, it might even imply the "inevitability" of new revolutions in Soviet society. This was the last thing he had intended to suggest, as he hastens to explain in his letter to A. I. Notkin. In his characteristic desire to invest every one of his moves with the merits of an absolute socialist "truth," Stalin has simply projected a conflict which afflicts present Soviet society on to the Marxist vision of fully fledged socialism and communism. He has put his finger on a current and potentially explosive issue and has hastened to add that the issue is not explosive at all, for in one form or another it is bound to reappear at every stage of human development.

3

Throughout his argument Stalin repeatedly puts his finger on some potentially explosive issue, then asserts that no issue can be explosive under the Soviet system and then again, forgetting this assertion, insists on the highly explosive nature of the issue in question. It would take us too far to go into all the scholastic twists and turns of his reasoning—only one or two illustrations will suffice.

The dichotomy between the planned sector of the economy and the market, coincides broadly with the contradiction between town and country in the Soviet Union. Stalin begins with denying the mere fact of the contradiction. The country, he says, is no longer exploited by the town as it used to be under capitalism and therefore "not a trace" has been left of their former antagonism. What has survived is a "difference" between town and country, not a "contradiction."

The critic might be tempted to ask when a "difference" becomes a "contradiction." The *kolkhoznik* sells food, the town-dweller buys it directly or through the medium of a State or co-operative trading organization. The seller aims at selling dearly, the buyer at buying cheaply. This remains so even if the State, which acts as the middleman, pays the peasant low prices and charges the town-dweller high prices for food. The "difference" between the rural seller and the urban buyer is obviously a "contradiction." The "difference" between national ownership and State planning (prevalent in town) and "group" and private ownership and market relations (prevalent in the country) is surely also a "contradiction"—otherwise group ownership and market relationships would not impede planning. The distinction between "differences" and "contradictions" is merely a formula of bureaucratic scholasticism designed to conceal the gulf between the various sections of Soviet society.

Eventually, however, Stalin is driven back to realities and then he reveals that gulf once again. When some of his correspondents suggest to him that it might be advisable to transfer the Machine Tractor Stations from State ownership to collective farm ownership he argues against this proposal strongly and in part very convincingly. He puts forward two arguments. He points out, first, that the technical equipment of farming (tractors and heavy machines) must be constantly renewed if agriculture is to keep pace with the industrial revolution. The collective farms, he goes on, would not be in a position to finance their own re-equipment:

"What does it mean to withdraw hundreds of thousands of wheeled tractors and to replace them by caterpillar tractors, to replace tens of thousands of obsolescent combines and to produce new machines, say, for technical cultures? This involves expenses running into milliards which could return only over six to eight years. Only the State can take upon itself such expenditure, because it and it alone is in a position to bear the losses resulting from the withdrawal and replacement of obsolescent machinery, because it and it alone is in a position to bear such losses over six to eight years in expectation of eventual returns."

We are thus told that the collective farms are not in a position to undertake medium-term investment necessary for the periodical modernization of their equipment. This is a somewhat specious argument, because the financial capacity of the *kolkhozy* depends largely on the government's price- and credit-policies. Stalin perhaps intended to say that the *kolkhozy* could not be relied upon to make the investments rather than to claim that they were economically absolutely in no position to make them. More relevant than this is, however, Stalin's second argument:

"Let us suppose for a moment that we have adopted comrades Sanina's and Venzher's proposals and have begun to sell . . . Machine Tractor Stations to the *kolkhozy*. What would be the consequence?

"In the first instance the *kolkhozy* would become owners of essential means of production. They would thus find themselves in an exceptional position such as no business concern in our country enjoys, for, as is well known, even our nationalized business concerns are not the owners of their means of production. How could this exceptional situation of the *kolkhozy* be justified, by what consideration of progress and advance? Could it be said that this situation would be conducive to raising *kolkhoz* property to the level of national property, that it would speed up the transition of our society from socialism to communism? Would it not be more correct to say that this would only lengthen the distance between *kolkhoz* property and national property and that it would not bring [our economy] closer to communism, but, on the contrary, take it further away from communism.

"The result would, secondly, be that the sphere of commodity circulation would be widened, because a colossal number of the means of agricultural production would find itself within the orbit of commodity circulation."

In other words, if the allegedly socialist *kolkhozy* were to own the Machine Tractor Stations, the result would be an enormous strengthening of the antisocialist elements in the Soviet economy. In this Stalin is undoubtedly right. *En passant* he reveals, however, that after more than two decades of collectivization Soviet policy vis-à-vis the peasantry is still saddled with the old dilemma: an impoverished peasantry does not produce enough food and raw materials for the town; but a peasantry enjoying material incentives which ensure high production, accumulates more property than is safe for the regime and imparts to the market economy more momentum than is safe for the planned sector of the economy. Between the lines of Stalin's argument there lurks the fear of the *kulak-kolkhoz*. The idea of the transfer of Machine Tractor Stations to collective farms is probably more than the brainwave of a few economists. It is only natural that the wealthier *kolkhozy* should cast covetous glances on the Machine Tractor Stations. The acquisition of those Stations by them might indeed mark the beginning of a powerful development of modern capitalism in Russian farming. Alas, Stalin has not told his correspondents whether he is afraid here of a contradiction or of a mere difference between town and country; but he has left them in no doubt that the party will continue to stand, with all its might, between the collective farms and the Machine Tractor Stations.

4

Stalin's recent writings offer a glimpse of the movement of ideas going on in the Soviet ruling circles behind the half-real and half-deceptive façade of uniformity. It is this movement that distinguishes present-day Russia from the Russia of the late thirties which was from head to foot stunned and petrified after the shock of the great purges. The movement of ideas reflects conflicting social aspirations and pressures which even a monolithic regime is not in a position to eliminate for good. Despite the rigid orthodox terms in which ideas are formulated, the present discussions are in some respects well ahead of earlier controversies within the Bolshevik Party, because they center on issues which have arisen on a much higher level of economic development. New questions demand new answers, and Stalinism is vitally interested in finding these, even if orthodoxy compels it to look for the answers by roundabout ways and to formulate them in circumlocution and "double-talk."

The "transition from socialism to communism" is at present the chief "double-talk" formula for the discussion of real problems. All views are framed in its terms. Since the formula refers to a future and hypothetical state of society, it sanctions up to a point exploration and experimental thinking, which were almost totally absent from an earlier phase of Stalinism. To the student of Soviet affairs who has followed over the years the violent campaigns against *uravnilovka* (egalitarianism) it is fascinating to watch how in the course of the arguments about the "transition" some economists draw cautiously, timidly yet quite distinctly the vistas of a society which will no longer be afflicted by the economic inequality now prevailing in the Soviet Union. Ideas and notions which were banished as heresies not so long ago seem to creep back into visions of the future and there to experience a quasi rehabilitation. The guesses about the future sometimes sound like reflections on the present—this is not the first time that Utopia is either an implied critique of existing society or an escape from it. Things being in Russia what they are, authority's sudden and angry reactions against flights of experimental thought are inevitable. Yet this particular dream, the dream about the higher phase of communism, has been officially licensed and encouraged; and the Soviet citizen has even sometimes been led to believe that the "transition" is not a matter for his "children and grandchildren" but something which his own generation can and must achieve.

There is something profoundly paradoxical in all this. The present rulers of the Soviet Union require on the one hand the Soviet citizen to show a blind faith in, and a pious devotion to, Soviet institutions and policies such *as they are.* In this respect the Soviet rulers are more conservative than even the most conservative governments, for none require from their citizens quite as much faith in and enthusiasm for the established order. On the other hand, Stalinism also instills in the Soviet people the revolutionary conviction that most of these exalted institutions and policies deserve to be scrapped or radically changed in the transition from socialism to communism. Thus Stalinism works to impose a standstill upon the minds and the thoughts of the people and at the same time it desires to keep those thoughts and minds on the move, searching for new worlds.

Stalin has now sounded a note of caution. He has warned the "young cadres," lured by the "higher phase," that the transition from socialism to communism is a long uphill road. Years ago he used to scold those who spoke about "objective laws" setting limits to governmental action. "There are no fortresses which the Bolsheviks cannot seize" was his slogan then. Now he scolds those who ignore the "objective laws" of a socialist economy or aspire to modify them. His insistence on the validity of economic laws under socialism has, for all its turgid scholasticism, symptomatic significance. When Stalin speaks so emphatically about the objective laws and warns against "economic adventurers," he surely applies the brake to economic policy. His invocation of the economic laws is his substitute for the cry: Moderation! Moderation!

"With us," Stalin says, "commodity production and trade are as necessary at present as they were, say, thirty years ago." Thirty years ago N.E.P. had just been introduced; farming was broken up into twenty-odd million farms; and some industries were just being transferred to capitalist ownership. Stalin's obvious overstatement serves an "educational" purpose. It amounts to a warning against overhasty experiments with farming and the market economy. *En passant* Stalin has made the startling revelation that "some comrades"—is it Voznessensky again?—have advocated the complete nationalization of all farming. Stalin agrees that national or social ownership of the whole economy, including farming, is the precondition for communism which will know no market economy and no money. But he gives to understand that this will be a protracted process to be completed perhaps only in that remote future when capitalism will have vanished in most countries and even the State will have withered away. He explores two methods for the solution of the problems of farming and of the market economy. He rejects direct absorption of farming by the State on grounds of political and social impracticability; and he foreshadows the gradual extension of planning by a single authority to both sectors of the economy and also to the distribution of farm produce.

In his article, dated February 1, 1952, Stalin did not go beyond this general conclusion. He did not specify how he envisaged the gradual extension of planning to collective farming and to the distribution of farm produce. In the letter to Sanina and Benzher dated eight months later (September 28, 1952), he offers a more specific plan. The collective farmer, he argues, cannot be brought to accept social ownership as long as he finds trade in farm produce profitable. The government cannot "abolish" trade, but it must offer to the peasantry something more profitable than trade, namely the direct exchange of industrial goods for farm produce, the exchange of products (*produkto-obmen*) instead of the exchange of commodities. A modest beginning has been made with farms specializing in the cultivation of technical plants. The government buys up their entire crops and pays them partly in money and partly in industrial goods. This practice should be gradually extended to other farms and money should gradually be eliminated from the transactions. Stalin points to the limiting factor which does not allow for a large-scale extension of the practice in the near future: the government is not in a position to offer the collective farmers industrial goods in quantities and assortments that would induce them to give up trade. The key to the solution is to be found in the town, not in the countryside; but the town has not yet produced it. "Such a system," Stalin writes, "requires an enormous increase in the output of goods which the town supplies to the country and therefore we shall have to introduce it without especial haste, only as urban output grows. But introduce it we must, unflaggingly, without wavering, step by step, thus reducing the sphere of commodity circulation. . . ."

As is usual with Stalin, the seriousness of what he has to say grows as he leaves theory and dogma for practical policy. What he foreshadows here may well prove the most significant economic reform contemplated in the Soviet Union since the collectivization of farming. In a nutshell these passages may be said to contain a broad plan for the gradual elimination of the market economy. Unlike collectivization, the reform is envisaged as an evolutionary process, the tempo of which will be dictated by the pace of further industrialization and the extent to which the growth of the Soviet national income may allow the government simultaneously to participate in the armaments race, to go on with massive investment in heavy industry, and to increase rapidly the output of consumer goods especially for rural consumption. Its multiple economic and political commitments may yet force the government to postpone the reform to an indefinite future. But even in the most favorable circumstances, a reform of this kind would require a decade or two for its successful completion. A great abundance of industrial consumer goods is only the first condition of its success. There still remain the imponderables, the mental habits, the social customs, and the economic "prejudices" of the peasantry which have all to be overcome before the *kolkhoznik* gives up the *kolkhoz* market for *produkto-obmen*. Although it has proved possible to drive the *muzhik* into the collective farm and to compel and induce him to stay in it, it has so far proved impossible to drive out of him his attachment to property, as Stalin now implicitly admits. The peasant's individualism has been kept within bounds and subdued but not destroyed. In a poverty-stricken nation, amid the miseries of the first decades of collectivization, it has still been property and trade that have offered or promised the peasant relative well-being and security. Not before planned economy can offer him much greater well-being and security can it begin to undo the rural market. Stalin's cautious approach to this problem seems therefore well justified.

The note of caution rings even more broadly in Stalin's "three conditions" for the transition to communism. In Stalin's own words—"in order to *prepare* the *transition* to communism in reality and not merely in declarations it is necessary to fulfil *at least* three essential *preliminary* conditions" (my italics). This sounds quite different from the glib assurances that Soviet society is already in the process of that transition. The "three conditions" include: (1) the continued intensive development of the country's industrial resources; (2) the slow and gradual adjustment of collective farming to the nationalized sector of the economy and the gradual abolition of trade;[2] and (3) the raising of the standards of living and of the cultural standards, the reduction of the working day "*at least*" to six or rather to five hours, the doubling (again "*at least*") of real wages, and the spread of education which would allow the contradiction between brainwork and manual labor to be abolished. As this statement appeared on the eve of the Nineteenth Congress of the party, it led commentators to expect an imminent shortening of the working day, which at eight hours is still longer than it was in the 1930's. The congress, however, has not reduced working hours, which also indicates that Stalin's "three conditions" are regarded as a long-term program.

Stalin had intended to give the "young cadres" the measure of the great distance which separates Soviet society from communism and to indicate in what way that distance might be shortened. What he has actually indicated is, in Marxist terms, the distance that still separates the Soviet Union not from communism but from socialism.

---

[2] "It is necessary, secondly, by way of *gradual transitions,* effected with benefit to the collective farms and consequently to the whole of society, to raise collective property to the level of national property and to replace commodity circulation by the system of *produkto-obmen,* also by way of *gradual transitions,* so that the central government or some other socialeconomic directing body should be able to encompass the whole output of social production in the interest of society."

Part Three

HISTORICAL ESSAYS

1. Two Revolutions [1]

An eminent French historian once wrote: "Consider the revolutions of the Renaissance: in them you will find all the passions, all the spirit, and all the language of the French revolution." With some reservations, one might also say that if one considers the Great French revolution, one can find in it the passions, the spirit, and the language of the Russian revolution. This is true to such an extent that it is absolutely necessary for the student of recent Russian history to view it every now and then through the French prism. (The student of the French revolution, too, may gain new insights if occasionally he analyzes his subject in the light of the Russian experience.) Historical analogy by itself is, of course, only one of the many angles from which he ought to approach his subject; and it may be downright misleading if he merely contents himself with assembling the points of formal resemblance between historical situations. "History is concrete"; and this means, among other things, that every event or situation is unique, regardless of its possible similarity to other events and situations. In drawing any analogy, it is therefore important to know where the analogy ends. I hope

[1] The publication of a French edition of *Stalin: A Political Biography* (English ed., New York and London, Oxford University Press, 1949) has given me an opportunity to comment on one aspect of that book, the analogies between the Russian and the French revolutions. These comments, written in 1950, appear here in substantially the same form as in the introduction to the French edition of *Stalin* (Paris, Gallimard).

143

that I shall not offend badly against this rule; and I would like to acknowledge my great debt to the eminent French historians whose works on the French revolution have helped me to gain new insights into the Russian revolution.

It is well known that the controversy over the "Russian Thermidor" played in its time a great role in the struggles inside the Bolshevik Party. Trotsky placed his thesis about the Russian Thermidor in the very center of his denunciation of the Stalinist regime. This issue was dealt with only indirectly in my political biography of Stalin. (In my view, the Russian counterparts to the Jacobin, Thermidorian, and Bonapartist phases of the revolution have in a curious way overlapped and merged in Stalinism.) A critical examination of this whole problem will be found in my forthcoming *Life of Trotsky*, where it properly belongs. For the present I will concentrate on another perspective on recent Russian history, a perspective somewhat similar to that which was drawn by Albert Sorel in relation to the French revolution in his monumental *L'Europe et la Révolution Française*. I have in mind the reassertion of national tradition in a revolutionary society.

The Bolshevik revolution of 1917 was in intention a radical break with Russia's past, a break with her old social outlook, with her old methods of government, with her customs, habits, and traditions. It was a great and stormy funeral of all the anachronisms inherited from centuries of backwardness, serfdom, and tyranny. The three postrevolutionary decades, however, saw a complex and contradictory development: on the one hand, Russia's advance, with gigantic strides, in industrialization and education, and a release of national energies such as only a great revolution can produce; on the other hand, an amazing resurrection of Russia's buried past, and the revenge of that past upon the present. It is as the embodiment of this contradictory development that I wish to consider Stalin. To an almost equal degree, Stalin represents the impetus given to Russia by the revolution and the triumph of the traditions of the *ancien régime* over the original spirit of the revolution. Yet, did not Napoleon I represent a similar phenomenon? Were not the revolutionary and the *Roi Soleil* blended in his personality as much as the Leninist and Ivan the Terrible (or Peter the Great) are blended in Stalin?

Those who are interested mainly in the individual psychology of historical personalities may be outraged by this comparison. Stalin, they may object, has none of the *élan*, the *esprit*, the charm, and nothing of the originality of mind and expression with which nature so richly endowed Bonaparte. This is willingly admitted. But we are concerned here with something else, with the respective functions of the two personalities in the history of their countries; and these ought to be viewed in the light of broader, impersonal factors, of the moving forces, the motives and objectives of the two revolutions, and in the light of their different social backgrounds and national traditions. Incidentally, even the contrast between the individual characteristics of the two men fits in with and can up to a point be explained by the contrast between their national backgrounds and traditions. Napoleon, the Emperor, descended indirectly from an absolute monarchy, the chief representative of which appears, in historical idealization, as the *Roi Soleil.* The Czar who in a sense is Stalin's political ancestor could earn, even from his apologists, no brighter epithet than *Grozny*—the Awe-inspiring. Napoleon has the clear air, bright color, and elegance of Versailles and Fontainebleau as his background; while Stalin's figure harmonizes with the grim *ambiance* of the Kremlin. Thus, even the individual temper of the two men seems to reflect something impersonal.

Albert Sorel describes how heavily tradition weighed upon the revolution: "Events hurled them [the members of the Convention] abruptly into power: if they had had a taste for liberty, they would have had no spare time to serve an apprenticeship in it." [2] The leaders of the Russian Soviets had just as little spare time in which to serve an apprenticeship in liberty as had the leaders of the Convention. "At the beginning of the revolution, the minds of men rushed towards the ideal: everything was destroyed, everything was renewed; France was re-created, so to speak, after having been annihilated. . . . Disorder, anarchy, civil war ensued. Foreign war was added. The revolution was threatened, France invaded. The Republicans had to defend at one and the same time the independence of the nation, the territory of the homeland, the principles of the revolution, the supremacy of their party, even their own lives. . . . With pure reason confounded, they fell back brutally on empiricism: they turned from instinct to custom, to routine, to precedents: none were for liberty, countless numbers were for despotism. Thus all the processes of government of the *ancien régime* were seen to insinuate themselves, in the name of expedience, into the revolution. Once having regained their place, they remained there as masters. All the theoreticians' art consisted of nothing more than masking and disguising them." [3] How admirably these words suit the fortunes of the Russian revolution as well!

Yet, while it is right to point to this reassertion of tradition, a reassertion that some may regard as natural and sound and others may view as a distortion of the revolution, it would be wrong to see in the postrevolutionary regime nothing but a prolongation of the *ancien régime*. Under the Empire, French history did not merely pick up the threads that had been violently snapped by the Convention; it wove the pattern of a new France and it worked the threads of tradition into that new pattern. The same may be said of Stalinist Russia. She may feel the revenge of the past on her-

---

[2] Albert Sorel, *L'Europe et la Révolution Française* (third ed., Paris, 1893), Part 1, p. 224.
[3] *Ibid.*, pp. 224–225.

self, but she does not revert to that past. The Bourbon monarchy could never have produced anything like the Napoleonic Code, that legal-philosophical mirror of a bourgeois society. Similarly, planned economy could never have come into existence within the framework of the old Russia. To make it possible, nothing less than the October Revolution was needed; and in it, in the principle and the practice of the planned economy, the October Revolution has survived and developed, despite the insinuation of "all the processes of government of the *ancien régime*."

In the case of the Russian revolution, it would be even more unrealistic than in that of the French to deny or overlook what is essentially new and epoch-making in its achievement. There may have been some justification for Sorel's view that if the French revolution had not taken place, the *ancien régime* would, in the course of time, have done some of the work that was accomplished only after its overthrow.[4] The point is that within the shell of France's *ancien régime* the elements of a modern bourgeois society had achieved a relatively high degree of maturity; the revolution merely broke the shell and thereby facilitated and speeded up the organic growth and development of those elements. Even so, historians like Michelet, Jaurés, and others, who stressed the essentially new and creative work of the revolution, seem nearer the truth than Sorel, whose emphasis on historical continuity, so original and illuminating in many respects, appears in others to be exaggerated and essentially conservative. In the case of Russia, the limits within which the law of historical continuity operates are undoubtedly much narrower. The elements of the present collectivist society, with its planned economy—let us leave aside whether this society deserves to be called socialist or not—hardly existed under the surface of Russia's *ancien régime*. They are largely the conscious creation of the revolution and of the post-

---

[4] This idea was, of course, developed before Sorel by Alexis de Tocqueville in *L'Ancien Régime*.

revolutionary government. As a builder of a new economy and a pioneer of new social techniques, Stalin, for all his limitations and vices—the limitations of an empiricist and the vices of a despot—is likely to leave deeper marks on history than any single French revolutionary leader. Here perhaps is the point at which the difference in the very nature of the two revolutions tends to make further comparisons misleading.

Let us now try to investigate how far the analogy holds good in a different field—in the French revolution's foreign policy, in its impact on the world and the world's impact on it. Sorel, who surveyed this vast field with the greatest thoroughness and understanding, tells us that "To come to terms with the French revolution, the old Europe abdicated its principles; to come to terms with the old Europe, the French revolution falsified its own. France had solemnly renounced conquests. . . . Victory made the revolution bellicose. The war, begun for the defence of French territory, continued for the invasion of neighbouring territories. After having conquered in order to liberate, France partitioned in order to retain." [5] Reading this, one cannot help thinking of Yalta and Potsdam, where by acquiescing in the expansion of Stalinist Russia, the statesmen of the capitalist West so clearly abdicated their principles, while Stalinist Russia, by insisting on strategic frontiers and on the absorption of most of the neighboring lands which had once been conquered by the Czars, so flagrantly falsified her own. Is it really true that history does not repeat itself? Or that in the repetition the original drama becomes a farce? Is it not rather that in its Russian repetition the French tragedy appears magnified and intensified, projected as it is from the European to the global scale and from an epoch preceding the steam engine to the age of atomic energy?

Let us once again compare the original with the repetition: "Not being able to destroy all the monarchies, she

[5] Albert Sorel, *L'Europe et la Révolution Française*, p. 3.

[the revolution] was forced to come to terms with the monarchs. She vanquished her enemies, she pursued them on their own territory, she effected magnificent conquests; but to keep them at peace, it was necesssary to treat: to treat, it was necessary to negotiate, and to negotiate was to return to custom. The *ancien régime* and the revolution compromised not on principles which were irreconcilable, but on frontiers which were changeable. There existed only one idea in common on which the old Europe and Republican France could understand each other and come to an agreement: it was *raison d'état*. It ruled their treaties. The territories not having changed their places, and the ambitions of States remaining what they were, all the traditions of the old statecraft were reborn in the negotiations. These traditions accorded only too well with the designs of the revolutionaries . . . they placed at the service of the victorious revolution the methods of the *ancien régime*." [6] While from the angle of the internal development of the revolution it may be said that up to a point the phases corresponding to Jacobinism, Thermidorianism, and Bonapartism have merged in Stalinism, in its foreign policy during the Second World War victorious Stalinism simply put to its service the methods of the *ancien régime*. I have described in my book how at Potsdam and Yalta Stalin's "conduct, aspirations, methods of action, even his gestures and caprices vividly resembled the behaviour, the aspirations, and gestures of Tsar Alexander I at the conclusion of the Napoleonic wars." [7] And what was Stalin's conception of the preponderance of the Great Powers and of the division between them of spheres of influence if not that old *raison d'état*, the only idea which he held in common with Churchill and Roosevelt? That this *raison d'état* agreed, in a way, with a revolutionary design subsequent events were to reveal.

Russia, like France before her, has carried her revolution

[6] *Ibid.*, pp. 544–545.
[7] *Stalin*, p. 530.

abroad. It was not, let us note, in the Jacobin and Republican period that Europe caught the revolutionary infection from France. And it was not in the heroic, Leninist period that the Bolshevik revolution spread beyond Russian frontiers. The two revolutions were carried abroad by rulers who had first tamed those revolutions at home. "The revolution was arrested in France and in a way congealed in military despotism; but, by the very action of that despotism, it continued to propagate itself in Europe. Conquest spread it among the peoples. Although greatly degenerated, it retained enough appeal to excite them. . . ." [8] And again: "It was in that form that the revolution appeared to have arrested itself and fixed itself in France; it was in that form that Europe understood it and imitated it." [9] It is in its Stalinist, and not in its Leninist and Trotskyist form that the revolution has come to a halt and has fixed itself in Russia, and it is in this form that it has spread, to the amazement of disillusioned ex-Communists who have difficulty understanding how a revolution so "greatly degenerated" has been able to retain so much appeal.[10]

Like Bonapartist France, Stalinist Russia has created a whole system of satellites. In this Stalin might find a grave warning to himself. It was the revolt of its own satellites that contributed so signally to the downfall of the Bonapartist empire. Two of these satellites, Prussia and Italy, inflicted on France some of its most severe setbacks. It was an Italian patriot who wrote in 1814 the following significant words: "It is painful for me to say it, for no one feels more than I the gratitude which we owe Napoleon; no one appreciates better than I the value of each drop of that generous French blood which watered the Italian soil and redeemed it; but I must be permitted to say it, for it is the truth: to see the French depart was an immense, an ineffable joy." We have

---

[8] Albert Sorel, *L'Europe et la Révolution Française*, pp. 4–5.
[9] *Ibid.*, p. 548.
[10] The reader will find a more detailed discussion of this point in *Stalin*, Chapters XIII and XIV.

heard Tito uttering similar words about the Russians, and who knows how many Eastern European Communists would be happy to utter them if they could? To Bonaparte, and many of his compatriots, the behavior of Italy and Prussia looked like the height of ingratitude. So does the behavior of Tito to Stalin. But what is it that gives rise to that "ingratitude"?

Neither of these systems of satellites has lacked redeeming features. "In the countries which France united with her territory or constituted in her image," says Sorel, "she proclaimed her principles, destroyed the feudal system, and introduced her laws. After the inevitable disorders of war and the first excesses of conquest, this revolution constituted an immense benefit to the peoples. This is why the conquests of the Republic could not be confused with the conquests of the *ancien régime*. They differed in the essential characteristic that, despite the abuse of principles and the deviations of ideas, the work of France was accomplished for the nations." [11] Without repeating here my analysis of our contemporary counterpart to this phenomenon, I shall only say that I do not believe that the verdict of history on the Stalinist system of satellites will in this respect be more severe than it has been on the Bonapartist system.[12] However, the French system of satellites was not saved by its redeeming features. It would be difficult to find a more brilliant and more convincing explanation of this fact than the one offered by Sorel:

"The French republicans believed themselves to be cosmopolitans, but they were that only in their speeches; they felt, they thought, they acted, they interpreted their universal

---

[11] Albert Sorel, *L'Europe et la Révolution Française*, p. 547.
[12] I was brought up in Poland, one of Napoleon's satellite countries, where even in my day the Napoleonic legend was so strongly alive that, as a schoolboy, I wept bitter tears over Napoleon's downfall, as nearly every Polish child did. And now I live in England, where most school children, I am sure, still rejoice over the story of the defeat of Napoleon, that villain of the English traditionalist historians.

ideas and their abstract principles in accordance with the
traditions of a conquering monarchy. . . . They identified
humanity with their homeland, their national cause with the
cause of all the nations. Consequently and entirely naturally,
they confused the propagation of new doctrines with the
extension of French power, the emancipation of humanity
with the grandeur of the Republic, the reign of reason with
that of France, the liberation of peoples with the conquest of
States, the European revolution with the domination of the
French revolution in Europe . . . they established subservient and subordinate republics which they held in a sort of
tutelage. . . . The revolution degenerated into an armed
propaganda, then into conquest. . . ." [13] In the same way,
the Russian Stalinists think of themselves as internationalists,
but they feel, think, and act with the tradition of a conquering monarchy behind them; and so they, too, confuse the
emancipation of mankind with the grandeur of their republic and the reign of reason with the rule of Russia. No wonder that the reaction of the satellite peoples tends to take a
familiar form: "The peoples easily understood this language
[of emancipation spoken by the revolution]. . . . What they
did not understand at all was that, using this language, . . .
she [France] aimed at enslaving them and exploited them.
They made no distinction, moreover, between her and the
man who governed her; they did not investigate the phases
through which the French revolution had passed, and how
the Republic had transformed itself into an empire; they
knew the revolution only in the form of conquest . . . and
it was in that form that, even by virtue of its principles,
they came to abhor it. They rose against its domination." [14]
We are not prophesying here a rising of the peoples against
Stalinist domination. But there can be little doubt that the
peoples of Eastern and Central Europe, who might have
understood well the language of social emancipation spoken

[13] Albert Sorel, *L'Europe et la Révolution Française,* pp. 541–42.
[14] *Ibid.,* p. 5.

by Russia, cannot understand why they should become subordinate to Russia; that they, and others, make no distinction now between the Russian revolution and "the man who governs her"; that they are not interested in the stages by which the Republic of the Workers' and Peasants' Councils has become transformed into something like an empire; and that they know the Russian revolution largely in the form of conquest.

Having indulged in these comparisons, I cannot but point out where and why this broad historical analogy ceases to apply. I shall not dwell on the obvious differences—in some respects important, in others irrelevant—between two revolutions, one of which was bourgeois in character and the other proletarian, at least in origin. Nor shall I expatiate on the major differences between the international scene as it looks now and as it looked a century and a half ago. But a few words ought perhaps to be said on one important development—the Chinese revolution—which has come to light only very recently.

The lightning collapse of the Kuomintang and the absolute victory of the Communist armies have clearly altered the international balance of power. In the long run, the Chinese revolution must also have its repercussions inside Russia. This revolution obviously deserves to be placed in a different category from the "revolutions from above" that took place in Eastern and Central Europe in the years 1945-1948. The latter were mainly the by-products of Russia's military victory: "Although the local Communist Parties were its immediate agents and executors, the great party of the revolution, which remained in the background, was the Red Army." [15] In contrast to this, even though it may have drawn moral inspiration from Russia, Chinese communism can rightly claim that its revolution has been its own work and its own achievement. The very magnitude of the Chinese revolution and its intrinsic momentum have been such that it is ludicrous to

[15] *Stalin*, p. 554.

consider it as anybody's puppet creation. This is not a satellite of the Russian revolution, but another great upheaval
in its own right. For this phenomenon we find no parallel in
the epoch of the French revolution. To its very end the
French revolution stood alone. One can only think of an imaginary analogy: one may wonder what Europe would look
like if, at the turn of the eighteenth and nineteenth centuries,
Germany, then disunited and backward, had carried out
more or less independently its own version of the French
revolution. A combination of a Jacobin or Bonapartist
France with a unified, Jacobin Germany might have given
history a direction different from that which France alone
could impart to it. Perhaps there would have been no Wa-
terloo. Or perhaps the antirevolutionary forces of Europe
would have joined hands much earlier and more resolutely
than they did against France alone.

Both Stalinists and anti-Stalinists have recently begun to
foster the legend that Stalin has been the actual inspirer of
the Chinese revolution. How is this to be reconciled with
his role in the events in China in 1925-1927? How is this
to be squared with Stalin's own statement at Potsdam that
"the Kuomintang is the only political force capable of ruling
China"? [16] It may be argued that at Potsdam he was ostensibly disavowing the Chinese Communists only to trick his
Western allies. But this was hardly the case. The version of
events which seems much nearer to the truth is that until
very late in the day Stalin had a low opinion of the ability
of the Communist Party to bring China under its control,
and that he went so far as to attempt, even in 1948, to dis-
suade Mao Tse-tung from launching the series of offensives
which was to bring victory to Chinese communism. A letter
from Stalin to Mao to this effect was apparently read at the
Conference of the Chinese Communist Party that took place

[16] For instance, see James F. Byrnes, *Speaking Frankly* (New York, 1947),
p. 228.

shortly before the opening of the offensive; but the Conference rejected Stalin's advice.[17]

In his untimely skepticism about the Chinese revolution, Stalin appears true to character. He made a similar miscalculation in the middle 1920's, before Chiang Kai-shek started his great march to the north. In March 1926, the Russian Politburo discussed whether it should encourage Chiang (then still Moscow's ally and honorary member of the Executive of the Comintern) in his plans for the conquest of the whole of China. Stalin insisted that Chiang be advised to content himself with the area in the south, where he was in actual control, and to seek a *modus vivendi* with Chang Tso-lin's government which still controlled the north. Chiang disregarded this advice and shortly thereafter established his control over all of China. More than two decades later, Stalin again seems to have overrated the stability of an old and decaying regime and underrated the revolutionary forces opposed to it. With much more justification than Tito, Mao Tse-tung might therefore say that not only was his regime not created by force of Russian arms, but that he secured its triumph against Moscow's explicit advice.

Whatever the truth about Stalin's role in these events, the Chinese revolution is likely to affect strongly the fortunes of Stalinism. In my book, Stalinism was shown to be primarily the product of the isolation of Russian Bolshevism in a capitalist world and of the mutual assimilation of the isolated

[17] In *The Times,* a Special Correspondent wrote on his return from Peking: '. . . there is much evidence to suggest that the Kremlin did not anticipate the sweeping victory which Chinese Communism was so soon to gain. . . . As late as July 1948 the Russians neither expected nor desired an immediate Communist victory in China. In that month the Chinese Communist Party held a conference to discuss plans for the coming autumn campaign. The advice from Russia was to continue guerrilla warfare for the coming year in order to weaken America, who was expected to continue to pour arms into China in support of the Kuomintang. Russia opposed any plan to end the civil war by taking the large cities. Russian advice was rejected by this conference, the contrary policy was adopted. . . .' *The Times,* 27 June 1950. Similar reports have appeared in many other papers.

revolution with the Russian tradition. The victory of Chinese communism marks the end of that isolation; and it does so much more decisively than did the spread of Stalinism in Eastern Europe. Thus, one major precondition for the emergence of Stalinism now belongs to the past. This should stimulate processes inside Russia, tending to overcome that strange ideology and frame of mind which formed themselves in the period of isolation. Yet we know how often in history effects do outlast causes; and for how long they do so!

While in one of its repercussions the Chinese revolution tends to deprive Stalinism of its *raison d'être,* in another it tends to strengthen and consolidate it. Stalinism has not only been the product of isolated Bolshevism; it has also reflected the ascendancy of the Oriental, semi-Asiatic and Asiatic, over the European element in Russia, and consequently in the revolution. Mao Tse-tung's victory enhances that element and imparts to it immense additional weight. How much more real must his own *Ex Oriente Lux* sound to Stalin himself now than it did in 1918, when he published it! So much indeed has the Oriental element come to predominate in the whole international Communist movement that the struggle between communism and anticommunism is more and more becoming identified, not only geographically, with the antagonism between East and West. The fact that communism is in its origin a Western idea *par excellence* and that the West exported it to Russia is almost forgotten. Having conquered the East and absorbed its climate and traditions, communism in its Stalinist form not only fails to understand the West, but itself becomes more and more incomprehensible to the West. In Russia, the Greek Orthodox and Byzantine tradition has refracted itself in the revolution. Will the Confucian tradition now similarly refract itself through Chinese communism?

The political history of Stalin is a tale not lacking in grimness and cruelty, but one ought perhaps to be cautioned against drawing from it a moral of disillusionment or despair, for the story is not yet finished. Nearly every great revolution has destroyed as many hopes as it has fulfilled; every revolution therefore has left behind it an aftermath of frustration and cynicism. As a rule, men have been able to do full justice to the whole experience only from a long perspective of time. "What do we know, after all?" Louis Blanc once wrote in a similar context. "In order that progress be realized, perhaps it is necessary that all evil alternatives be exhausted. The life of mankind is very long, and the number of possible solutions very limited. All revolution is useful, in this sense at least, that every revolution takes care of one dangerous alternative. Because from an unfortunate state of affairs societies sometimes tumble into a worse state, let us not hasten to conclude that progress is a chimera." [18] Let us not hasten to do so.

[18] Louis Blanc, *Histoire de Dix Ans* (10th ed., Paris, n.d.), I, 135.

2. Marx and Russia *

The attitudes of Marx and Engels towards Russia and their views on the prospects of Russian revolution form a curious topic in the history of socialism. Did the founders of scientific socialism have any premonition of the great upheaval in Russia that was to be carried out under the sign of Marxism? What results did they expect from the social developments inside the Czarist Empire? How did they view the relationship between revolutionary Russia and the West? One can answer these questions more fully now on the basis of the correspondence between Marx, Engels, and their Russian contemporaries, published by the Marx-Engels-Lenin Institute in Moscow last year. This correspondence covers nearly half a century. It opens with Marx's well-known letters to Anenkov of 1846. It closes with the correspondence between Engels and his Russian friends in 1895. The volume also contains nearly fifty letters published for the first time.

Among the Russians who kept in touch with Marx and Engels there were men and women belonging to three generations of revolutionaries. In the forties the revolutionary movement in Russia had an almost exclusively intellectual and liberal character. It was based on no social class or popular force. To that epoch belonged Marx's early correspondents, Anenkov, Sazonov, and a few others. Marx explained to them his philosophy and his economic ideas, but engaged

* B.B.C. Third Programme talk, November 1948.

in no discussion on revolution in Russia. For this it was too early. Broadly speaking, in those years Russia was to Marx still identical with Czardom, and Czardom was the hated "gendarme of European reaction." His and Engels' main preoccupation was to arouse Europe against that gendarme, for they believed that a European war against Russia would hasten the progress of the West towards socialism.

In the sixties another generation of Russian revolutionaries came to the fore. They were the Narodniks or Populists or Agrarian socialists. It was, curiously enough, with the Russian intellectuals of that school advocating a pure peasant socialism that the two founders of the Western, strictly proletarian, socialism established ties of the closest friendship. Russia possessed no industry yet, no modern working class, almost no bourgeoisie. The intelligentsia and the peasantry were the only forces inside Russia to whom the two sworn enemies of Czardom could look. There was, of course, also Bakunin's anarchism. Marx first co-operated with Bakunin and then quarreled with him. But I shall not discuss that controversy, to which only casual references occur in the correspondence under review. Incidentally, *vis-à-vis* Marx, Bakunin acted more as the spokesman of Italian, Swiss, and Spanish anarchists than as a Russian revolutionary.

The Narodniks in Russia and in exile eagerly responded to the theories of Marx and Engels. Russian was the first language into which *Das Kapital* was translated from the original. Based on English classical economy and German philosophy and on a thorough study of Western industrial capitalism, this great work seemed to bear no direct relation to the social conditions then prevailing in Russia. And yet right from the beginning when it was making no impression on the Western European public, Marx's *opus* exercised an enormous influence upon the Russian intelligentsia. Danielson, the translator of *Das Kapital*, himself a prominent Narodnik and economist, wrote to Marx that the Russian censor passed the book, believing it to be too strictly scientific to be suppressed. The book, so the censor thought, made in any case too heavy reading to have any subversive influence. He was more afraid of the frontispiece of the Russian edition with Marx's portrait, and, allowing Marx's ideas to reach the Russian public, he confiscated his picture. Some years later the Russian censor passed the second volume of *Das Kapital* too, even though he had shortly before confiscated a Russian edition of the works of good old Adam Smith. Nine hundred copies of *Das Kapital* were sold out in St. Petersburg within a few weeks after its publication in 1872, a very large number considering the character of the book, the time, and the place. But even before that Marx received striking proof of strange Russian enthusiasm for his ideas, when on March 12, 1870, a group of Russian revolutionaries asked him to represent Russia on the General Council of the first International.

Marx was slightly puzzled by this unexpected Russian enthusiasm; "A funny position for me," he wrote to Engels, "to be functioning as the representative of young Russia! A man never knows what he may come to, or what strange fellowship he may have to submit to." But ironical amusement was only one part, perhaps the least essential, of Marx's reaction to Russian admiration. His mind was agitated by Russia as a social phenomenon. At the age of fifty he and Engels began to learn Russian. They watched the development of Russian literature and swallowed volume after volume of Russian statistics and sociology. Marx even intended to rewrite a portion of *Das Kapital* so as to base it on his Russian findings, an intention he was never able to carry out. Although amusement at some Russian eccentricities never left them, both Marx and Engels acquired a profound respect for the Russian intellectual achievement. Chernyshevsky, then serving his term of slave labor in Siberia, impressed Marx as the most original contemporary thinker and economist. He planned to arouse protests in Western Europe against the victimization of Chernyshevsky, but Chernyshevsky's friends feared that foreign protest and intervention might do more harm than good to the great convict. Dobrolyubov, who had died at the age of twenty-five, was another Russian thinker highly valued by Marx as "a writer of the stature of a Lessing or a Diderot." Finally, in 1884, Engels wrote to Madame Papritz, a Russian singer, and translator of Engels:

"We both, Marx and myself, cannot complain about your countrymen. If in some groups there was more revolutionary muddle than scientific research, there was also, on the other hand, critical thought and disinterested investigation in the field of pure theory, worthy of the nation of Dobrolyubov and Chernyshevsky . . . I have in mind not only the active revolutionary socialists, but also the historical and critical school in Russian literature, which is infinitely superior to anything achieved by respectable historians in Germany and France."

But the main issue of the correspondence was Russia's road to socialism. In the West, capitalist industrialization was, according to Marx and Engels, paving the way for socialism. The industrial working class was the main force interested in socialism. But what about Russia, where capitalist industry had not even begun to strike roots? The Narodniks argued that Russian socialism would be based on the primeval rural commune or the *obshchina,* which had existed alongside feudalism. Even after the emancipation of the serfs in 1861, the peasant land was still owned by the rural commune, in some respects the forerunner of the present Russian *kolkhoz.* Russia, said the Narodniks, need not go through the trials and tribulations of capitalist industrialism to attain socialism. She finds socialism in her native rural tradition, which she only needs to cleanse of feudal remnants. This then was to be Russia's road to socialism, very different from that by which Western Europe was expected to travel.

Most, though not all, Narodniks were Slavophils and believed in Russia's peculiar socialist mission. Marx, as we know, rejected Slavophilism; and nothing made him more furious than the talk about Russia's socialist mission. He did not believe, he once said, that old Europe needed to be rejuvenated by Russian blood. But he did, nevertheless, share some of the hopes that the Narodniks placed on the Russian rural commune. Here, he said, in a famous letter to a Russian periodical in 1877, here was "the finest chance ever offered by history to any nation" the chance to escape capitalism and to pass from feudalism straight into socialism. True, Marx added important qualifications: the rural commune had begun to disintegrate, and if that process were to continue Russia would miss her "finest chance." Moreover, a stimulus from outside, the socialist transformation of Western Europe, was needed to enable Russia to build socialism on the rural commune. In his eyes Western Europe had the birthright of socialist revolution, while Russia's role could be secondary only. Nevertheless, Russia might have her own short cut to socialism.

He and Engels also sympathized with the terrorism of the Narodniks, with their attempts on the life of the Czar and his satraps. When, in 1881, revolutionaries assassinated Czar Alexander II, Marx and Engels applauded the deed. In a message to a Russian meeting commemorating the tenth anniversary of the Paris Commune, they expressed the hope that the assassination of the Czar foreshadowed "the formation of a Russian Commune." Here we reach the most dramatic point in the whole correspondence. By the time of the assassination of Alexander II a new generation of revolutionaries, the first real Russian Marxists, had entered politics. Their chief spokesmen were George Plekhanov, Vera Zasulich, and Paul Axelrod, the future founders of Russian social democracy. These first Russian Marxists were bitterly opposed to the Narodniks precisely on those points in which Marx and Engels had supported them. The young Marxists opposed terrorism. Plekhanov in particular had regarded the planned assassination of the Czar as a senseless adventure. He believed that the task of Russian revolutionaries was to abolish the autocratic system, not to kill an autocrat. The Russian Marxists further believed that like Western Europe Russia had to go through capitalist industrialization and the experience of democratic self-government before she could even begin to evolve in the direction of socialism. They held that the rural commune was irretrievably disintegrating and was of no use to socialism. They placed their hopes not on the peasants but on the industrial working class now beginning to grow, not on agrarian but on proletarian socialism.

Both Narodniks and Marxists quoted *Das Kapital* as their authority. The Marxists had reason to expect that the two great Western socialists would agree with them that Russia was destined to go through the same evolution that Western Europe had gone through. One can therefore imagine their disappointment when Marx himself cold-shouldered them. In a letter to Vera Zasulich of 1881 Marx told them that it was no use to quote *Das Kapital* against the Narodniks and the rural commune, for in *Das Kapital* he had analyzed the social structure of Western Europe only—Russia might well evolve toward socialism in her own way. Marx admitted that the rural commune had begun to decay, but on balance he still subscribed to the Narodnik view that the commune had a great future. Nor was Marx impressed by indignant arguments against Narodnik terrorism, although he regarded it as a "specifically Russian and historically inevitable method about which there is no reason . . . to moralize for or against." He would, of course, have none of that terrorism in Western Europe.

In 1883 Marx died and Engels took over the correspondence. The Russian Marxists tried to convert the surviving founding father of the Marxist school to their view. At first they were unsuccessful. Engels persisted in the hope that the Narodnik terrorist attempts would lead to the overthrow of Czardom. In 1884 and 1885 he expected dramatic political changes inside Russia. Russia, he wrote, was approach-

ing her 1789. Recalling the assassination of the Czar four
years after the event, he said that this was "one of the exceptional cases in which a handful of men could make a revolution," a view that the young Russian Marxists, hoping for
revolution by a social class and not by a "handful of men,"
had already derided as a dangerous illusion. "Every month
now," Engels wrote to Vera Zasulich in 1884, "ought to ag-
gravate Russia's domestic difficulties. If some constitution-
ally minded and courageous Grand Duke were to appear
now, even the Russian upper classes would find that a palace
revolution was the best way out of the impasse." One can
imagine the ironical smile with which Plekhanov and Zasulich tried to disillusion him but in vain. We now know that in
this controversy it was the Russian Marxists and not Marx
and Engels whom events proved to be right. The assassination of Alexander II in fact entailed the disintegration and
demoralization of the Narodnik movement and a prolonged
period of reaction. This cool attitude of Marx and Engels towards their Russian followers was marked by intellectual inconsistency. But it was understandable and very human.
The Narodniks had been Marx's close and admired friends,
the first to raise the banner of popular revolution, the first
to respond, in their own Slavonic manner, to Marxism. The
Narodnik views had now become outdated. But an old loyalty and, no doubt, remoteness from the Russian scene, prevented Marx and Engels from grasping this as quickly as
their young Russian pupils had done it.

Only in the early nineties, towards the end of his life, Engels at last realized that Plekhanov and Zasulich had been
right, that the rural commune was doomed, that capitalism
was invading Russia and that the agrarian brand of socialism had to give way to the industrial one. He tried to impress
his new view upon the old Narodniks, especially upon Danielson, the translator of *Das Kapital*. The letters that now
passed between Danielson and Engels make melancholy
reading. Danielson vented his disappointment with Engels'

new attitude. He described very eloquently the evils of capitalism in Russia, suggesting that by its insistence on the need
for Russia to go through the capitalist phase Marxism acted
as *advocatus diaboli*. He reminded Engels what great store
Marx had set by the Russian rural commune. In reply Engels argued seriously, patiently, and gently, very gently indeed, that new social processes had taken place, that in the
meantime the rural commune had become part of a "dead
past," and that though the evils of capitalism were so great,
Russia could unfortunately not escape them. "History,"
said Engels, "is the most cruel of all goddesses. She drives
her triumphal chariot over heaps of corpses, not only during
war, but even in times of 'peaceful' economic development."

This was a reference to the disastrous Russian drought
and famine of 1891, which Danielson had blamed on incipient capitalist disorganization in agriculture. The rural commune, Engels went on, would have become the basis for
Russian socialism, if in the industrial West socialism had
won "some ten or twenty years ago. Unfortunately, we [that
is the West] have been too slow." Which were the symp-
toms? The loss by England of her industrial monopoly, the
industrial competition between France, Germany, and England. "America," Engels wrote in 1893, "bids fair to drive
them all out of the world's markets. . . . The introduction of an at least relative free-trade policy in America is sure
to complete the ruin of England's industrial position and to
destroy, at the same time, the industrial export trade of Germany and France; then the crisis must come. . . ." Meanwhile capitalism still dominated the West, and Russia, too,
must come within its orbit. This delay in the march of socialism was deplorable. But, said Engels, "we . . . are unfortunately so stupid that we never can pluck up courage for a
real progress unless urged to it by sufferings that seem almost out of proportion" to the goal to be achieved.

It is now easy to see that in this controversy both sides
were right and wrong at the same time. Engels, converted to

the view of his young Russian disciples, was of course right when he said that Russia could not avoid becoming capitalist. But the old Narodnik Danielson was also right in his insistence that Russian capitalism would have little scope for development because the terrifying poverty of the Russian peasants would limit to a minimum its home market and because Russia was too weak to compete with other nations in foreign markets. It was precisely this weakness in Russian capitalism, a weakness not clearly seen either by Engels or by the early Russian Marxists, that led in the last instance to the Bolshevik revolution of 1917. It was this weakness that was to make of Russia, in Lenin's words, the "weakest link in the chain of capitalism."

Nevertheless, Engels had a strong premonition of the coming Russian revolution. Repeatedly he stated that "Russia was the France of the new age." On his dying bed almost, in 1895, he watched the first moves of the new, and the last, Russian Czar Nicolas II, and in a letter to Plekhanov he prophesied: "If the devil of revolution has taken anybody by the scruff of the neck then it is Tsar Nicolas II." But what Engels apparently expected to occur in Russia was "another 1789," another antifeudal, bourgeois revolution, not a socialist one.

Even towards the end of his life, after he had intellectually detached himself from the Narodniks, Engels still refused to criticize them in public. Plekhanov and Zasulich repeatedly urged him to do so and thus to further the cause of Russian Marxism. Engels then somewhat apologetically explained to Plekhanov his extremely delicate attitude towards the old Narodniks:

"It is quite impossible to argue with Russians of that generation . . . who still believe in the spontaneously communistic mission, which allegedly distinguishes Russia, the true holy Russia, from all other infidel countries. . . . Incidentally, in a country like yours . . . surrounded by a more or less solid intellectual Chinese Wall, erected by despotism, one should not be surprised by the appearance of the most incredible and queer combinations of ideas."

With this note of an almost sorrowful understanding for the limitations of his old Narodnik friends, Engels' correspondence came to an end.

3. Trotsky on Stalin *

Trotsky's "appraisal" of Stalin is one of the tragic documents in modern literature. The contemporary reader cannot yet look either at the hero of this book or at its author in the perspective of history, and hence it is not easy to define its value as a document. The train of events, to which the feud of the two men belongs, has not yet run its full course. Even the publication of the book has, regardless of its author's intentions, become a minor incident in the contemporary controversy between East and West. The book was ready for publication in the United States as early as 1941. It was then withheld from print by the American publishers, in deference to the leader of a mighty allied nation. It first saw the light (in the United States) only in 1946, after the Foreign Secretaries of the former allies had fallen out, and opinion had made the remarkable swing from wartime admiration of Russia to acute peacetime suspicion. Thus Trotsky's testimony is being used for discrediting Stalin. *Pro captu lectoris habent sua fata libelli.*

This adventitious use of the book makes it the more necessary to attempt its criticism as a historical document, and nothing else. Imagine that Danton, after his conviction, had been given a lease of life which enabled him to write a biography of Robespierre. His evidence would certainly have in-

* This review of Trotsky's *Stalin* appeared in *The* (London) *Times Literary Supplement* on July 17, 1948.

fluenced posterity's judgment on Robespierre. Yet it is doubtful whether posterity would have accepted that evidence wholly as it stood.

Such an analogy—if an imaginary one—is as imperfect as any comparison drawn between two real and historic situations. Stalin is, and is not, the Robespierre of Bolshevism. In the actual making of the revolution his role was incomparably slighter—the title of the Russian Robespierre goes not to Stalin but to Lenin. It is in the postrevolutionary era that Stalin has loomed just as large, or even larger, than Robespierre; he has even combined his traits with those of the First Consul. On the other hand, Trotsky's resemblance to Danton will hardly be disputed. Both represented the same type of revolutionary leadership, oratorical genius, and tactical brilliance. Both gave expression to the whole *élan* of a revolution so long as popular enthusiasm was its chief motive force and both suffered eclipse when that enthusiasm ebbed away.

If, at times, Stalin appears to combine some traits of Robespierre with some of Bonaparte, in Trotsky also two characters at least seem to have blended—Danton's and Babeuf's. Only a few years after his resounding triumphs the universally acclaimed tribune of the people was already the hunted leader of a new Conspiracy of Equals, raising the cry for the regeneration of the revolution and defying the implacable builders of a half-revolutionary and half-conservative empire. The tide of history ran against Trotsky as powerfully as it had run against Babeuf.

What Trotsky's publishers have now produced is not a biography but an indictment of Stalin. It is a book that bears all the marks of the tremendous nervous pressure under which its author lived his last tragic years. When he wrote it he had behind him more than ten years of a frustrating isolation from the world, ten years in the course of which he wandered uneasily, in constant danger of sudden death, from one uncertain asylum to another. He was oppressed by the nightmare of the Moscow purge trials, in which he had been depicted as the center of a most sinister conspiracy. All his children had died in mysterious circumstances which led him to believe that they had fallen victims to Stalin's vengeance. Finally, while he was still working on this book, on August 20, 1940, he was struck down by an assassin, who presumably was carrying out a verdict passed in Moscow. Only the first seven chapters were finished by him. The others were pieced together from his notes and edited, though not always in strict accordance with Trotsky's trend of thought. Trotsky would have protested against Mr. Malamuth's phrase, "the trend towards centralization, that sure precursor of totalitarianism" or against his description of Marshal Pilsudski as "Poland's Liberator." Small wonder, therefore, that this posthumous book lacks the sweep and brilliance which distinguished his monumental *History of the Russian Revolution*. As a piece of writing it is disappointingly inchoate and at times incoherent. Even so, it must be said that many of its pages are illumined by flashes of genius, epigrams, and sayings that may go down to history:

"Of Christ's twelve apostles [says Trotsky on page 416, referring to the purge trials] Judas alone proved to be a traitor. But if he had acquired power, he would have represented the other eleven apostles as traitors, and also all the lesser apostles, whom Luke numbers as seventy."

And this is how Trotsky sums up his indictment of Stalin:

" '*L'État, c'est moi*' is almost a liberal formula by comparison with the actualities of Stalin's totalitarian regime. Louis XIV identified himself only with the State. The Popes of Rome identified themselves with both the State and the Church—but only during the epoch of temporal power. The totalitarian State goes far beyond Caesaro-Papism, for it has encompassed the entire economy of the country as well. Stalin can justly say, unlike the *Roi Soleil*, '*La Société, c'est moi.*' " . . .

In the conflict of the two men, principles, ideas, and policies were at stake; but the conflict of temperaments was
also important. Two so extremely contrasting personalities would have clashed in any party, in any circumstances.
Stalin's mind is shrewd, strictly practical, cautious, and
pedestrian. Only in an atmosphere overcharged with revolution like that of Czarist Russia could so cautious a mind as
his be attracted by the Marxian doctrine. Where his actions
have the sweep of the boldest social experimentation they reflect less the qualities of that mind than the extraordinary
pressures of a revolution which compel a most circumspect
leader to jump over precipices, in a neck-breaking manner.
As a rule, Stalin makes such jumps *contre-cœur,* when the
situation in which he finds himself allows neither retreat nor
advance by any normal way. Thus in many ways this most
adventurous of contemporary statesmen at heart fears and
abhors adventure. His inclinations are those of the stickler
for the "middle of the road," for "safety first," even though
events have consistently thrown him off the middle of the
road, now toward one and now toward another most unsafe
extreme. Feared by conservatives as the very embodiment of
revolution, he himself has been a conservative in the revolution.

Not so Trotsky. Revolution was his proper element. He
had been drawn to it by his temperament and outlook. The
dialectical philosophy, which views life as the continuous
conflict of opposites, continuous change and movement, was
to him not merely a doctrine to be intellectually absorbed—
it permeated his instinctive behavior. While Stalin distrusts
generalizations, Trotsky was in constant search for them.
Stalin may often miss the wood for the trees. Trotsky had
little or no interest for trees that would not make a wood.
There is no end to such contrasts. Stalin shows an absolute
lack of artistic sense and imagination; he relies exclusively
on his solid mechanics of power. In Trotsky the artist was as
strong as the political leader; he is obviously sincere when

he confesses in his autobiography that he "felt the mechanics of power as an inescapable burden rather than as a spiritual satisfaction." He was ebullient, eloquent, generous, and picturesque, while Stalin's main characteristics are cool reserve, taciturnity, and suspiciousness. Trotsky was the *émigré* steeped in Western European culture, while Stalin breathed the air of Russia only. Small wonder that from their very first personal contact there was suspicion between them. Trotsky recalls the "yellow glint" of animosity which he noticed in Stalin's eyes during their first conversation in Vienna, in 1913. From the beginning he treated Stalin with the contempt that he never abandoned for a moment while he was writing this book.

Trotsky's bitterness towards Stalin is unlimited. Yet the statement that bitterness too often directed his pen must be qualified. As a historian and biographer, Trotsky treats facts, dates, and quotations with almost pedantic conscientiousness. Where he goes wrong is in the constructions put on the facts; he errs in his inferences and guesses. Not rarely his evidence is based on dubious hearsay. To this category belongs his dark, vague, and self-contradictory suggestion that Stalin, in his striving for power, may have speeded up Lenin's death. Yet the historian's conscience, as a rule, does make him draw a clear line of distinction between the facts and his own constructions and guesses, so that the discriminating reader is able to sift the enormous biographical material and form his own opinions.

English readers may find the book's method of exposition extremely wearisome, repetitive, and pedantic. The author delves with unrelenting suspicion into every detail of his adversary's life. Armed with a formidable array of quotations and documents, he polemizes at great length. He often expresses agreement or disagreement with Stalin's other biographers, many of whom hardly deserve to be taken seriously, and it is pathetic that this great political and literary warrior should turn all his big guns on the hares and rabbits roaming the field in front of him.

He was not, however, writing his book with an eye to any English-speaking, or other Western, public. Nor was he greatly interested in its immediate success. Rather, in his thoughts, he addressed a Russian public whom he hoped his words would eventually reach, not, perhaps, in his lifetime: a new Russian generation inured from its cradle to the cult of Stalin and brought up on histories of the revolution, from which Trotsky's name and all that it stood for had been carefully expunged. It was for the benefit of this generation that he set out, step by step, to destroy the Stalinist cult, to reassert his own role in the revolution, and to restate what he regarded as the pristine principles of Bolshevism. The future will show whether his labor was lost or not. In ten or twenty years his *Stalin* may become a great spiritual experience for the Russian intelligentsia, a stimulus for some sweeping, unpredictable "transvaluation of values." A new Russian generation may find in Trotskyism (side by side with an obviously quixotic attempt to put the clock of Russian history back to 1917) a starting-point for a new trend of ideas, just as the progenitors of French socialism found such a starting-point in Babeuf.

Nevertheless, the weakness of Trotsky's indictment is not difficult to see. It appears clearly in, for example, the following passages from page 336:

"This fundamental dissimilarity [between Stalin and the fascist dictators] is illustrated . . . by the uniqueness of Stalin's career by comparison with the careers of . . . Mussolini and Hitler, each the initiator of a movement, each an exceptional agitator, a popular tribune. Their political rise, fantastic though it seems, proceeded on its own momentum in full view of all, in unbreakable connection with the growth of the movements they headed. . . . Altogether different was the nature of Stalin's rise. It is not comparable with anything in the past. He seems to have no pre-history. The process of his rise took place somewhere behind an impenetrable political curtain. At a certain moment his figure, in the full panoply of power, suddenly stepped away from the Kremlin wall, and for the first time the world became aware of Stalin as a ready-made dictator. . . .

"The current official comparisons of Stalin to Lenin are simply indecent. If the basis of comparison is sweep of personality, it is impossible to place Stalin even alongside Mussolini or Hitler. However meagre the 'ideas' of Fascism, both the victorious leaders of reaction, the Italian and the German, from the beginning of their respective movements, displayed initiative, roused the masses to action, pioneered new paths through the political jungle. Nothing of the kind can be said about Stalin."

These words, written while Russia was entering into the second decade of planned economy—i.e., several years after the collectivization of twenty-odd million farms—had a sufficiently unreal ring even eight or nine years ago; today they sound fantastic. Trotsky's view of Stalin is colored by the familiar but unwise contempt of an original thinker and man of letters for a grayish, dullish but yet very powerful man of action. Trotsky underrated his adversary so much that he came to see Stalin's figure, like a *deus ex machina*, "suddenly stepping away from the Kremlin wall, in the full panoply of power." But Stalin did not come to the fore like that. It is clear from Trotsky's own revelations that ever since the October Revolution Stalin was one of the very few (the three or five) men who exercised power; and that his practical, though not ideological, influence in the ruling group was second only to Lenin's and Trotsky's.

It was not only Stalin's personality which Trotsky underrated. He underrated also the depth and strength of the social developments which had brought Stalin to the fore, though he himself had been the first to interpret those very developments to the world. He viewed Stalin as the leader of a "Thermidorian reaction" from the revolution, the chief of a new bureaucratic hierarchy, the originator of a new nationalist trend epitomized in Socialism In One Country. Throughout the twenties and the thirties he blamed Stalin's leadership for all the defeats that communism suffered all over the world. In these criticisms there was truth, especially in his devastating criticisms of the Comintern's policies in Germany on the eve of the Nazi era. But the sum total of his charges betrays a degree of "subjectivism" in Trotsky which is at cross-purposes with his Marxian method of analysis. In his conception Stalin appears almost as the demiurge, the evil demiurge, of contemporary history, the one man whose vices have dominated the fortunes of international revolution. At this point Trotsky's polemics smack less of Marx than of Carlyle.

Was Stalin the leader of the Soviet Thermidor? In France the Thermidorian reaction put an end to the Terror. It did not undo the economic and social work of the revolution, but it brought that work to a stop. After Thermidor no major change occurred in the social structure of France as it had been so far wrought by the revolution. The political power moved from the *plebs* to the *bourgeois* Directory. In Russia, however, the social revolution did not come to a stop with Stalin's rise to power. On the contrary, its most comprehensive and radical acts, the expropriation and collectivization of all individual farmers, the initiation of planned economy, took place only after Stalin's ascendancy.

There is much more truth in Trotsky's other charge that Stalin came forward as the leader of a new bureaucracy which had risen above the people. Against the rigid, totalitarian outlook of Stalin's hierarchy Trotsky invoked the program of Soviet democracy—i.e., of government by the revolutionary people—which the Bolsheviks had advanced when they seized power. Here the precedent of his argument is unmistakable to the historian: under the Directory Babeuf advocated the return to the Jacobin Constitution of 1793. However, government by the revolutionary people was as impossible in Russia in 1925 or 1930 as it had been in France in 1797. The revolutionary masses had spent their political energy in the civil war and played out their role. The "heroic" phase of the revolution had given place to weariness and apathy; the nation's progress could no longer be prompted by impulses coming from below, but only by direction from above. In this point the analogy between Stalin's regime and the Thermidorian reaction is correct.

What Trotsky understated was the extent to which the change from "Soviet democracy" to "bureaucratic control" had occurred in the Leninist period. He distinguishes between the two phases of the revolution, but is reluctant fully to admit connection between them. It is true that Leninism was essentially nontotalitarian; but it is also true that by the end of the civil war (say, 1920 and 1921) it had, under the pressure of events, gradually, gropingly, almost unconsciously evolved towards totalitarianism. The birth of Bolshevik totalitarianism can be traced, with a high degree of precision, to the Tenth Congress of the party in 1921. It was on the foundations laid by the 1921 congress that Stalin built up his regime in later years. Both Lenin and Trotsky thought of going back to a more democratic order; but it may be doubted whether, even if Lenin had lived longer, they would have been able to do so. Leaving aside the contemporary fascist counterrevolutions, which have been predominantly political in character and totalitarian *a priori*, no historic social revolution—Cromwellian, Jacobin, or Bolshevik—has escaped the phase of "totalitarian degeneration."

It is the main count in Trotsky's indictment that Stalin gave up world revolution for Socialism In One Country. To non-Marxists the dispute over this point between Trotskyism

and Stalinism looks like a scholastic squabble, even if the
heads of many Bolshevik leaders have rolled in the course
of it. Yet, it was more than that. What in fact divided the two
antagonists was not that the one "wanted" and the other
"did not want" world revolution, but a fundamental difference in their estimate of the revolutionary potential of the
working classes in the Western countries.

Underlying Trotskyism was the firm belief that at least
Europe was "ripe for socialism." This was the thesis that had
been enunciated by Karl Kautsky, the "Pope" of international social democracy, at the beginning of the century.
From this standpoint the Russian revolution was the prelude
to a far wider upheaval. In Trotsky's eyes the achievements
of Socialist construction in Russia alone ranked little in comparison with the grand crescendo of material prosperity,
cultural advance, and spiritual freedom which could be expected from a socialist economy based and planned on a
European scale. Trotsky was convinced that European capitalism had lost its vitality, and that, at heart, the European
working classes were willing to give up the meretricious benefits of reformism in favor of revolution. Wherever the capitalist order succeeded in achieving a measure of stabiliza-
tion, either by means of fascist surgery or by mild reformist
cure, the blame, in Trotsky's eyes, lay on the shoulders of
communist or social democratic leadership. He often argued
that even were the victory of socialism in Europe still to be
remote, it was nevertheless closer than the achievement of
a truly socialist, classless society in "backward, uncivilized"
Russia. He regarded Russia as upon a periphery of modern
civilization. That periphery, to be sure, contained a powerful force; it was the pioneer of socialism. But eventually the
forms of the new society would not be forged upon the periphery but in the center of modern civilization.

Upon this aspect of affairs Stalin has never formulated his
mind very explicitly. First he lacks Trotsky's gift for the ex-

position of ideas; but, more significantly, his attitude marks a departure from Marxian tradition. Thus his real, though quasi-esoteric view, has merely been implied in his doctrine of Socialism In One Country. He never shared Trotsky's optimism concerning Europe's "ripeness" for socialism, but estimated the powers of resistance left in the capitalist order as, on the whole, still very formidable. In the many crises of international politics between the wars—e.g., the British crisis of 1926, the rise of Nazism in Germany, the Popular Front in France, and the civil war in Spain—Stalin was much less sanguine than Trotsky regarding the receptiveness of the working classes to the ideas of proletarian revolution. To Stalin his peculiar brand of socialism in Russia was, and still is, of incomparably greater importance than the possibility of socialism in the West. He declined to regard Russia as existing upon a peripheral area of modern civilization, and was confident that Russia was destined to become the citadel of the new socialist civilization. It was Stalin's plan to build up and safeguard that citadel, even if the means used for that purpose clashed (as, for example, the Russo-German pact of 1939), or seemed to clash, with the interests of foreign working classes. While Trotsky thought in terms of a double impact, first of Russia upon the West and then of the socialist West upon Russia, Stalin sees in Russia's one-sided impact upon the West the primary and decisive factor in the fortunes of communism or socialism.

The doctrines of Trotsky and Stalin both view contemporary history as a world-wide rivalry between capitalism and socialism, a rivalry historically as legitimate as was the old struggle between the feudal and the bourgeois systems of society. Stalin has, on balance, been inclined to rely on a peaceful development of that rivalry as allowing growth and consolidation of the Russian citadel of socialism. Trotsky laid stress upon its "cataclysmic" forms and emphasized, especially, the "pressure of the capitalist world," under which the isolated edifice of Russian socialism might collapse long before it had been completed. In addition, that edifice, built as it had been on narrow and shaky foundations in a "backward, semi-Asiatic" country, was, in his view, so dangerously misshapen as in many respects to be a caricature of socialism.

Ever since the controversy began, nearly a quarter of a century ago, events have submitted the two antagonistic doctrines of communism to continual test. The controversy is unconcluded though it is no longer thrashed out in the ranks of communism, for Trotsky's Fourth International has been stillborn. But indirectly the tenets of Stalinism and Trotskyism are being submitted to new tests at the conference tables of international diplomacy and in the social turmoil of Europe and Asia.

On the showing of these tests, Stalin's skepticism regarding the revolutionary temper of the European working classes has so far seemed better justified than Trotsky's confidence. To be sure, that temper has as often been damped as it has been stimulated by Stalin's policies. But this is no answer to the fundamental problem. No social class with a real and significant momentum of its own will allow itself to be diverted from its essential objectives by any outside influence. If Trotsky's view that the influence of Moscow had acted as the decisive brake on European revolution were correct, it would merely testify to the relative weakness of the revolutionary proletarian element in Western Europe. Moreover, Russia can no longer be regarded today as upon the periphery of Europe. Much of Europe has, on the contrary, become peripheral to Russia. This radical shift in the international balance of power alone may be held by some to vindicate, in terms of communism, the Stalinist doctrine.

But from the standpoint of the Marxist, the Trotskyist argument has by no means been finally disposed of. There still remains the problem of Stalin's regime, on the origins of which Trotsky's posthumous work has shed keen, if one-sided, illumination. Can that regime, with its leader's implicit maxim, *"La Société, c'est moi,"* really lead the Russian people to a free and classless society? Or will that regime continue, as Trotsky feared, to "degenerate," until it turns into an unequivocal negation of socialism? Or will it, as he sometimes forecast, eventually clash with the noncommunist world, seek salvation in the spread of revolution or perish? To these questions history has yet to give its answer.

4. Mr. E. H. Carr as Historian
of the Bolshevik Regime

The publication of the fourth volume of Mr. Carr's *History of Soviet Russia* offers a welcome opportunity for a general survey of his work and for an appraisal of the place it occupies in the field of Soviet studies.

It is difficult not to begin these remarks with a reflection on the state in which the writing of the history of the Russian revolution finds itself at present.[1] It is an almost incredible fact that not a single work deserving the name of a History has yet been produced inside the Soviet Union. True, the first decade of the Soviet regime brought a vast number of valuable contributions to a History, many special monographs, and collections of documents. In the intellectual *Sturm und Drang* of that period Soviet historians initiated ambitious projects of research. This, they thought, was the first time that Marxists were going to write history in all seriousness, backed up by the resources of a great State and the abundance of all the State archives recently thrown open, and sure to find response in the intense curiosity for history which had been awakened in the young generation. When if not under such circumstances should Marxism prove its unrivaled merits as a method of historical inquiry and analysis?

However, the advent and consolidation of Stalinism cast a blight upon the whole field of historical study. The Stalinist

[1] 1954.

State intimidated the historian, and dictated to him first the pattern into which he was expected to force events and then the ever new versions of the events themselves. At the outset the historian was subjected to this pressure mainly when he dealt with the Soviet revolution, the party strife which had preceded and which had followed it, and especially the struggles inside the Bolshevik Party. All these had to be treated in a manner justifying Stalin as the Leader of monolithic Bolshevism. Later the rewriting of history extended backward to past centuries, and outward to the history of other countries, until Clio was degraded to be not just the dignified servant of Politics—a role to which she is well accustomed—but their slave. The verve and passion with which historians had thrown themselves on the archives found a deadly enemy in secrecy which barred access to documentation. The historians could not be allowed to inquire into the facts because free inquiry was incompatible with falsification. Finally, all the chronicles of the party and the revolution, even those written in the Stalinist spirit, were banned, until at every level of teaching, from the rural party cells to the academic seminaries, students were allowed to draw from one fount only, the *Short Course of the History of the C.P.S.U.*, that bizarre and crude compendium of Stalinist myths, written or inspired by Stalin himself.

This deterioration of historical standards was not without precedent. For a long time the French revolution fared no better with its historians. Napoleon and his Prefects and Censors kept a suspicious eye on those "ideologues" who tried to delve into the great revolutionary drama which preceded the Empire. The security of the Empire required that a curtain should descend upon the great revolution, that its ghosts be laid, and its republican and plebeian ideas be banished from people's minds. Napoleon could afford to vent openly his antipathy for ideologies and ideologues; and so, unlike Stalin, he did not even bother to dabble with history writing. He had no need to falsify history—he suppressed it.

The first histories of the revolution began to appear only during the Restoration, and they were written by the enemies of the Bourbons. Stalin, placed as he was at the head of a party proud of its *historical* materialism, could not even attempt openly to suppress the history of the revolution: all the more savagely did he have to cripple and mutilate it.

Curiously enough, none of the many Russian *émigré* groups has used its enforced and long-lasting political idleness to produce anything like a history. There exists no serious Monarchist version of the revolution, no Cadet version, no Menshevik account, and no social revolutionary interpretation. The White Guards produced their accounts of the civil war, among which Denikin's five volumes are still the most important, despite all their lack of sophistication. Miliukov wrote his *History* in the heat of the civil war; but it was little more than an inflated pamphlet indicting all anti-Cadet parties; and Miliukov himself was too great a scholar not to realize this. In the Preface to his work he virtually disavowed as a historian the account of events which he had given as a leader of his party. Nor have the Mensheviks, among whom there were more gifted writers and theorists than in any other *émigré* group, made any notable historical contribution. The apologetic books by Kerensky and Chernov contain no serious attempt at a reconstruction of the historical process; and even Dan's posthumous work *Proiskhozhdenie Bolshevisma* offers a certain interest as a retrospective self-criticism of Menshevism but not as a History. To all these parties and groupings involved in the struggles of 1917 the revolution was such an unmitigated disaster and their role in it appeared to themselves so incongruous and inexplicable that their theorists and writers preferred not to return as historians to the scene of those struggles. A notable exception is Trotsky's *History*, which alone transcends the limitations of apologetic writing and is a lasting literary-historical monument to 1917.

Nor can Western historiography be proud of its achievements. This is so not merely because *wer den Dichter will verstehen muss in Dichter's Lande gehen,* although it will certainly be the Russians themselves, who, after they have recovered from the intellectual slump of the Stalin era, will eventually write the great and revealing histories of the revolution. The failure of Western historians to produce an adequate interim account has also been due mainly to preoccupation with current politics. Western historiography has rarely been guilty of wholesale falsification, but it has not been innocent of suppression of facts. It has as a rule shown little or no insight into the motives and minds of the social classes and political parties and leaders engaged in the Russian struggle; and most recently the cold war has had almost as blighting an effect on research as had Stalinism itself.

It is Mr. Carr's enduring and distinguished merit that he is the first genuine historian of the Soviet regime. He has undertaken a task of enormous scope and scale; and he has already performed a major portion of it. He views the scene with the detachment of one who stands if not *au dessus de la mêlée,* then at least *au delà de la mêlée.* He wishes to leave his readers with understanding and he searches for both the facts and the trends, the trees and the wood. He is as austerely conscientious and scrupulous as penetrating and acute. He has a flair for seeing the scheme and order of things and is lucid in the presentation of his findings. His *History* must be judged a truly outstanding achievement.

To be sure, Mr. Carr has been able to use only such sources as have long been available to students: he has had no access to unpublished documentation. But from these admittedly limited sources he has been able to extract the utmost; and to weave it into a close-textured narrative. For the period he has covered so far the published documentation is indeed so abundant and reliable that it is doubtful whether archives, when they are opened, will compel the historian to revise fundamentally the view which can be formed now on the basis of materials already published. This, incidentally, is my own experience with the Trotsky Archives which I have studied at Harvard. These contain a great number of important documents, and their knowledge causes me to disagree with Mr. Carr on certain specific points. But on the whole these disagreements, in so far as they concern the facts, are not fundamental.[2] It may therefore be assumed that Mr. Carr's study of Soviet Russia up to 1924 is as definitive as any historical work can be.

Mr. Carr is a historian primarily of institutions and policies, of which he traces the origins and the development in minute detail. He shows the Soviet State *in statu nascendi;* and this he does with a masterly grasp. But he is preoccupied primarily with the State, not with the nation and society behind it. Moreover, his interest is focused on the very top of the State machinery so that it might be said that his *History of the Soviet Union* is primarily a history of its ruling group. In part this is unavoidable: a historian reconstructs the historical process on the basis of documentary evidence which emanates mostly from the rulers, although in the years of the revolutionary upheaval Soviet society was by no means as amorphous and inarticulate as to form merely a mute background. But this characteristic of Mr. Carr's work is also in part due to his basic approach. Whenever he refers to developments in the social background, his references are subsidiary to his analysis of what was going on inside the ruling group. He tends to see society as the object of policies made and decreed from above. He is inclined to view the State as the maker of society rather than society as the maker of the State.

This approach creates *a priori* certain difficulties for the historian of a revolution, because a revolution is the break-

[2] The importance of the Trotsky Archives for the years after 1924 is incomparably greater.

down of the State and demonstrates that in the last resort it is society which makes the State, not vice versa. Mr. Carr approaches the revolutionary upheaval with the mind of the academic scholar interested above all in constitutional precepts, political formulas, and machinery of government, and less in mass movements and revolutionary upheavals. His passion is for statecraft, not for "subversive" ideas. He studies diligently the subversive ideas but only in so far as they may provide a clue to the statecraft of the triumphant ex-revolutionists. If he had chosen to epitomize his work in some epigrammatic motto he might have opened his *History* in the Churchillian manner with the following text: "How Russian Society Collapsed Through the Folly and Ineptitude of its Old Ruling Classes and Through the Utopian Dreams of Bolshevik Revolutionaries, and How These Revolutionaries in The End saved Russia by Giving up Their Quixotic Delusions and Learning Arduously and Painfully the ABC of Statecraft."

This approach is reflected even in the composition of Mr. Carr's work. The major part of his introductory volume deals with Bolshevik Constitution making, which seems to me to have been the least important, the most shadowy, aspect of the story. Another major portion of the same volume is devoted to "policy, doctrine, machinery"; and still another, by far the best, describes the "dispersal" of the Czarist Empire and its "Reunion" under the Soviet flag. What is lacking almost completely is the social background of 1917. To the academic scholar steeped in the study of constitutions, this is of course the most natural line of approach, but it is not one which is best suited for the study of a society in the throes of revolution. As he proceeds with his work Mr. Carr progressively overcomes the limitations of this approach to quite a remarkable extent. By an almost heroic, self-critical effort of his analytical mind, he has come much closer to the understanding of the strange phenomenon of the Russian revolution than his starting-point allowed to expect. But that starting-point is still reflected in his treatment of the subject and underlies much of his reasoning.

Mr. Carr has been censured by academic critics for his attitude towards Leninism and his alleged worshiping of Lenin. One of the critics has remarked that Lenin occupies in his work the place which Caesar holds in Mommsen's History. This criticism seems to me groundless. Mr. Carr is too skeptical, too acute, and too strongly aware of Lenin's inconsistencies to be his worshiper. What is true is that in his presentation Lenin's figure dominates and overshadows the revolution, the Bolshevik Party, the Soviet State. It does so in part because of the inadequate picture of the social background, and in part because Mr. Carr is not sufficiently aware of the formative processes by which Lenin's political thought was shaped and of the extent to which, even in the years of his mature leadership and ascendancy, Lenin's mind was formed by his environment and influenced by the ideas of his followers. In this respect Mr. Carr's work suffers from a certain lack of political and psychological insight.

But what is more important is that Mr. Carr's "apotheosis" of Lenin applies to Lenin the statesman and the self-taught master of statecraft as distinct from the Marxist revolutionary and thinker. It is the Lenin who *builds* a State that evokes his admiration, not the one who *overthrows* a State, and certainly not the one who obstinately *dreams* about the eventual "withering away" of the State of his own making. Mr. Carr views the story of Lenin the revolutionary as the indispensable prelude to Lenin the statesman, and he has little more than a polite smile of condescending irony for the Lenin who, at the summit of power, still had his gaze fixed on the remote vision of a classless and Stateless society. Yet these different and seemingly conflicting aspects of Lenin's personality were so closely integrated that neither of them can be isolated and understood in isolation. To the reader of Mr. Carr's *History* it must remain something of a puzzle how Lenin came to achieve the stature of statesman which Mr.

Carr ascribes to him. Did he perhaps even as builder of a State find his strength in the resources of his revolutionary thought and dream?

By implication, and sometimes explicitly, Mr. Carr answers this question in the negative. He is impressed by those features which Lenin may have had in common with, say, Bismarck, rather than by those in which his affinity with Marx, the French Communards, or Rosa Luxemburg shows itself.

Reading Mr. Carr's pages I could not help thinking of a confession once made by the eminent Polish liberal publicist Konstanty Srokowski, who knew Lenin during the latter's stay in Cracow before the First World War. Having spent much time with Lenin, arguing about politics and social affairs and playing chess, Srokowski confessed later that in 1912-1914 he regarded Lenin as a well-meaning but utterly impractical man with no chance whatsoever to make any impact on practical politics. "Whatever subject we approached," Srokowski related, "Lenin would begin with expounding one of the tenets of Marxist philosophy. He never stopped quoting Marx as if he deluded himself that he had found in Marx's writings a master-key to all problems preoccupying mankind. I could only shrug shoulders. It was interesting to argue with Lenin for he was a man of intellect and education. But he seemed to me a quixotic visionary. I was sure that every one of our minor socialist politicians and trade union leaders was superior to him as *a man of action*. When I then learned that the same Lenin was the leader of a revolution and the head of a great State I was dumbfounded. I lost confidence in my judgment. How, I wondered, could I have committed so cardinal an error in appraising the man. There must have been something wrong in my approach to him and to politics in general." The old Polish publicist had, of course, an exaggerated respect for practical politics and all too little regard for "revolutionary romanticism." Sometimes I wonder whether Mr. Carr's view of Lenin would have been any different, if he had met Lenin, say, in 1912. Essentially it is not very far removed from that view even in the *History* where it is only Lenin the successful masterbuilder of Soviet Russia who seems to redeem in Mr. Carr's eyes Lenin the revolutionary dreamer.

It is not difficult to detect that Mr. Carr has formed his view of the Bolshevik revolution, at least partly, in opposition to the outlook of Western diplomacy in the years of the anti-Bolshevik intervention. The generation of Western diplomats that witnessed the rise of Bolshevism and resisted it with all its might was notoriously incapable of comprehending the phenomenon against which it struggled. Mr. Carr may be described as an intellectual expatriate from that diplomacy—a rebel criticizing its tradition from the inside, as it were. We know of no other man of Mr. Carr's background who has proved capable of even a small part of that enormous mental effort which Mr. Carr has made to grasp the inner logic of Leninism. Even so, the peculiar limitations of the diplomatic mind can sometimes be sensed between the lines of his *History*.

Watching the earthquake of the Russian revolution, Mr. Carr surveys the landscape to see what has happened to so familiar a landmark as the Russian Ministry of Foreign Affairs. He is puzzled, bewildered, and worried by its disappearance. He cannot believe that the breakdown of diplomacy, brought about by the revolution, can serve any useful purpose, or that it can last. And he is relieved to find that when the dust settles diplomacy and its landmarks seem to be back where he expected them to be. The rare moments when he gives vent to irritation with the Bolshevik leaders are those in which he relates their initial hostility towards conventional diplomacy and their indulging in "the illusion that foreign policy and diplomacy were no more than an evil legacy of capitalism." The Bolshevik Utopians could well reply that they were forced to take up diplomacy only because the "evil legacy of capitalism" was much heavier than they had feared. If one views the prospect of an international socialist society as utterly unreal, and if one sees the future of mankind as a perpetual rivalry between nation-States, then, of course, one must consider diplomacy, its institutions and its procedures, to be inseparable from the history of mankind. The Leninists believed that the national diplomacies of our age would one day appear as anachronistic as the diplomacies of the particularist, feudal and postfeudal, princedoms appear today; and that the unifying historical process which had merged those particularist entities into nation-States would eventually merge nation-States into an international community which will have no use for diplomacy. Mr. Carr will have none of this nonsense, and he is glad to get away from it, and to applaud generously the Bolsheviks when, like repentant prodigal sons, they give up their "haughty contempt for the ordinary conceptions and procedures of foreign policy" and reopen a normal chancellery. Of this he repeatedly speaks as of the "normalization" of Soviet policy, although what may seem normal by one standard may be highly abnormal by another.

How self-revealing is, for instance, Mr. Carr's description of the scene of Trotsky's departure from the Soviet Foreign Office on the conclusion of the Brest-Litovsk Treaty. "The fiery revolutionary agitator was succeeded by a scion of the old diplomacy whose early [?] conversion to Bolshevism had not effaced a certain ingrained respect for traditional forms. . . . After Trotsky's whirlwind career at Narkomindel, Chicherin sat down to a patient and less spectacular task of organization." This contrast between Trotsky, the fiery agitator, and Chicherin in whom the virtues of the conventional diplomat had survived despite his Bolshevism, is somewhat dubious. Chicherin was as unconventional a Bohemian as one can imagine; and he was anything but a patient organizer. Trotsky, on the other hand, was in personal behavior and habits much less eccentric than Chicherin; he easily switched from fiery revolutionary agitation to the most correct diplomatic negotiations; and he was certainly a patient organizer. Nor would the suggestion be well-founded that Chicherin's influence came to supersede Trotsky's in the conduct of Soviet diplomacy. Mr. Carr is aware that Chicherin was a mere executor of the Politbureau's decisions on which, in so far as they concerned diplomacy, Trotsky's influence was second only to Lenin's or equal to it. We now know from the documentary evidence in Trotsky's Archives that it was Trotsky who in 1920 strove, much more insistently than Lenin, for British-Soviet agreement, for peace with Poland, for a normalization of Russia's relations with the small Baltic States;[3] and Mr. Carr himself relates some of the preliminaries to the Rapallo Treaty from which it is clear that he was also one of the chief inspirers of Rapallo, probably its chief initiator. But this scene of Trotsky's departure and Chicherin's arrival, drawn with such unmistakable relish, illustrates a conception according to which the Soviet regime gained its *raison d'être* only when it discovered its *raison d'état*.

I do not intend to deny that there was an element of unreal dream in Bolshevik attitudes or the subsequent reassertion of the concepts and procedures of traditional government and diplomacy. But how we view these is a matter of proportion and evaluation; and my criticism applies to Mr. Carr's overemphasis on the Bolshevik return to the conventional concepts and procedures and to his inadequate grasp of the revolutionary ethos of the epoch.

Mr. Carr is a great respecter of policies and—sometimes—a despiser of revolutionary ideas and principles. Again, this shows itself even in the composition of his monumental work. He relegates the ideas and principles of Bolshevism to Appendixes and Notes, treating them implicitly as points of only marginal interest, while his narrative is concerned primarily with policies. In Volume I he deals with Lenin's Theory of the State in a Note, whereas one-third of the

[3] See I. Deutscher, *The Prophet Armed*, pp. 461–471.

volume is devoted to constitution-making, although Soviet
constitutions were honored mainly in their breach and had
little practical significance. Another Note deals with the
"Doctrine of Self-determination." In the second and the
third volumes the Appendixes deal with the Marxist attitude
toward the peasantry and the Marxist view of war. Yet
these views and ideas were active and crucial elements in the
developments described in the main body of the *History*,
because they animated its characters. Mr. Carr is, of course,
familiar with the Marxian saying that an idea, when it gets
hold of human minds, itself becomes a power. Historical
realism cannot therefore consist in playing down the power
of ideas, for this can only narrow and impoverish the historian's perspective.

The validity of this criticism can be illustrated by Mr.
Carr's treatment of the inner Bolshevik controversy over the
Peace of Brest-Litovsk. His account of this is disappointing.
Other writers, who lack Mr. Carr's scholarship and ability,
have rendered this momentous episode with much greater
insight and sense of drama. This is not mainly or even primarily a question of literary style. The Brest-Litovsk controversy may be seen as a clash between political expediency
and revolutionary idealism in which expediency gains the
upper hand. This is a simplified but essentially correct view;
and it is the one adopted by Mr. Carr. But he grasps much
more acutely the arguments of political expediency than the
motives of revolutionary idealism; and he is not quite sensitive to the full force of the conflict between the two. Moreover, his predilections lead him astray as a historian: he
describes accurately and in great detail Lenin's arguments
for peace, but he omits to give even a bare summary of the
views held by the opponents of peace, who, as he knows, at
first had behind them the majority of the party and repeatedly outvoted Lenin. Had Mr. Carr given a little patient attention to Bukharin's, Radek's, Yoffe's, and Dzerzhinsky's
views, he might have found in them more than mere en-

thusiastic flamboyance and revolutionary phrasemongering, of which there was admittedly no lack; he might also have found considerable realism and far-sightedness. Even if this should not be so, his omission to give an adequate idea of the arguments of the Left communists results in a curious gap.

On several occasions Mr. Carr refers sarcastically to the Bolsheviks' "Wilsonian" "appeal from wicked governments to enlightened peoples." But was that appeal so quixotic as Mr. Carr suggests? Was it so impractical even from the viewpoint of the analyst of power politics? After all, the victorious revolution was nothing else but one great appeal "from a wicked government to an enlightened people." Because of his contempt for that appeal, Mr. Carr misses the revolution's climate, its emotional atmosphere, its mass enthusiasms, its moral tensions, the high flights of its hopes, and the deep depressions of its disillusionments, all of which derived from the ardent belief of both the revolutionaries and the people in the reality of that "appeal." Sometimes Mr. Carr's characters seem to move through an airless space and an emotional vacuum as if they were nothing but disembodied political conceptions and formulas. In part this is due to the author's preoccupation with scientific history writing, which to him seems to imply the exclusion of the emotional and spiritual coloring of the events. As an historian Mr. Carr superbly surveys and scrutinizes his period, but he does not relive it. Perhaps he does not consider it important and necessary or even admissible for the historian to do so. His approach has certainly its justification and validity: there are at least several legitimate ways of writing history, although the best histories are those that are works of imaginative insight and art as well as of science. But even within Mr. Carr's approach and style his insight would have gained in depth if it had not been held in check too strongly by his impatience with Utopias, dreams, and revolutionary agitation.

Mr. Carr is fascinated by the subtlety and flexibility with

which Lenin adjusted his policies to events and circumstances. Sometimes, however, he magnifies the element of the opportunist in Lenin out of its real proportion and to the exclusion of other elements. Lenin, the Marxist, appears rather dimly in his pages. Mr. Carr is not sufficiently aware of the strength of the Marxist tradition in Lenin. When he does refer to that tradition he seems out of his depth and makes curious errors of fact. (Thus he claims that Lenin based in part his *Imperialism* on R. Luxemburg's *Accumulation of Capital*, which is patently incorrect. Lenin's *Imperialism* was entirely based on Hilferding's *Finanzkapital;* and Lenin's own economic thought, from his earliest writings to his final evaluation of Rosa Luxemburg's ideas after her death, was strongly opposed to Luxemburg's theory.) What Mr. Carr describes as the "Wilsonian" element in Leninism was indeed part and parcel of the Marxist internationalist tradition; and Mr. Carr, misled by the outward similarity of some Wilsonian and Bolshevik slogans, tends to overlook the realities behind the slogans and the different and incompatible trains of thought from which political watchwords had sprung. Implicitly, Mr. Carr treats the early Bolshevik internationalism as a purely ideological conviction, unrelated to the economic trend of the epoch, if not simply as a sentimental weakness. Marxists had always argued that the needs of capitalist development had been the main motive power behind the formation of nation-States; and that one of the central "contradictions" of capitalism consists in the fact that the productive forces of modern society outgrow their national frameworks. According to this view, the conflict between the productive forces and the nation-State manifests itself in various forms: negatively—in the imperialist search for *Grossraumwirtschaft;* and positively, in the internationalist outlook of the proletarian revolution, which cannot settle down within the framework of any nation-State.

Stalinism neglected and then suppressed this aspect of Marxist internationalism and it sought to elevate the isolation of the Russian revolution to a virtue and a theoretical principle. For all his conscious effort to resist the insinuating influence of the Stalinist way of thought, Mr. Carr unwittingly sometimes views Marxism through the Stalinist prism, because his interest in Marxism is only secondary to his study of the Soviet State. But Stalinism itself carried with it its own self-refutation for in its last expansive phase it bore reluctant but conclusive testimony to the conflict between the development of the productive forces of Soviet Union and its national boundaries. Yet, the habits of thought associated with Socialism In One Country, habits formed and consolidated in the course of a quarter of a century, persist; and they color the thought even of a student as critical and detached as Mr. Carr. In the heyday of Stalinism it may have appeared that Bolshevik internationalism had no more economic and historic substance behind it than had the abstract cosmopolitanism of the French revolution (to which Mr. Carr indeed relates it). But at present it should no longer be possible to take this view: it is more than clear that the Russian revolution, unlike the French, has initiated not just a new type of the nation-State, but—for good or evil—a new and expanding international economy and society.

The vantage point from which history is written is of great consequence. It would have been natural for an historian of Mr. Carr's background to treat the early Bolshevik internationalism as Wilsonian and Utopian in, say, 1932, although even then this would not have been proof of great historical realism. But it is a positive anachronism to treat it so twenty years later. In the retrospective light of the Chinese revolution and even of the expansion of Stalinism in Eastern and Central Europe, the early Bolshevik hopes for the spread of revolution appear to have been tragically ahead of their time, but by no means Utopian.

Perhaps the main weakness of Mr. Carr's conception is that he sees the Russian revolution as virtually a national phenomenon only. He does not deny its international significance or its Impact on the West. But he treats it as an historical process essentially national in character and self-sufficient within the national framework. He thinks in terms of statecraft and statecraft is national. His Lenin is a Russian super-Bismarck achieving the Titanic work of rebuilding the Russian State from ruin, and of reuniting its dissolved component parts. This view is correct and incorrect at the same time—it misses the broader perspective within which Lenin's achievement places itself.

A Lenin shorn of his unmanageable revolutionary internationalism and shown as master of national statecraft may appear plausibly as nothing but Stalin's legitimate ideological forebear. In the *History* Mr. Carr has done very much to reconstruct the authentic picture of Leninism and to free it from Stalinist accretions. He has succeeded admirably in his presentation of facts which is, on the whole, irreproachable; but he has only half succeeded in some of the finer shadings of emphasis and interpretation. Unwillingly he overdraws those features through which Lenin may be seen as resembling Stalin and he blurs the others in which the dissimilarity and contrast are striking. Here, too, I would like to qualify the criticisms and to add that Mr. Carr's understanding of the subject deepens with the progress of his research; and that in this respect, too, his latest volume, *The Interregnum*, represents a notable advance. When he reaches the threshold of the Stalin era, Mr. Carr is much more aware of the discontinuity between Leninism and Stalinism than he was while he analyzed Leninism.

This is perhaps the most difficult and complex problem by which the student of the Soviet Union is confronted. The historian's mind grappling with this issue inevitably oscillates over the years; and as a fellow worker in the same field I do not claim to have struck any faultless balance between the factors making for the continuity and the discontinuity of Leninism and Stalinism. Unlike the Stalinists, the Trotsky-ists, and the vast majority of the anti-Communist writers, for whom this problem does not even exist, Mr. Carr comes to grips with it. To the Stalinist Stalin is the legitimate heir to the apostolic succession of Marx-Engels-Lenin. To the Trotskyist he is the traitor, gravedigger, and renegade of Leninism. The great majority of anti-communist "Sovietologists" also see in Stalinism a straight continuation of Leninism, while a minority accepts the Trotskyist version because it is polemically so convenient to denounce Stalinism as a devilish betrayal of the "true" communism as well as a menace to Western values. Each of these schools is trading in half-truths, and refuses to face the fact that in some respects Stalinism is the "legitimate" development of Leninism, while in others it is its negation. Mr. Carr's work is free from such simplifications and half-truths; but it nevertheless still seems to overdraw the Stalin in Lenin.

This inclination induces Mr. Carr to antedate certain trends in Soviet foreign policy and to project back the Russian traditionalism of Stalin's diplomacy on to Lenin's conduct of foreign affairs. The antedating is noticeable in several instances, into which I cannot go here; but it is most striking when he surveys the Rapallo Treaty and the preliminaries to it—there he unwittingly injects the flavor of 1939 into the situation of 1921-1922 and tends to treat Lenin as the straight precursor of the Stalin who was to share out Polish spoils with Hitler. Mr. Carr sees an "ultimate alliance between Bolshevik Russia and a Germany of the Right" as an historic inevitability manifesting itself in both situations. "Assuming that the Bolshevik regime survived, such an alliance would give the Reichswehr what it would one day need—a free hand against the West; and it would also give Germany heavy industry its indispensable market" (Vol. III, p. 310). The argument about the market cuts both ways, to say the least: twice within a quarter of a century German heavy industry backed not an alliance but an invasion of Russia in order to obtain control of that "market" or, to put it more accurately, of Russian and Ukrainian sources of raw materials. Superimposing the pattern of 1939 on 1921-1922 Mr. Carr suggests that the Rapallo Treaty was directed against Poland and that underlying it was the perennial Russo-German striving for Poland's dismemberment. That the idea of Poland's dismemberment with Russian help lured the German Right even in 1920-1922 is true, of course; but it is not true that it evoked any response in Soviet diplomacy or in the Bolshevik leadership of the Lenin era.

Indeed, nothing would show better the gulf between two phases of Soviet diplomacy than a careful comparison between Rapallo and the Nazi-Soviet pact. In both pacts Russia strove to strengthen her position by "exploiting the contradiction" between Germany and the West while the West either ostracized Russia or worked to exclude her influence from European diplomacy. But in 1922 Russia joined hands with a Germany vanquished and outlawed, not with the imperialist incendiary run amok of 1939. At Rapallo the Bolsheviks made a sober deal without compromising their principles and their integrity and dignity: there was in their whole behavior not even a hint of that state of mind in which, seventeen years later, Molotov could send Hitler the ill-famed telegram assuring the Führer of a "friendship cemented by blood." And the Rapallo pact was not concluded at the expense of weaker neighbors: even in its secret parts it contained not a single arrangement made at the expense of Poland, for instance. Outwardly Rapallo and the Nazi-Soviet pact may look like two consecutive phases of the same policy; but they are set apart by the imponderable difference between the political morality of Leninism and that of Stalinism, a difference which Mr. Carr tends to overlook.[4]

[4] It is my duty to use this opportunity for explaining a curious incident in the preliminaries to the Rapallo pact. In his little book *German-Soviet Re-*

In spite of these flaws and limitations Mr. Carr's work will remain a great and enduring landmark in historical writing devoted to the Bolshevik revolution. Its merits are so obvious that they need no further underlining in a journal for specialists. Even the criticisms made here testify to its high standard, for they could not apply to a work less distinguished than this *History* is by consistency of method and unity of approach. In the future various schools of historians will study the Russian revolution with the same interest and passion with which the records of the French revolution have been searched for the last 130 years; and each generation and each school of historians will uncover new sources and throw new shafts of light on the great epic. But future historians will

---

lations, published in 1951, Mr. Carr quoted Lenin as instructing his diplomats to "play the Polish card" in negotiations with Germany. Mr. Carr referred to the Trotsky Archives, and quoted myself as the source of the information. I feel therefore co-responsible for this error and obliged to put it right especially because the version given in *German-Soviet Relations* has been widely quoted by other writers.

Among several documents bearing on the preliminaries to the Rapallo Treaty, the Trotsky Archives contain a "strictly secret" memorandum addressed, on December 10, 1921, to Moscow by a cryptic German "negotiator." The author of the memorandum, apparently an official German personality favoring agreement with Russia, surveyed the factors that operated in Germany against such an agreement and went on to advise the Bolsheviks what counteraction they should, in his view, take in order to prepare the ground for a diplomatic deal. Among other things, he suggested that the Bolsheviks should "play the Polish card" especially in connection with the conflict which flared up over Upper Silesia. It was that German "well-wisher" that used the phrase about "the Polish card," not Lenin. In all the highly confidential and illuminating documents of the Trotsky Archives relating to this episode, there is not the slightest indication that Lenin's government paid any heed to this advice. In those years the Politbureau had not yet sufficiently freed itself from "idealistic illusions" to respond to such promptings. This was still Lenin's not Stalin's Politbureau; and its members could only contemptuously shrug shoulders over the "playing of the Polish card." Mr. Carr certainly can not treat as historical evidence for the opposite view the gossipy third-hand account of Enver Pasha, an adventurer-interloper who tried in vain to build himself up into a sort of mediator between Moscow and Berlin and to whom the Bolshevik leaders made no confidences, as can be seen even from his own "report." In the *History* Mr. Carr himself corrects the version given in the *Soviet-German Relations;* but somehow that version still seems to reverberate in his reasoning.

probably turn to Mr. Carr as their first guide as the French historians still turn to the work of Thiers, with which Mr. Carr's *History* has quite a few features in common. This comparison gives perhaps a measure of Mr. Carr's achievement.

Part Four

HERETICS AND RENEGADES

1. The Ex-Communist's Conscience *

Ignazio Silone relates that he once said jokingly to Togliatti, the Italian Communist leader: "The final struggle will be between the communists and the ex-communists." There is a bitter drop of truth in the joke. In the propaganda skirmishes against the U.S.S.R. and communism, the ex-Communist or the ex-fellow traveler is the most active sharpshooter. With the peevishness that distinguishes him from Silone, Arthur Koestler makes a similar point: "It's the same with all you comfortable, insular, Anglo-Saxon anticommunists. You hate our Cassandra cries and resent us as allies—but, when all is said, we ex-communists are the only people on your side who know what it's all about."

The ex-Communist is the problem child of contemporary politics. He crops up in the oddest places and corners. He buttonholes you in Berlin to tell the story of *his* "battle of Stalingrad," fought here, in Berlin, against Stalin. You find him in de Gaulle's entourage: none other than André Malraux, the author of *Man's Fate*. In America's strangest political trial the ex-Communist has, for months, pointed his finger at Alger Hiss. Another ex-Communist, Ruth Fischer, denounces her brother, Gerhart Eisler, and castigates the British for not having handed him back to the United States. An ex-Trotskyite, James Burnham, flays the American businessman for his real or illusory lack of capitalist class con-

* This essay appeared as a review of *The God That Failed* in *The Reporter* (New York) in April 1950.

sciousness, and sketches a program of action for nothing less than the world-wide defeat of communism. And now six writers—Koestler, Silone, André Gide, Louis Fischer, Richard Wright, and Stephen Spender—get together to expose and destroy *The God That Failed.*

The "legion" of ex-Communists does not march in close formation. It is scattered far and wide. Its members resemble one another very much, but they also differ. They have common traits and individual features. All have left an army and a camp—some as conscientious objectors, some as deserters, and others as marauders. A few stick quietly to their conscientious objections, while others vociferously claim commissions in an army which they had bitterly opposed. All wear threadbare bits and pieces of the old uniform, supplemented by the quaintest new rags. And all carry with them their common resentments and individual reminiscences.

Some joined the party at one time, others at another; the date of joining is relevant to their further experiences. Those, for instance, who joined in the 1920's went into a movement in which there was plenty of scope for revolutionary idealism. The structure of the party was still fluid; it had not yet gone into the totalitarian mold. Intellectual integrity was still valued in a Communist; it had not yet been surrendered for good to Moscow's *raison d'état.* Those who joined the party in the 1930's began their experience on a much lower level. Right from the beginning they were manipulated like recruits on the party's barrack squares by the party's sergeant majors.

This difference bears upon the quality of the ex-Communist's reminiscences. Silone, who joined the party in 1921, recalls with real warmth his first contact with it; he conveys fully the intellectual excitement and moral enthusiasm with which communism pulsated in those early days. The reminiscences of Koestler and Spender, who joined in the 1930's, reveal the utter moral and intellectual sterility of the party's first impact on them. Silone and his comrades were intensely concerned with fundamental ideas before and after they became absorbed in the drudgery of day-to-day duty. In Koestler's story, his party "assignment," right from the first moment, overshadows all matters of personal conviction and ideal. The Communist of the early drafts was a revolutionary before he became, or was expected to become, a puppet. The Communist of the later drafts hardly got the chance to breathe the genuine air of revolution.

Nevertheless, the original motives for joining were similar, if not identical, in almost every case: experience of social injustice or degradation; a sense of insecurity bred by slumps and social crises; and the craving for a great ideal or purpose, or for a reliable intellectual guide through the shaky labyrinth of modern society. The newcomer felt the miseries of the old capitalist order to be unbearable; and the glowing light of the Russian revolution illumined those miseries with extraordinary sharpness.

Socialism, classless society, the withering away of the State —all seemed around the corner. Few of the newcomers had any premonition of the blood and sweat and tears to come. To himself, the intellectual convert to communism seemed a new Prometheus—except that he would not be pinned to the rock by Zeus's wrath. "Nothing henceforth [so Koestler now recalls his own mood in those days] can disturb the convert's inner peace and serenity—except the occasional fear of losing faith again. . . ."

Our ex-Communist now bitterly denounces the betrayal of his hopes. This appears to him to have had almost no precedent. Yet as he eloquently describes his early expectations and illusions, we detect a strangely familiar tone. Exactly so did the disillusioned Wordsworth and his contemporaries look back upon their first youthful enthusiasm for the French revolution:

Bliss was it in that dawn to be alive,
But to be young was very heaven!

The intellectual Communist who breaks away emotion-
ally from his party can claim some noble ancestry. Beethoven
tore to pieces the title page of his *Eroica,* on which he had
dedicated the symphony to Napoleon, as soon as he learned
that the First Consul was about to ascend a throne. Wordsworth called the crowning of Napoleon "a sad reverse for all
mankind." All over Europe the enthusiasts of the French
revolution were stunned by their discovery that the Corsican
liberator of the peoples and enemy of tyrants was himself a
tyrant and an oppressor.

In the same way the Wordsworths of our days were
shocked at the sight of Stalin fraternizing with Hitler and
Ribbentrop. If no new *Eroicas* have been created in our days,
at least the dedicatory pages of unwritten symphonies have
been torn with great flourishes.

In *The God That Failed,* Louis Fischer tries to explain
somewhat remorsefully and not quite convincingly why he
adhered to the Stalin cult for so long. He analyzes the variety
of motives, some working slowly and some rapidly, which
determine the moment at which people recover from the in-
fatuation with Stalinism. The force of the European disillusionment with Napoleon was almost equally uneven and
capricious. A great Italian poet, Ugo Foscolo, who had been
Napoleon's soldier and composed an *Ode to Bonaparte the
Liberator,* turned against his idol after the Peace of Campo-
formio—this must have stunned a "Jacobin" from Venice as
the Nazi-Soviet Pact stunned a Polish Communist. But a man
like Beethoven remained under the spell of Bonaparte for
seven years more, until he saw the despot drop his republican mask. This was an "eye-opener" comparable to Stalin's
purge trials of the 1930's.

There can be no greater tragedy than that of a great revolution's succumbing to the mailed fist that was to defend it
from its enemies. There can be no spectacle as disgusting as
that of a post-revolutionary tyranny dressed up in the banners of liberty. The ex-Communist is morally as justified as

was the ex-Jacobin in revealing and revolting against that spectacle.

But is it true, as Koestler claims, that "ex-communists are the only people . . . who know what it's all about?" One may risk the assertion that the exact opposite is true: Of all people, the ex-Communists know least what it is all about.

At any rate, the pedagogical pretensions of ex-Communist men of letters seem grossly exaggerated. Most of them (Silone is a notable exception) have never been inside the real Communist movement, in the thick of its clandestine or open organization. As a rule, they moved on the literary or journalistic fringe of the party. Their notions of Communist doctrine and ideology usually spring from their own literary intuition, which is sometimes acute but often misleading.

Worse still is the ex-Communist's characteristic incapacity for detachment. His emotional reaction against his former environment keeps him in its deadly grip and prevents him from understanding the drama in which he was involved or half-involved. The picture of communism and Stalinism he draws is that of a gigantic chamber of intellectual and moral horrors. Viewing it, the uninitiated are transferred from politics to pure demonology. Sometimes the artistic effect may be strong—horrors and demons do enter into many a poetic masterpiece; but it is politically unreliable and even dangerous. Of course, the story of Stalinism abounds in horror. But this is only one of its elements; and even this, the demonic, has to be translated into terms of human motives and interests. The ex-Communist does not even attempt the translation.

In a rare flash of genuine self-criticism, Koestler makes this admission:

"As a rule, our memories romanticize the past. But when one has renounced a creed or been betrayed by a friend, the opposite mechanism sets to work. In the light of that later knowledge, the original experience loses its innocence, becomes tainted and rancid in recollection. I have tried in these pages to recapture the mood in which the experiences [in the Communist Party] related were originally lived—and I know that I have failed. Irony, anger, and shame kept intruding; the passions of that time seem transformed into perversions, its inner certitude into the closed universe of the drug addict; the shadow of barbed wire lies across the condemned playground of memory. Those who were caught by the great illusion of our time, and have lived through its moral and intellectual debauch, either give themselves up to a new addiction of the opposite type, or are condemned to pay with a lifelong hangover."

This need not be true of all ex-Communists. Some may still feel that their experience has been free from the morbid overtones described by Koestler. Nevertheless, Koestler has given here a truthful and honest characterization of the type of ex-Communist to which he himself belongs. But it is difficult to square this self-portrait with his other claim that the confraternity for which he speaks "are the only people . . . who know what it's all about." With equal right a sufferer from traumatic shock might claim that he is the only one who really understands wounds and surgery. The most that the intellectual ex-Communist knows, or rather feels, is his own sickness; but he is ignorant of the nature of the external violence that has produced it, let alone the cure.

This irrational emotionalism dominates the evolution of many an ex-Communist. "The logic of opposition at all cost," says Silone, "has carried many ex-communists far from their starting-points, in some cases as far as fascism." What were those starting-points? Nearly every ex-Communist broke with his party in the name of communism. Nearly every one set out to defend the ideal of socialism from the abuses of a bureaucracy subservient to Moscow. Nearly every one began by throwing out the dirty water of the Russian revolution to protect the baby bathing in it.

Sooner or later these intentions are forgotten or abandoned. Having broken with a party bureaucracy in the name of communism, the heretic goes on to break with communism itself. He claims to have made the discovery that the root of the evil goes far deeper than he at first imagined, even though his digging for that "root" may have been very lazy and very shallow. He no longer defends socialism from unscrupulous abuse; he now defends mankind from the fallacy of socialism. He no longer throws out the dirty water of the Russian revolution to protect the baby; he discovers that the baby is a monster which must be strangled. The heretic becomes a renegade.

How far he departed from his starting-point, whether, as Silone says, he becomes a fascist or not, depends on his inclinations and tastes—and stupid Stalinist heresy-hunting often drives the ex-Communist to extremes. But, whatever the shades of individual attitudes, as a rule the intellectual ex-Communist ceases to oppose capitalism. Often he rallies to its defense, and he brings to this job the lack of scruple, the narrow-mindedness, the disregard for truth, and the intense hatred with which Stalinism has imbued him. He remains a sectarian. He is an inverted Stalinist. He continues to see the world in white and black, but now the colors are differently distributed. As a Communist he saw no difference between fascists and social democrats. As an anti-Communist he sees no difference between nazism and communism. Once, he accepted the party's claim to infallibility; now he believes himself to be infallible. Having once been caught by the "greatest illusion," he is now obsessed by the greatest disillusionment of our time.

His former illusion at least implied a positive ideal. His disillusionment is utterly negative. His role is therefore intellectually and politically barren. In this, too, he resembles the embittered ex-Jacobin of the Napoleonic era. Wordsworth and Coleridge were fatally obsessed with the "Jacobin danger"; their fear dimmed even their poetic genius. It was Coleridge who denounced in the House of Commons a bill for the prevention of cruelty to animals as the "strongest instance of legislative Jacobinism." The ex-Jacobin became the prompter of the anti-Jacobin reaction in England. Directly or indirectly, his influence was behind the Bills Against Seditious Writings and Traitorous Correspondence, the Treasonable Practices Bill, and Seditious Meetings Bill (1792-1794), the defeats of parliamentary reform, the suspension of the Habeas Corpus Act, and the postponement of the emancipation of England's religious minorities for the lifetime of a generation. Since the conflict with revolutionary France was "not a time to make hazardous experiments," the slave trade, too, obtained a lease on life—in the name of liberty.

In quite the same way our ex-Communist, for the best of reasons, does the most vicious things. He advances bravely in the front rank of every witch hunt. His blind hatred of his former ideal is leaven to contemporary conservatism. Not rarely he denounces even the mildest brand of the "welfare State" as "legislative Bolshevism." He contributes heavily to the moral climate in which a modern counterpart to the English anti-Jacobin reaction is hatched.

His grotesque performance reflects the impasse in which he finds himself. The impasse is not merely his—it is part of a blind alley in which an entire generation leads an incoherent and absent-minded life.

The historical parallel drawn here extends to the wider background of two epochs. The world is split between Stalinism and an anti-Stalinist alliance in much the same way it was split between Napoleonic France and the Holy Alliance. It is a split between a "degenerated" revolution exploited by a despot and a grouping of predominantly, although not exclusively, conservative interests. In terms of practical politics the choice seems to be now, as it was then, confined to these alternatives. Yet the rights and the wrongs of this controversy are so hopelessly confused that whichever the choice, and whatever its practical motives, it is almost certain to be wrong in the long run and in the broadest historical sense.

An honest and critically minded man could reconcile himself to Napoleon as little as he can now to Stalin. But despite
Napoleon's violence and frauds, the message of the French
revolution survived to echo powerfully throughout the
nineteenth century. The Holy Alliance freed Europe from
Napoleon's oppression; and for a moment its victory was
hailed by most Europeans. Yet what Castlereagh and Metternich and Alexander I had to offer to "liberated" Europe
was merely the preservation of an old, decomposing order.
Thus the abuses and the aggressiveness of an empire bred by
the revolution gave a new lease on life to European feudalism. This was the ex-Jacobin's most unexpected triumph.
But the price he paid for it was that presently he himself,
and his anti-Jacobin cause, looked like vicious, ridiculous
anachronisms. In the year of Napoleon's defeat, Shelley
wrote to Wordsworth:

In honoured poverty thy voice did weave
Songs consecrate to truth and liberty—
Deserting these, thou leavest me to grieve,
Thus having been, that thou shouldst cease to be.

If our ex-Communist had any historical sense, he would
ponder this lesson.

Some of the ex-Jacobin prompters of the anti-Jacobin reaction had as few scruples about their *volte-face* as have the
Burnhams and the Ruth Fischers of our days. Others were
remorseful, and pleaded patriotic sentiment, or a philosophy
of the lesser evil, or both, to explain why they had sided with
old dynasties against an upstart emperor. If they did not
deny the vices of the Courts and the governments they had
once denounced, they claimed that those governments were
more liberal than Napoleon. This was certainly true of Pitt's
government, even though in the long run the social and political influence of Napoleonic France on European civiliza-

tion was more permanent and fruitful than that of Pitt's England, not to speak of the influence of Metternich's Austria or Alexander's Russia. "O grief that Earth's best hopes rest all in thee!"—this was the sigh of resignation with which Wordsworth reconciled himself to Pitt's England. "Far, far more abject is thy enemy" was his formula of reconciliation.

"Far, far more abject is thy enemy" might have been the text for *The God That Failed*, and for the philosophy of the lesser evil expounded in its pages. The ardor with which the writers of this book defend the West against Russia and communism is sometimes chilled by uncertainty or residual ideological inhibition. The uncertainty appears between the lines of their confessions, or in curious asides.

Silone, for instance, still describes the pre-Mussolini Italy, against which, as a Communist, he had rebelled, as "pseudo-democratic." He hardly believes that post-Mussolini Italy is any better, but he sees its Stalinist enemy to be "far, far more abject." More than the other co-authors of this book, Silone is surely aware of the price that Europeans of his generation have already paid for the acceptance of lesser-evil philosophies. Louis Fischer advocates the "double rejection" of communism and capitalism, but his rejection of the latter sounds like a feeble face-saving formula; and his newly found cult of Gandhiism impresses one as merely an awkward escapism. But it is Koestler who, occasionally, in the midst of all his affectation and anti-Communist frenzy, reveals a few curious mental reservations: ". . . if we survey history [he says] and compare the lofty aims, in the name of which revolutions were started, and the sorry end to which they came, we see again and again how a *polluted civilization pollutes its own revolutionary offspring*" (my italics). Has Koestler thought out the implications of his own words, or is he merely throwing out a *bon mot?* If the "revolutionary offspring," communism, has really been "polluted" by the civilization against which it has rebelled, then no matter how repulsive the offspring may be, the source of the evil is not in it but in that civilization. And this will be so regardless of how zealously Koestler himself may act as the advocate of the "defenders" of civilization *à la* Chambers.

Even more startling is another thought—or is this perhaps also only a *bon mot?*—with which Koestler unexpectedly ends his confession:

"I served the Communist Party for seven years—the same length of time as Jacob tended Laban's sheep to win Rachel his daughter. When the time was up, the bride was led into his dark tent; only the next morning did he discover that his ardors had been spent not on the lovely Rachel but on the ugly Leah.

"I wonder whether he ever recovered from the shock of having slept with an illusion. I wonder whether afterwards he believed that he had ever believed in it. I wonder whether the happy end of the legend will be repeated; for at the price of another seven years of labor, Jacob was given Rachel too, and the illusion became flesh.

"And the seven years seemed unto him but a few days, for the love he had for her."

One might think that Jacob-Koestler reflects uneasily whether he has not too hastily ceased tending Laban-Stalin's sheep, instead of waiting patiently till his "illusion became flesh."

The words are not meant to blame, let alone to castigate, anybody. Their purpose, let this be repeated, is to throw into relief a confusion of ideas, from which the ex-Communist intellectual is not the only sufferer.

In one of his recent articles, Koestler vented his irritation at those good old liberals who were shocked by the excess of anti-Communist zeal in the former Communist, and viewed him with the disgust with which ordinary people look at "a defrocked priest taking out a girl to a dance."

Well, the good old liberals may be right, after all: this peculiar type of anti-Communist may appear to them like a defrocked priest "taking out," not just a girl, but a harlot. The ex-Communist's utter confusion of intellect and emotion makes him ill-suited for any political activity. He is haunted by a vague sense that he has betrayed either his former ideals or the ideals of bourgeois society; like Koestler, he may even have an ambivalent notion that he has betrayed both. He then tries to suppress his sense of guilt and uncertainty, or to camouflage it by a show of extraordinary certitude and frantic aggressiveness. He insists that the world should recognize his uneasy conscience as the clearest conscience of all. He may no longer be concerned with any cause except one—self-justification. And this is the most dangerous motive for any political activity.

It seems that the only dignified attitude the intellectual ex-Communist can take is to rise *au-dessus de la mêlée*. He cannot join the Stalinist camp or the anti-Stalinist Holy Alliance without doing violence to his better self. So let him stay outside any camp. Let him try to regain critical sense and intellectual detachment. Let him overcome the cheap ambition to have a finger in the political pie. Let him be at peace with his own self at least, if the price he has to pay for phony peace with the world is self-renunciation and self-denunciation. This is not to say that the ex-Communist man of letters, or intellectual at large, should retire into the ivory tower. (His contempt for the ivory tower lingers in him from his past.) But he may withdraw into a *watchtower* instead. To watch with detachment and alertness this heaving chaos of a world, to be on a sharp lookout for what is going to emerge from it, and to interpret it *sine ira et studio*—this is now the only honorable service the ex-Communist intellectual can render to a generation in which scrupulous observation and honest interpretation have become so sadly rare. (Is it not striking how little observation and interpretation, and how much philosophizing and sermonizing, one finds in the books of the gifted pleiad of ex-Communist writers?)

But can the intellectual really now be a detached observer of this world? Even if taking sides makes him identify himself with causes that, in truth, are not his, must he not take sides all the same? Well, we can recall some great "intellectuals" who, in a similar situation in the past, refused to identify themselves with any established Cause. Their attitude seemed incomprehensible to many of their contemporaries: but history has proved their judgment to have been superior to the phobias and hatreds of their age. Three names may be mentioned here: Jefferson, Goethe, and Shelley. All three, each in a different way, were confronted with the choice between the Napoleonic idea and the Holy Alliance. All three, again each in a different manner, refused to choose.

Jefferson was the stanchest friend of the French revolution in its early heroic period. He was willing to forgive even the Terror, but he turned away in disgust from Napoleon's "military despotism." Yet he had no truck with Bonaparte's enemies, Europe's "hypocritical deliverers," as he called them. His detachment was not merely suited to the diplomatic interest of a young and neutral republic; it resulted naturally from his republican conviction and democratic passion.

Unlike Jefferson, Goethe lived right inside the storm center. Napoleon's troops and Alexander's soldiers, in turn, took up quarters in his Weimar. As the Minister of his Prince, Goethe opportunistically bowed to every invader. But as a thinker and man, he remained noncommittal and aloof. He was aware of the grandeur of the French revolution and was shocked by its horrors. He greeted the sound of French guns at Valmy as the opening of a new and better epoch, and he saw through Napoleon's follies. He acclaimed the liberation of Germany from Napoleon, and he was acutely aware of the misery of that "liberation." His aloofness, in these as in other matters, gained him the reputation of "the Olympian"; and the label was not always meant to be flattering. But his Olympian appearance was due least of all to an inner indifference to the fate of his contemporaries. It veiled his drama: his incapacity and reluctance to identify himself with causes, each an inextricable tangle of right and wrong.

Finally, Shelley watched the clash of the two worlds with all the burning passion, anger, and hope of which his great young soul was capable: he surely was no Olympian. Yet, not for a single moment did he accept the self-righteous claims and pretensions of any of the belligerents. Unlike the ex-Jacobins, who were older than he, he was true to the Jacobin republican idea. It was as a republican, and not as a patriot of the England of George III, that he greeted the fall of Napoleon, that "most unambitious slave" who did "dance and revel on the grave of Liberty." But as a republican he knew also that "virtue owns a more eternal foe" than Bonapartist force and fraud—"old Custom, legal Crime, and bloody Faith" embodied in the Holy Alliance.

All three—Jefferson, Goethe, and Shelley—were in a sense outsiders to the great conflict of their time, and because of this they interpreted their time with more truthfulness and penetration than did the fearful—the hate-ridden partisans on either side.

What a pity and what a shame it is that most ex-Communist intellectuals are inclined to follow the tradition of Wordsworth and Coleridge rather than that of Goethe and Shelley.

2. The Tragic Life of
a Polrugarian Minister *

Polrugaria need not be exactly located on the map. Enough
that it lies somewhere in the eastern reaches of Europe. Nor
need the name of Vincent Adriano, a high Polrugarian official, be looked up in any *Who's Who,* for he is a half-real
and half-imaginary character. Adriano's features and traits
can be found in some of the people who now rule the Russian satellite countries, and not a single one of his experiences related here has been invented. It need not be specified
what post Vincent Adriano holds in his government. He may
be the President or the Prime Minister or the Vice-Premier,
or he may be only the Minister of the Interior or the Minister of Education. In all likelihood he is a member of the
Politbureau, and is known as one of the pillars of the People's Democracy in Polrugaria. His words and doings are reported in newspapers all over the world.

It is common to refer to men of Adriano's kind as "Stalin's
henchmen," "Russian puppets," and "leaders of the Comin-
form fifth column." If any of these labels described him
adequately, Adriano would not be worth any special attention. To be sure, he is unavoidably something of a puppet
and an agent of a foreign power, but he is much more than
that.

Vincent Adriano is in either his late forties or early fifties
—he may be just fifty. His age is significant because his form-

* Written in 1950.

ative years were those of the revolutionary aftermath of the
First World War. He came from a middle-class family that
before 1914 had enjoyed a measure of prosperity and believed in the stability of dynasties, governments, currencies,
and moral principles. In his middle or late teens, Adriano
saw three vast empires crumble with hardly anybody shed-
ding a tear. Then he watched many governments leap into
and tumble out of existence in so rapid and breath-taking a
succession that it was almost impossible to keep account of
them. On the average, there were a dozen or a score of them
every year. The advent of each was hailed as an epoch-making event; each successive Prime Minister was greeted as a
savior. After a few weeks or days, he was booed and hissed
out of office as a misfit, scoundrel, and nincompoop.

The currency of Polrugaria, like the currencies of all
neighboring countries, lost its value from month to month,
then from day to day, and finally from hour to hour. Adriano's father sold his house at the beginning of one year; with
the money he received he could buy only two boxes of
matches at the end of that year. No political combination, no
institution, no established custom, no inherited idea seemed
capable of survival. Moral principles, too, were in flux.
Reality seemed to lose clear-cut outline, and this was reflected in the new poetry, painting, and sculpture.

The young man was easily convinced that he was witness-
ing the decay of a social order, that before his very eyes
capitalism was succumbing to the attack of its own deep-
seated insanity. He was aroused by the fiery manifestos of
the Communist International signed by Lenin and Trotsky.
Soon he became a member of the Communist Party. Since in
Polrugaria the party was savagely persecuted—the penalties
for membership ranged from five years' imprisonment to
death—the people who joined it did not do so, in those days,
for selfish or careerist motives.

Adriano, at any rate, gave up without hesitation the prospect of a secure career in the academic field to become a professional revolutionary. He was prompted by idealistic sympathy with the underdog and by something he called "scientific conviction." Studying the classics of Marxism, he became firmly convinced that private ownership of the means of production and the concept of the nation-state had outlived their day, and further, that they were certain to be replaced by an international socialist society which could be promoted only by a proletarian dictatorship.

Proletarian dictatorship meant not the dictatorial rule of a clique, let alone of a single leader, but the social and political predominance of the working classes, "the dictatorship of an overwhelming majority of the people over a handful of exploiters, semi-feudal landlords, and big capitalists." Far from disowning democracy, the proletarian dictatorship, so he thought, would represent its consummation. It would fill the empty shell of formal equality, which was all that bourgeois democracy could offer, with the content of social equality. With this vision of the future he plunged deep into the revolutionary underground.

We need not relate in detail Adriano's revolutionary career—its pattern was, up to a point, typical. There were the years of his dangerous work in the underground, when he lived the life of a hunted man without name or address. He organized strikes, wrote for clandestine papers, and traveled all over the country studying social conditions and setting up organizations. Then came the years of prison and torture and of longing in solitude. The vision of the future that had inspired him had to be somewhat adulterated with expedients, tactical games, and tricks of organization—the daily business of every politician, even of one who serves a revolution. For all that, his idealism and enthusiasm had not even begun to evaporate.

While imprisoned he helped sustain in his comrades their conviction, their hope, and their pride in their own sacrifices. Once he led several hundred political prisoners in a hunger strike. The strike, lasting six or seven weeks, was one of the longest ever known. The governor of the prison knew that in order to break it he had first to break Vincent Adriano. Guards dragged the emaciated man by his legs from a cell on the sixth floor down the iron staircase, banging his head against the hard and rusty edges of the steps until he lost consciousness. Vincent Adriano became a legendary hero.

With some of his comrades, he at last managed to escape from prison and make his way to Russia. Inasmuch as he spent several years in Moscow, it is now often said and written about him that he belongs to that "hard core of Moscow-trained agents who control Polrugaria." Such words, when he happens to read them, bring a sadly ironical smile to his lips.

When Adriano arrived in Moscow in the early 1930's, he was not among the chief leaders of the Polrugarian party. Nor was he greatly concerned with his place in the hierarchy. He was more preoccupied with the confusion in his own mind that arose when he first compared his vision of the society of the future with life in the Soviet Union under Stalin. He hardly dared admit, even to himself, the extent of his disillusionment. This, too, has been so typical in the experiences of men of his kind that we need not dwell on it. Typical, too, were the truisms, the half-truths, and the self-delusions with which he tried to soothe his disturbed Communist conscience. Russia's inherited poverty, her isolation in a capitalist world, the dangers threatening her from outside, the illiteracy of her masses, their laziness and lack of civic responsibility—all this and more he evoked to explain to himself why life in Russia fell appallingly short of the ideal.

"Oh," he sighed, "if only the revolution had first been victorious in a more civilized and advanced country! But history has to be taken as it is, and Russia is at least entitled to the respect and gratitude due the pioneer, whatever that pioneer's faults and vices." He did his utmost not to see the realities of life around him.

Then came the great purges of 1936-8. Most leaders of the Polrugarian party who had lived as exiles in Moscow were shot as spies, saboteurs, and agents of the Polrugarian political police. Before they died, they (and even their wives, brothers, and sisters) were made to bear witness against one another. Among the dishonored and the executed was one who more than anybody else had aroused Adriano's enthusiasm and sustained his courage, who had initiated him into the most difficult problems of Marxist theory, and to whom Adriano had looked up to as a friend and spiritual guide.

Adriano, too, was confronted with the usual charges. By a freak of fortune, however, or perhaps by the whim of the chief of the G.P.U., Yezhov, or of one of Yezhov's underlings, he was not made to face a firing-squad. Instead, he was deported to a forced-labor camp somewhere in the sub-polar north. With many others—Trotskyites, Zinovievites, Bukharinites, kulaks, Ukrainian nationalists, bandits and thieves, former generals, former university professors and party organizers—he was employed in felling trees and transporting them from a forest to a depot. Frost, hunger, and disease took their toll of the deportees, but the ranks were constantly filled with newcomers.

Adriano saw how people around him were first reduced to an animal-like struggle for survival, how they next lost the will to struggle and survive, and how finally they collapsed and died like flies. Somehow his own vitality did not sag. He went on wielding the ax with his frostbitten fingers. Every third or fourth day it was his turn to harness himself, along with fellow prisoners, to the cart loaded with timber and to drag it across the snow- and ice-covered plain to the depot several miles away. Those were the worst hours. He could not reconcile himself to the fact that he, the proud revolutionary, was being used as a beast of burden in the country of his dream.

Even now he still feels a piercing pain in his heart whenever he thinks of those days—and that is why he reads with a melancholy smile the stories about the mysterious "training in fifth-column activity" he received in Russia.

With a shred of his mind he tried to penetrate the tangle of circumstances behind his extraordinary degradation. At night he argued about this with the other deportees. The problem was vast and confused beyond comprehension. Some of the deported Communists said that Stalin had carried out a counterrevolution in which every achievement of Lenin's revolution had been destroyed.

Others held that the foundations of the revolution—public ownership and a collectivist economy—had remained intact, but that instead of a free socialist society, a terrifying combination of socialism and slavery was being erected on those foundations. The outlook was therefore more difficult than anything they could have imagined, but there was perhaps some hope, if not for this generation then for the next. Stalinism, it was true, was casting grave discredit upon the ideal of socialism, but perhaps what was left of socialism might still be salvaged from the wreckage. Adriano could not quite make up his mind, but he was inclined to adopt this latter view.

Events now took a turn so fantastic that even the most fertile imagination could not have conceived it. One day, towards the end of 1941 (Hitler's armies had just been repulsed from the gates of the Russian capital), Adriano was freed from the concentration camp and taken with great honors straight to Moscow. The Kremlin urgently needed East and Central European Communists capable of broadcasting to the Nazi-occupied lands and of establishing liaison with the underground movements behind the enemy lines. Because of their country's strategic importance, Polrugarians were especially wanted. But not a single one of the chief leaders of the Polrugarian party was alive. The few less prominent ones who had been dispersed in various places of deportation were hurriedly brought back to Moscow, rehabilitated, and put to work. The rehabilitation took the form of an apology from the Security Police to the effect that the deportation of Comrade So-and-So had been a regrettable mistake.

Several times a week, Adriano, facing the microphone, shouted into the ether his confidence in the Land of Socialism, extolled Stalin and his achievements, and called on the Polrugarians to rise behind the enemy lines and prepare for liberation.

He sensed sharply the incongruity of his situation. He was now a propaganda agent for his jailers and torturers, for those who had denigrated and destroyed the leaders of Polrugarian communism, his friend and guide among them. At heart he could neither forget nor forgive the agony and the shame of the purges. And with a part of his mind he could never detach himself from the people he had left behind in the north.

But he could not refuse the assignment. Refusal would have amounted to sabotage of the war effort, and the penalty would have been death or deportation. Yet it was not merely for life's sake that he was doing his job. He was eager to help defeat the Nazis, and for this, he felt, it was right to join hands "with the devil and his grandmother"—and with Stalin.

Nor was this merely a matter of defeating nazism. Despite all he had gone through, he clung to his old ideas and hopes. He was still a Communist. He looked forward to the revolutionary ferment that would spread over the capitalist world after the war. The more severe his disillusionment with the Soviet Union, the more intense was his hope that the victory of communism in other countries would regenerate the movement and free it from the Kremlin's faithless tutelage.

The same motives prompted him to agree to a proposal,

which Stalin personally made to him a few months later, that he should organize a Polrugarian Committee of Liberation and become its secretary. It was certain that the Red Army would cross into Polrugaria sooner or later. The Committee of Liberation was to follow in its wake and to become the nucleus of a provisional government.

Adriano's hands were full of work. He was now in charge of liaison with the Polrugarian Resistance. He issued instructions to the emissaries who penetrated the enemy lines or were parachuted behind them. He received reports from the guerrillas in the occupied country and transmitted them higher up. He arranged that leaders of the non-Communist and even anti-Communist parties be smuggled out of the country and brought to Moscow. And he induced some of them to join the Committee of Liberation.

The sequel is known. The Committee of Liberation became the provisional government, and then the actual government of Polrugaria. The non-Communist parties were squeezed out one by one and suppressed. Polrugaria became a People's Democracy. Adriano is one of the pillars of the new government, and so far nothing seems to foreshadow his eclipse. He has not found the way out of the trap; neither has he been crushed in it.

There are two Vincent Adrianos now. One seems never to have known a moment of doubt or hesitation. His Stalinist orthodoxy has never been questioned, his devotion to the party has never flagged, and his virtues as leader and statesman are held to be unsurpassed. The other Adriano is almost constantly tormented by his Communist conscience, a prey to scruple and fear, to illusion and disillusionment. The former is expansive and eloquent, the latter broods in silence and hides even from his oldest friends. The former acts, the latter never ceases to ponder.

From 1945 to 1947 the two Adrianos were almost reconciled with each other. In those years the Polrugarian party carried out some of the root-and-branch reforms that for decades had been inscribed in its program. It attacked the problem of Polrugarian landlordism. It divided the large semifeudal estates among the land-hungry peasants. It established public ownership of large-scale industry. It initiated impressive plans for the further industrial development of a sadly underdeveloped country. It sponsored a great deal of progressive social legislation and an ambitious educational reform. These achievements filled Adriano with real joy and pride. It was, after all, for these things that he had languished in Polrugarian prisons.

In those years, too, Moscow, for its own reasons, was telling the Polrugarians that they should not look too much to Russia as their model, that they ought to find and follow their own "Polrugarian road to socialism." To Adriano this meant that Polrugaria would be spared the experience of purges and concentration camps, of abject subservience and fear. Communism, intense industrial and educational development, and a measure of real freedom to argue with one's fellow and to criticize the powers that be—this seemed to be the achievement of an ideal.

What disturbed him even then was that the people of Polrugaria were showing little enthusiasm for the revolution. To be sure, they saw the advantages and on the whole approved them. But they resented the revolution that was being carried out over their heads by people whom they had not chosen and who did not often bother to consult them and who looked like stooges of a foreign power.

Adriano knew to what extent the presence of the Red Army in Polrugaria had facilitated the revolution. Without it, the forces of the counterrevolution, with the assistance of the Western bourgeois democracies, might have reasserted themselves in bloody civil war, as they had done after the First World War. But he reflected that a revolution without genuine popular enthusiasm behind it is half defeated. It is inclined to distrust the people whom it should serve. And distrust may breed dark fear and terror as it had done in Russia.

Yet, although he saw these dangers, he hoped that through honest and devoted work for the masses, the new Polrugarian government could eventually win their confidence and arouse their enthusiasm. Then the new social order would stand on its own feet. Sooner or later the Russian armies would go back to Russia. Surely, he thought, there must be another road to socialism, perhaps not exactly a Polrugarian one, but not a Russian and a Stalinist road either.

In the meantime, Vincent Adriano did a few things that were understood only by the initiated. He sponsored in Polrugaria a cult to glorify the memory of his old friend and guide who had perished in Russia, although Moscow had not officially rehabilitated the latter's memory. The biography of the dead leader can even now be seen displayed in Polrugarian bookshops, side by side with the official life of Stalin. Since the circumstances of the martyr's death are not mentioned in the biography, only the older Communists are aware of the hidden implications of this homage.

Adriano has also set up a special institute which looks after the families of all the Polrugarian Communists who perished in Moscow as "spies and traitors." The institute is called the Foundation of the Veterans and Martyrs of the Revolution. Such gestures give Adriano a measure of moral satisfaction, but he knows that politically they are irrelevant.

As the two camps, East and West, began to marshal their forces and as the leaders on both sides, each in their own ways, confronted everybody with a categorical "who-is-not-with-me-is-against-me," Adriano's prospects darkened. If he could have had his way, Adriano's answer would have been a hearty "plague o' both your houses." He who has been an outcast in Stalin's Russia, a beast of burden in one of his concentration camps, he to whom every copy of *Pravda*, with its demented hymns to Stalin, gives an acute sensation of nausea, has watched with a shudder as his "Polrugarian road to socialism" has become more and more the Stalinist road. Yet he does not see how he can depart from it.

He takes it for granted that all the West can offer to East and Central Europe is counterrevolution. The West may extol freedom and the dignity of man (and who has explored the meaning of these ideals as tragically and thoroughly as Adriano?), but his gaze is fixed on the gulf he sees between Western promise and fulfillment. He is convinced that in his part of the world every new upheaval will bring more rather than less oppression, more rather than less degradation of man.

He is willing to concede that those who speak for the West may be quite sincere in their promises, but he adds that he has retained his old Marxist habit of disregarding the wishes and promises of statesmen and of keeping his eyes on social and political realities. Who among the Polrugarians, he asks, are ready to rally to the banners of the West? There may be a few well-meaning people among them, but these will be the dupes.

The most active and energetic allies of the West in Polrugaria are those who have had a stake in the old social order, the privileged men of the prewar dictatorship, the old *soldateska,* the expropriated landlords and their like. These, should the West win, will form the new government, and, in the name of freedom and of the dignity of man, let loose a White terror the like of which has never been seen. Adriano had known *their* terror once, also. But that was at a time when the old ruling class believed that their rule would last for ever, and when their self-confidence prevented their terror from becoming altogether insane. Now, if they came back, they would be mad with fear and revenge. The real choice, as he sees it, is not between tyranny and freedom, but between Stalinist tyranny, which is in part redeemed by economic and social progress, and a reactionary tyranny which would not be redeemed by anything.

At times Adriano would be happy to give up his high office and withdraw into obscurity. But the world has become too small. He cannot seek asylum in the West. This, in his eyes, would be not much better than treason—not to Russia, but to his ideal of communism. Nor can he withdraw into obscurity. Resignation and withdrawal on his part would be a gesture of opposition and defiance, and this the regime he has helped to build would not allow.

How much is there in common between the young man who once set out with Promethean ardor to conquer history's insanity as it manifested itself in capitalism and the middle-aged Cabinet Minister who vaguely feels that history's irrational forces have overpowered the camp of the revolution, too, and, incidentally, driven him into a trap? He does his best to bolster his own self-respect and to persuade himself that as statesman, dignitary, and leader he is still the same man he was when he championed the cause of the oppressed and suffered for it in the prisons of his native land. But sometimes, while he solemnly receives delegations of peasants or salutes a colorful parade, a familiar sharp pain pierces his heart; and suddenly he feels that he is merely a pathetic wreck, a subpolar beast of burden.

postscript

When this character sketch was first published in 1951, the Editor of a very serious and intelligent publication expressed to me his surprise that "so scholarly a writer should produce such facetious stuff." The story of Vincent Adriano seemed then quite unreal—it seemed indeed to be an incongruous invention even to well-informed people in the West. In recent years, however, the men whose experiences and dilemmas were epitomized in this "half-real and half-imaginary character" have been much in the limelight and at last their life stories have become widely known; and so it can be seen plainly that "Adriano's features and traits can be found in some of the people who ruled the Russian satellite countries" and that "not a single one of his experiences has been invented."

Adriano was a composite type, of course. I have used for his character sketch the real features and biographical data of several leaders of that party which I knew best—the Communist Party of Poland. There is in Adriano something of Rokossovsky who, before gaining fame on the battlefields and becoming one of Stalin's Marshals and his Polish Viceroy, had spent several years in Stalin's prisons and concentration camps; something of the late Polish Foreign Minister Modzelewski, likewise a victim of the purges of the 1930's; and something also of Boleslaw Bierut, the late "Stalinist" President of Poland. Indeed, Adriano's profile was so realistic and typical that, as I have learned since, at least several other Polish Communist leaders have been startled to find themselves mirrored in it; and a few old Hungarian Communists also could not help wondering which of them has served as prototype for Adriano.

It is hardly necessary or even possible to bring Adriano's story quite up to date. Under the pressure of his dilemmas and conflicting aspirations his personality has disintegrated recently and broken up into its component parts. The disintegration may be exemplified by the present fortunes of two men: Imre Nagy and Janos Kadar, both old Communists and both one-time victims of the Stalinist terror, who are now separated from each other by a gulf—in each of them a different part of Adriano's political character has asserted itself. Or is it perhaps possible that Adriano's tortured personality should still have survived in, say, Janos Kadar?

April 2, 1957.

3. "1984"—The Mysticism of Cruelty [1]

Few novels written in this generation have obtained a popularity as great as that of George Orwell's *1984*. Few, if any, have made a similar impact on politics. The title of Orwell's book is a political byword. The terms coined by him—"Newspeak," "Oldspeak," "Mutability of the Past," "Big Brother," "Ministry of Truth," "Thought Police," "Crimethink," "Doublethink," "Hate Week," etc.—have entered the political vocabulary; they occur in most newspaper articles and speeches denouncing Russia and communism. Television and the cinema have familiarized many millions of viewers on both sides of the Atlantic with the menacing face of Big Brother and the nightmare of a supposedly Communist Oceania. The novel has served as a sort of an ideological superweapon in the cold war. As in no other book or document, the convulsive fear of communism, which has swept the West since the end of the Second World War, has been reflected and focused in *1984*.

The cold war has created a "social demand" for such an ideological weapon just as it creates the demand for physical superweapons. But the superweapons are genuine feats of technology; and there can be no discrepancy between the uses to which they may be put and the intention of their producers: they are meant to spread death or at least to threaten utter destruction. A book like *1984* may be used without much regard for the author's intention. Some of its

[1] Written in December 1954.

features may be torn out of their context, while others, which do not suit the political purpose which the book is made to serve, are ignored or virtually suppressed. Nor need a book like *1984* be a literary masterpiece or even an important and original work to make its impact. Indeed a work of great literary merit is usually too rich in its texture and too subtle in thought and form to lend itself to adventitious exploitation. As a rule, its symbols cannot easily be transformed into hypnotizing bogies, or its ideas turned into slogans. The words of a great poet when they enter the political vocabulary do so by a process of slow, almost imperceptible infiltration, not by a frantic incursion. The literary masterpiece influences the political mind by fertilizing and enriching it from the inside, not by stunning it.

1984 is the work of an intense and concentrated, but also fear-ridden and restricted imagination. A hostile critic has dismissed it as a "political horror-comic." This is not a fair description: there are in Orwell's novel certain layers of thought and feeling which raise it well above that level. But it is a fact that the symbolism of *1984* is crude; that its chief symbol, Big Brother, resembles the bogieman of a rather inartistic nursery tale; and that Orwell's story unfolds like the plot of a science-fiction film of the cheaper variety, with mechanical horror piling up on mechanical horror so much that, in the end, Orwell's subtler ideas, his pity for his characters, and his satire on the society of his own days (not of 1984) may fail to communicate themselves to the reader. *1984* does not seem to justify the description of Orwell as the modern Swift, a description for which *Animal Farm* provides some justification. Orwell lacks the richness and subtlety of thought and the philosophical detachment of the great satirist. His imagination is ferocious and at times penetrating, but it lacks width, suppleness, and originality.

The lack of originality is illustrated by the fact that Orwell borrowed the idea of *1984*, the plot, the chief characters, the symbols, and the whole climate of his story from a Russian writer who has remained almost unknown in the West. That writer is Evgenii Zamyatin, and the title of the book which served Orwell as the model is *We*. Like *1984*, *We* is an "anti-Utopia," a nightmare vision of the shape of things to come, and a Cassandra cry. Orwell's work is a thoroughly English variation on Zamyatin's theme; and it is perhaps only the thoroughness of Orwell's English approach that gives to his work the originality that it possesses.

A few words about Zamyatin may not be out of place here: there are some points of resemblance in the life stories of the two writers. Zamyatin belonged to an older generation: he was born in 1884 and died in 1937. His early writings, like some of Orwell's, were realistic descriptions of the lower middle class. In his experience the Russian revolution of 1905 played approximately the same role that the Spanish civil war played in Orwell's. He participated in the revolutionary movement, was a member of the Russian Social Democratic Party (to which Bolsheviks and Mensheviks then still belonged), and was persecuted by the Czarist police. At the ebb of the revolution, he succumbed to a mood of "cosmic pessimism"; and he severed his connection with the Socialist Party, a thing which Orwell, less consistent and to the end influenced by a lingering loyalty to socialism, did not do. In 1917 Zamyatin viewed the new revolution with cold and disillusioned eyes, convinced that nothing good would come out of it. After a brief imprisonment, he was allowed by the Bolshevik government to go abroad; and it was as an émigré in Paris that he wrote *We* in the early 1920's.

The assertion that Orwell borrowed the main elements of *1984* from Zamyatin is not the guess of a critic with a foible for tracing literary influences. Orwell knew Zamyatin's novel and was fascinated by it. He wrote an essay about it, which appeared in the left-socialist *Tribune*, of which Orwell was Literary Editor, on 4 January 1946, just after the publication of *Animal Farm* and before he began writing *1984*. The essay is remarkable not only as a conclusive piece of evidence, supplied by Orwell himself, on the origin of *1984*, but also as a commentary on the idea underlying both *We* and *1984*.

The essay begins with Orwell saying that after having for years looked in vain for Zamyatin's novel, he had at last obtained it in a French edition (under the title *Nous Autres*), and that he was surprised that it had not been published in England, although an American edition had appeared without arousing much interest. "So far as I can judge," Orwell went on, "it is not a book of the first order, but it is certainly an unusual one, and it is astonishing that no English publisher has been enterprising enough to re-issue it." (He concluded the essay with the words: "This is a book to look out for when an English version appears.")

Orwell noticed that Aldous Huxley's *Brave New World* "must be partly derived" from Zamyatin's novel and wondered why this had "never been pointed out." Zamyatin's book was, in his view, much superior and more "relevant to our own situation" than Huxley's. It dealt "with the rebellion of the primitive human spirit against a rationalized, mechanized, painless world."

"Painless" is not the right adjective: the world of Zamyatin's vision is as full of horrors as is that of *1984*. Orwell himself produced in his essay a succinct catalogue of those horrors so that his essay reads now like a synopsis of *1984*. The members of the society described by Zamyatin, says Orwell, "have so completely lost their individuality as to be known only by numbers. They live in glass houses . . . which enables the political police, known as the 'Guardians,' to supervise them more easily. They all wear identical uniforms, and a human being is commonly referred to either as 'a number' or a 'unif' (uniform)." Orwell remarks in parenthesis that Zamyatin wrote "before television was invented." In *1984* this technological refinement is brought in as well as the helicopters from which the police supervise the homes of the citizens of Oceania in the opening passages of the novel. The "unifs" suggest the "Proles." In Zamyatin's society of the future as in 1984 love is forbidden: sexual intercourse is strictly rationed and permitted only as an unemotional act. "The Single State is ruled over by a person known as the Benefactor," the obvious prototype of Big Brother.

"The guiding principle of the State is that happiness and freedom are incompatible . . . the Single State has restored his [man's] happiness by removing his freedom." Orwell describes Zamyatin's chief character as "a sort of Utopian Billy Brown of London town" who is "constantly horrified by the atavistic impulses which seize upon him." In Orwell's novel that Utopian Billy Brown is christened Winston Smith, and his problem is the same.

For the main *motif* of his plot Orwell is similarly indebted to the Russian writer. This is how Orwell defines it: "In spite of education and the vigilance of the Guardians, many of the ancient human instincts are still there." Zamyatin's chief character "falls in love (this is a crime, of course) with a certain I-330" just as Winston Smith commits the crime of falling in love with Julia. In Zamyatin's as in Orwell's story the love affair is mixed up with the hero's participation in an "underground resistance movement." Zamyatin's rebels "apart from plotting the overthrow of the State, even indulge, at the moment when their curtains are down, in such vices as smoking cigarettes and drinking alcohol"; Winston Smith and Julia indulge in drinking "real coffee with real sugar" in their hideout over Mr. Charrington's shop. In both novels the crime and the conspiracy are, of course, discovered by the Guardians or the Thought Police; and in both the hero "is ultimately saved from the consequences of his own folly."

The combination of "cure" and torture by which Zamyatin's and Orwell's rebels are "freed" from the atavistic impulses, until they begin to love Benefactor or Big Brother, is very much the same. In Zamyatin: "The authorities announce that they have discovered the cause of the recent disorders: it is that some human beings suffer from a disease called imagination. The nerve centre responsible for imagination has now been located, and the disease can be cured by X-ray treatment. D-503 undergoes the operation, after which it is easy for him to do what he has known all along that he ought to do—that is, betray his confederates to the police." In both novels the act of confession and the betrayal of the woman the hero loves are the curative shocks.

Orwell quotes the following scene of torture from Zamyatin:

"She looked at me, her hands clasping the arms of the chair, until her eyes were completely shut. They took her out, brought her to herself by means of an electric shock, and put her under the bell again. This operation was repeated three times, and not a word issued from her lips."

In Orwell's scenes of torture the "electric shocks" and the "arms of the chair" recur quite often, but Orwell is far more intense, masochistic-sadistic, in his descriptions of cruelty and pain. For instance:

"Without any warning except a slight movement of O'-Brien's hand, a wave of pain flooded his body. It was a frightening pain, because he could not see what was happening, and he had the feeling that some mortal injury was being done to him. He did not know whether the thing was really happening, or whether the effect was electrically produced; but his body had been wrenched out of shape, the joints were being slowly torn apart. Although the pain had brought the sweat out on his forehead, the worst of all was the fear that his backbone was about to snap. He set his teeth and breathed hard through his nose, trying to keep silent as long as possible."

The list of Orwell's borrowings is far from complete; but let us now turn from the plot of the two novels to their underlying idea. Taking up the comparison between Zamyatin and Huxley, Orwell says: "It is this intuitive grasp of the irrational side of totalitarianism—human sacrifice, cruelty as an end in itself, the worship of a Leader who is credited with divine attributes—that makes Zamyatin's book superior to Huxley's." It is this, we may add, that made of it Orwell's model. Criticizing Huxley, Orwell writes that he could find no clear reason why the society of *Brave New World* should be so rigidly and elaborately stratified: "The aim is not economic exploitation. . . . *There is no power-hunger, no sadism, no hardness of any kind.* Those at the top have no strong motive for staying on the top, and though everyone is happy in a vacuous way, life has become so pointless that it is difficult to believe that such a society could endure." (My italics.) In contrast, the society of Zamyatin's anti-Utopia could endure, in Orwell's view, because in it the supreme motive of action and the reason for social stratification are not economic exploitation, for which there is no need, but precisely the "power-hunger, sadism, and hardness" of those who "stay at the top." It is easy to recognize in this the *leitmotif* of *1984*.

In Oceania technological development has reached so high a level that society could well satisfy all its material needs and establish equality in its midst. But inequality and poverty are maintained in order to keep Big Brother in power. In the past, says Orwell, dictatorship safeguarded inequality, now inequality safeguards dictatorship. But what purpose does the dictatorship itself serve? "The party seeks power entirely for its own sake. . . . Power is not a means, it is an end. One does not establish a dictatorship in order to safeguard a revolution; one makes the revolution in order to establish the dictatorship. The object of persecution is persecution. . . . The object of power is power."

Orwell wondered whether Zamyatin did "intend the Soviet regime to be the special target of his satire." He was not sure of this: "What Zamyatin seems to be aiming at is not any particular country but the implied aims of the industrial civilization. . . . It is evident from *We* that he had a strong leaning towards primitivism. . . . *We* is in effect a study of the Machine, the genie that man has thoughtlessly let out of its bottle and cannot put back again." The same ambiguity of the author's aim is evident also in *1984*.

Orwell's guess about Zamyatin was correct. Though Zamyatin was opposed to the Soviet regime, it was not exclusively, or even mainly, that regime which he satirized. As Orwell rightly remarked, the early Soviet Russia had few features in common with the supermechanized State of Zamyatin's anti-Utopia. That writer's leaning towards primitivism was in line with a Russian tradition, with Slavophilism and hostility towards the bourgeois West, with the glorification of the *muzhik* and of the old patriarchal Russia, with Tolstoy and Dostoyevsky. Even as an émigré, Zamyatin was disillusioned with the West in the characteristically Russian fashion. At times he seemed half-reconciled with the Soviet regime when it was already producing its Benefactor in the person of Stalin. In so far as he directed the darts of his satire against Bolshevism, he did so on the ground that Bolshevism was bent on replacing the old primitive Russia by the modern, mechanized society. Curiously enough, he set his story in the year 2600; and he seemed to say to the Bolsheviks: this is what Russia will look like if you succeed in giving to your regime the background of Western technology. In Zamyatin, as in some other Russian intellectuals disillusioned with socialism, the hankering after the primitive modes of thought and life was in so far natural as primitivism was still strongly alive in the Russian background.

In Orwell there was and there could be no such authentic nostalgia after the preindustrial society. Primitivism had no part in his experience and background, except during his stay in Burma, when he was hardly attracted by it. But he was terrified of the uses to which technology might be put by men determined to enslave society; and so he, too, came to question and satirize "the implied aims of industrial civilization."

Although his satire is more recognizably aimed at Soviet Russia than Zamyatin's, Orwell saw elements of Oceania in

the England of his own days as well, not to speak of the
United States. Indeed, the society of *1984* embodies all that
he hated and disliked in his own surroundings: the drabness
and monotony of the English industrial suburb, the "filthy
and grimy and smelly" ugliness of which he tried to match in
his naturalistic, repetitive, and oppressive style; the food ra-
tioning and the government controls which he knew in wartime Britain; the "rubbishy newspapers containing almost
nothing except sport, crime, and astrology, sensational five-
cent novelettes, films oozing with sex"; and so on. Orwell
knew well that newspapers of this sort did not exist in
Stalinist Russia, and that the faults of the Stalinist press were
of an altogether different kind. *Newspeak* is much less a satire
on the Stalinist idiom than on Anglo-American journalistic
"cablese," which he loathed and with which, as a working
journalist, he was well familiar.

It is easy to tell which features of the party of *1984* satirize
the British Labor Party rather than the Soviet Communist
Party. Big Brother and his followers make no attempt to in-
doctrinate the working class, an omission Orwell would have
been the last to ascribe to Stalinism. His Proles "vegetate":
"heavy work, petty quarrels, films, gambling . . . fill their
mental horizon." Like the rubbishy newspapers and the films
oozing with sex, so gambling, the new opium of the people,
does not belong to the Russian scene. The Ministry of Truth
is a transparent caricature of London's wartime Ministry of
Information. The monster of Orwell's vision is, like every
nightmare, made up of all sorts of faces and features and
shapes, familiar and unfamiliar. Orwell's talent and originality are evident in the domestic aspect of his satire. But in the
vogue which *1984* has enjoyed that aspect has rarely been
noticed.

1984 is a document of dark disillusionment not only with
Stalinism but with every form and shade of socialism. It is a
cry from the abyss of despair. What plunged Orwell into that
abyss? It was without any doubt the spectacle of the Stalinist

Great Purges of 1936-1938, the repercussions of which he ex-
perienced in Catalonia. As a man of sensitivity and integrity,
he could not react to the purges otherwise than with anger
and horror. His conscience could not be soothed by the Stalinist justifications and sophisms which at the time did soothe
the conscience of, for instance, Arthur Koestler, a writer of
greater brilliance and sophistication but of less moral resolution. The Stalinist justifications and sophisms were both *be-
neath* and *above* Orwell's level of reasoning—they were be-
neath and above the common sense and the stubborn
empiricism of Billy Brown of London town, with whom Orwell identified himself even in his most rebellious or revolutionary moments. He was outraged, shocked, and shaken in
his beliefs. He had never been a member of the Communist
Party. But, as an adherent of the semi-Trotskyist P.O.U.M.,
he had, despite all his reservations, tacitly assumed a certain
community of purpose and solidarity with the Soviet regime
through all its vicissitudes and transformations, which were
to him somewhat obscure and exotic.

The purges and their Spanish repercussions not only destroyed that community of purpose. Not only did he see the
gulf between Stalinists and anti-Stalinists opening suddenly
inside embattled Republican Spain. This, the immediate effect of the purges, was overshadowed by "the irrational side
of totalitarianism—human sacrifice, cruelty as an end in itself,
the worship of a Leader," and "the color of the sinister slave-
civilizations of the ancient world" spreading over contemporary society.

Like most British socialists, Orwell had never been a
Marxist. The dialectical-materialist philosophy had always
been too abstruse for him. From instinct rather than consciousness he had been a stanch rationalist. The distinction
between the Marxist and the rationalist is of some importance. Contrary to an opinion widespread in Anglo-Saxon
countries, Marxism is not at all rationalist in its philosophy:
it does not assume that human beings are, as a rule, guided

by rational motives and that they can be argued into socialism by reason. Marx himself begins *Das Kapital* with the
elaborate philosophical and historical inquiry into the "fet-
ishistic" modes of thought and behavior rooted in "commodity production"—that is, in man's work for, and depend-
ence on, a market. The class struggle, as Marx describes it, is
anything but a rational process. This does not prevent the
rationalists of socialism from describing themselves sometimes as Marxists. But the authentic Marxist may claim to be
mentally better prepared than the rationalist is for the manifestations of irrationality in human affairs, even for such
manifestations as Stalin's Great Purges. He may feel upset or
mortified by them, but he need not feel shaken in his *Weltanschauung*, while the rationalist is lost and helpless when
the irrationality of the human existence suddenly stares him
in the face. If he clings to his rationalism, reality eludes
him. If he pursues reality and tries to grasp it, he must part
with his rationalism.

Orwell pursued reality and found himself bereft of his
conscious and unconscious assumptions about life. In his
thoughts he could not henceforth get away from the Purges.
Directly and indirectly, they supplied the subject matter for
nearly all that he wrote after his Spanish experience. This
was an honorable obsession, the obsession of a mind not inclined to cheat itself comfortably and to stop grappling with
an alarming moral problem. But grappling with the Purges,
his mind became infected by their irrationality. He found
himself incapable of explaining what was happening in
terms which were familiar to him, the terms of empirical
common sense. Abandoning rationalism, he increasingly
viewed reality through the dark glasses of a quasi-mystical
pessimism.

It has been said that *1984* is the figment of the imagination
of a dying man. There is some truth in this, but not the
whole truth. It was indeed with the last feverish flicker of life
in him that Orwell wrote this book. Hence the extraordinary,

gloomy intensity of his vision and language, and the almost physical immediacy with which he suffered the tortures which his creative imagination was inflicting on his chief character. He identified his own withering physical existence with the decayed and shrunken body of Winston Smith, to whom he imparted and in whom he invested, as it were, his own dying pangs. He projected the last spasms of his own suffering into the last pages of his last book. But the main explanation of the inner logic of Orwell's disillusionment and pessimism lies not in the writer's death agonies, but in the experience and the thought of the living man and in his convulsive reaction from his defeated rationalism.

"I understand how: I do not understand why" is the refrain of *1984*. Winston Smith knows how Oceania functions and how its elaborate mechanism of tyranny works, but he does not know what is its ultimate cause and ultimate purpose. He turns for the answer to the pages of *"the* book," the mysterious classic of *Crimethink*, the authorship of which is attributed to Emmanuel Goldstein, the inspirer of the conspiratorial Brotherhood. But he manages to read through only those chapters of *"the* book" which deal with the how. The Thought Police descend upon him just when he is about to begin reading the chapters which promise to explain why; and so the question remains unanswered.

This was Orwell's own predicament. He asked the Why not so much about the Oceania of his vision as about Stalinism and the Great Purges. At one point he certainly turned for the answer to Trotsky: it was from Trotsky-Bronstein that he took the few sketchy biographical data and even the physiognomy and the Jewish name for Emmanuel Goldstein; and the fragments of *"the* book," which take up so many pages in *1984*, are an obvious, though not very successful, paraphrase of Trotsky's *The Revolution Betrayed*. Orwell was impressed by Trotsky's moral grandeur and at the same time he partly distrusted it and partly doubted its authenticity. The ambivalence of his view of Trotsky finds its counterpart in Winston Smith's attitude towards Goldstein. To the end Smith cannot find out whether Goldstein and the Brotherhood have ever existed in reality, and whether "*the* book" was not concocted by the Thought Police. The barrier between Trotsky's thought and himself, a barrier which Orwell could never break down, was Marxism and dialectical materialism. He found in Trotsky the answer to How, not to Why.

But Orwell could not content himself with historical agnosticism. He was anything but a skeptic. His mental make-up was rather that of the fanatic, determined to get an answer, a quick and a plain answer, to his question. He was now tense with distrust and suspicion and on the lookout for the dark conspiracies hatched by *them* against the decencies of Billy Brown of London town. *They* were the Nazis, the Stalinists, and—Churchill and Roosevelt, and ultimately all who had any *raison d'état* to defend, for at heart Orwell was a simple-minded anarchist and, in his eyes, any political movement forfeited its *raison d'être* the moment it acquired a *raison d'état*. To analyze a complicated social background, to try and unravel tangles of political motives, calculations, fears and suspicions, and to discern the compulsion of circumstances behind *their* action was beyond him. Generalizations about social forces, social trends, and historic inevitabilities made him bristle with suspicion. Yet, without some such generalizations, properly and sparingly used, no realistic answer could be given to the question which preoccupied Orwell. His gaze was fixed on the trees, or rather on a single tree, in front of him, and he was almost blind to the wood. Yet his distrust of historical generalizations led him in the end to adopt and to cling to the oldest, the most banal, the most abstract, the most metaphysical, and the most barren of all generalizations: all *their* conspiracies and plots and purges and diplomatic deals had one source and one source only—"sadistic power-hunger." Thus he made his jump from workaday, rationalistic common sense to the mysticism of cruelty which inspires *1984*.[2]

In *1984* man's mastery over the machine has reached so high a level that society is in a position to produce plenty for everybody and put an end to inequality. But poverty and inequality are maintained only to satisfy the sadistic urges of Big Brother. Yet we do not even know whether Big Brother really exists—he may be only a myth. It is the collective cruelty of the party (not necessarily of its individual members who may be intelligent and well-meaning people), that torments Oceania. Totalitarian society is ruled by a disembodied sadism. Orwell imagined that he had "transcended" the familiar and, as he thought, increasingly irrelevant concepts of social class and class interest. But in these Marxist generalizations, the interest of a social class bears at least some specific relation to the individual interests and the social position of its members, even if the class interest does not represent a simple sum of the individual interests. In Or-

---

[2] This opinion is based on personal reminiscences as well as on an analysis of Orwell's work. During the last war Orwell seemed attracted by the critical, then somewhat unusual, tenor of my commentaries on Russia which appeared in *The Economist, The Observer,* and *Tribune.* (Later we were both *The Observer's* correspondents in Germany and occasionally shared a room in a press camp.) However, it took me little time to become aware of the differences of approach behind our seeming agreement. I remember that I was taken aback by the stubbornness with which Orwell dwelt on "conspiracies," and that his political reasoning struck me as a Freudian sublimation of persecution mania. He was, for instance, unshakably convinced that Stalin, Churchill, and Roosevelt consciously plotted to divide the world, and to divide it for good, among themselves, and to subjugate it in common. (I can trace the idea of Oceania, Eastasia, and Eurasia back to that time.) *"They* are all power-hungry," he used to repeat. When once I pointed out to him that underneath the apparent solidarity of the Big Three one could discern clearly the conflict between them, already coming to the surface, Orwell was so startled and incredulous that he at once related our conversation in his column in *Tribune,* and added that he saw no sign of the approach of the conflict of which I spoke. This was at the time of the Yalta conference, or shortly thereafter, when not much foresight was needed to see what was coming. What struck me in Orwell was his lack of historical sense and of psychological insight into political life coupled with an acute, though narrow, penetration into some aspects of politics and with an incorruptible firmness of conviction.

well's party the whole bears no relation to the parts. The party is not a social body actuated by any interest or purpose. It is a phantomlike emanation of all that is foul in human nature. It is the metaphysical, mad and triumphant, Ghost of Evil.

Of course, Orwell intended *1984* as a warning. But the warning defeats itself because of its underlying boundless despair. Orwell saw totalitarianism as bringing history to a standstill. Big Brother is invincible: "If you want a picture of the future, imagine a boot stamping on a human face—for ever." He projected the spectacle of the Great Purges on to the future, and he saw it fixed there forever, because he was not capable of grasping the events realistically, in their complex historical context. To be sure, the events were highly "irrational"; but he who because of this treats them irrationally is very much like the psychiatrist whose mind becomes unhinged by dwelling too closely with insanity. *1984* is in effect not so much a warning as a piercing shriek announcing the advent of the Black Millennium, the millennium of damnation.

The shriek, amplified by all the "mass-media" of our time, has frightened millions of people. But it has not helped them to see more clearly the issues with which the world is grappling; it has not advanced their understanding. It has only increased and intensified the waves of panic and hate that run through the world and obfuscate innocent minds. *1984* has taught millions to look at the conflict between East and West in terms of black and white, and it has shown them a monster bogy and a monster scapegoat for all the ills that plague mankind.

At the onset of the atomic age, the world is living in a mood of Apocalyptic horror. That is why millions of people respond so passionately to the Apocalyptic vision of a novelist. The Apocalyptic atomic and hydrogen monsters, however, have not been let loose by Big Brother. The chief predicament of contemporary society is that it has not yet succeeded in adjusting its way of life and its social and political institutions to the prodigious advance of its technological knowledge. We do not know what has been the impact of the atomic and hydrogen bombs on the thoughts of millions in the East, where anguish and fear may be hidden behind the façade of a facile (or perhaps embarrassed?) official optimism. But it would be dangerous to blind ourselves to the fact that in the West millions of people may be inclined, in their anguish and fear, to flee from their own responsibility for mankind's destiny and to vent their anger and despair on the giant Bogy-cum-Scapegoat which Orwell's *1984* has done so much to place before their eyes.

"Have you read this book? You must read it, sir. Then you will know why we must drop the atom bomb on the Bolshies!" With these words a blind, miserable newsvender recommended to me *1984* in New York, a few weeks before Orwell's death.

Poor Orwell, could he ever imagine that his own book would become so prominent an item in the program of Hate Week?